WOMEN AND THE EVERYDAY CITY

Architecture, Landscape, and American Culture Series

KATHERINE SOLOMONSON AND ABIGAIL A. VAN SLYCK, Series Editors

WOMEN AND THE EVERYDAY CITY

PUBLIC SPACE IN SAN FRANCISCO, 1890–1915

Jessica Ellen Sewell

Architecture, Landscape, and American Culture Series

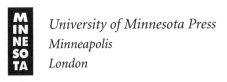

University of Minnesota Press
Minneapolis
London

This book is published with assistance from the Margaret S. Harding Memorial Endowment, which honors the first director of the University of Minnesota Press.

Portions of chapters 2 and 5 were originally published in *Constructing Image, Identity, and Place: Perspectives in Vernacular Architecture IX,* edited by Alison K. Hoagland and Kenneth A. Breisch (Knoxville: University of Tennessee Press, 2003); copyright 2003 by the University of Tennessee Press; reprinted with permission.

Contemporary maps drawn by Austin Porter.

Unless otherwise credited, photographs are from the author's collection.

Published by the University of Minnesota Press
111 Third Avenue South, Suite 290
Minneapolis, MN 55401-2520
http://www.upress.umn.edu

Library of Congress Cataloging-in-Publication Data

Sewell, Jessica Ellen.
  Women and the everyday city : public space in San Francisco, 1890-1915 / Jessica Ellen Sewell.
    p. cm. — (Architecture, landscape, and American culture series)
  Includes bibliographical references and index.
  ISBN 978-0-8166-6973-8 (hc : alk. paper)
  ISBN 978-0-8166-6974-5 (pbk. : alk. paper)
  1. Architecture and women—California—San Francisco. 2. Public spaces—Social aspects—California—San Francisco—History—19th century. 3. Public spaces—Social aspects—California—San Francisco—History—20th century. 4. Women—California—San Francisco—Social conditions—19th century. 5. Women—California—San Francisco—Social conditions—20th century. I. Title. II. Title: Public space in San Francisco, 1890-1915.
  NA2543.W65S47 2011
  711'.40820979461—dc22

                                                                    2010032668

Printed in the United States of America on acid-free paper

The University of Minnesota is an equal-opportunity educator and employer.

18 17 16 15 14 13 12 11   10 9 8 7 6 5 4 3 2 1

In memory of Ellen

CONTENTS

ACKNOWLEDGMENTS

THIS PROJECT has been possible with the support of a community of scholars who critiqued, applauded, nudged, edited, and otherwise helped me to turn my general ideas about women and space into this book. My writing partners Julian Carter, Zeynep Kezer, Marie-Alice L'Heureux, and especially Sibel Zandi-Sayek helped me to find the arguments in my story. The women of the Critical Feminist Inquiry Working Group at the University of California, Berkeley, and my fellow participants in the workshop "Taking Gender Seriously: Engendering Social Analysis" pushed my analysis and encouraged me to write for all feminist scholars. Conversations with Erik Klinenberg and Neil Brenner allowed me to place this project in the larger discourse of urban studies. Mary Ryan, Dell Upton, and Paul Groth were in on this project at its inception, and their insightful comments improved it in innumerable ways. The comments of Sarah Deutsch, a reader for the University of Minnesota Press, were invaluable. Abigail Van Slyck is the most generous and thoughtful editor I could imagine: her detailed feedback and provocative suggestions allowed me to turn this into the book that I hoped it could be.

The Bancroft Library Study Award and the Mellon Fellowship at the Huntington Library both supported my research financially and gave me the opportunity to immerse myself in the collections of these two institutions. A Junior Faculty Fellowship from the Boston University Humanities Foundation gave me precious time to complete my manuscript. The reference staff and archivists at the Bancroft, the Huntington, the Schlesinger Library at the Radcliffe Institute, the San Francisco History Room of the San Francisco Public Library, and the College of Environmental Design at UC Berkeley have been a joy to work with; none of this would have been possible without their help. I also thank my research assistants Jessica Roscio Ploetz and Karen Robbins.

My parents, Bill and Ellen Sewell, gave me love, support, and their expert points of view throughout this process, for which I am extremely grateful. A number of cats, including Max, Photon, Inky, Dudley, and Bob, gave me love and companionship and shredded my drafts. Most important, my husband, Andrew Johnston, lived with this project from start to finish, supporting me through thick and thin, including my mother's death and the birth of our son, Benjamin. I thank him with all my heart.

INTRODUCTION
WOMEN IN PUBLIC

IN THE EARLY TWENTIETH CENTURY, San Francisco boasted a thoroughly modern downtown, a specialized district of tall, densely packed commercial buildings. After the earthquake and fire of 1906, Market Street, San Francisco's spine and the center of its downtown, was quickly and substantially rebuilt with stylish buildings that made up an increasingly dedicated landscape of shopping and offices, displacing other prequake institutions, including museums and religious buildings. At the intersection of Market Street and Powell Street (Figure I.1), substantial stone-clad buildings created a relatively uniform street frontage along Market, lining the sidewalk with plate-glass show windows that created a landscape tailor-made for window shopping. Above this tall first story, regular rows of windows hinted at the warren of cellular offices necessary in the heart of any modern city. This landscape was punctuated by signature early skyscrapers, including the Flood Building (at center in Figure I.1) and the Call Building, visible down Market Street.

This image also suggests the lively mixture of uses and people that made up San Francisco's downtown. Businessmen in suits and coats; middle-class women shoppers in long dresses and large hats; suited women who might have worked in offices; children (including some boys who might have been hawking newspapers);

Figure I.1. View north on Powell (on the left) and east on Market Street, c. 1910, showing the men, women, and children who made up the crowds on the sidewalks of Market Street. Courtesy of The Bancroft Library, University of California, Berkeley.

and policemen, whose presence helped to maintain order—all share this intersection. Early-twentieth-century descriptions of Market Street emphasize this sort of bustling modernity and the cosmopolitan mixture of its crowds:

> Before noon Market Street is a bustle of business men. At noon the bright-eyed blooming youth of the office forces debouche for luncheon and a "how d'ye do." Then come the down-town cars to discharge shopping matrons, and forth come the butterflies of leisure and of pleasure. Towards the half light the bees buzz out again and turn drones for the hour before dinner (the five-o'clock promenade). Playtime has commenced. Actor, soubrette and ingenue, both professional and amateur, soldier and sailor, clerk and boulevardier, workingman and workingwoman, a dozen tongues, a dozen grades of color, a dozen national costumes—miner from the desert, cowboy from the range, chekako or sourdough from Alaska; upper, lower and half world; full of the joy of being, of forming one of the lively throng, exchange greetings more or less conventional, gaze in the brilliant store windows, buy—or hope to—and go to dinner, clubward, homeward, to restaurant and boarding-place.[1]

Writers at the turn of the nineteenth century presented Market Street as a space for all classes, ethnicities, and races—and for both sexes. This was "the thoroughfare alike of the strolling shopper and the hurrying businessman."[2]

While women were one component of this heterogeneous crowd, their presence in public was still problematic in the public imagination. As late-nineteenth-century etiquette books made clear, the heterogeneity of urban space offered serious challenges to female respectability. To retain their propriety, women were advised to avoid interaction with strangers, a job accomplished by making themselves inconspicuous, dressing modestly, never walking rapidly or talking loudly, and quickly entering the more sanitized space of department stores.[3]

In this book I explore how women in varying class positions experienced this urban environment, negotiating the gaps between the urban landscape as it was built and as it was imagined to be, concentrating on the case of San Francisco. Focusing on women's use of modern public spaces and how those spaces were built and managed in relation to women's presence within them, I explore the complicated relationship between gender structures and the built environment.[4] I concentrate on the everyday use of ordinary public spaces—streets, streetcars, shops, restaurants, and theaters—examining how women used them, which women used them, and how they were changed and expanded in response to women's presence within them, while also considering the larger social and political consequences of women's everyday occupation of these spaces. In doing so, I build on the work of a number of historians, including Christine Stansell, Mary Ryan, and Sarah Deutsch, who have explored the history of women in urban public spaces, illuminating the relationship between gendered ideology and experience and noting how women's relationship to public spaces has been inflected by class. Stansell explores the Bowery as a setting for working-class women's construction of a new culture of sociability not possible within the confines of their tenement homes, Ryan focuses on the gendered perils attached to the street and other public spaces and how middle-class women negotiated them, and Deutsch looks at both female reformers' and working-class women's struggles over the meanings and uses of public space.[5] These authors have looked carefully at the built environment of public urban space as a setting for women's experience and actions, but they do not, for the most part, use the built environment as historical evidence in its own right. In this book my focus on the built environment expands on their insights, but I move in new directions by considering the built environment as an active force in the construction of gender.

By looking at space and movement through it, we get a much fuller picture of women's everyday lives. This picture goes beyond what texts tell us about the ideal separation of spheres—a cultural ideal in which women were associated with the private space of the home and men with the public realm and the city—to understand how the public and private realms actually interacted. Similarly, a focus on space tells us a great deal about the experiences of women of different social positions. It shows how and where these experiences converge and differ and how women's spatial experiences help to construct varied women's relationships to the city. Even more important, looking at space and gender together reveals the ways that gender systems and the built environment are mutually constitutive. It demonstrates that changes in women's everyday lives shape the built environment of the city, and that built environment in turn shapes women's everyday experiences and the possible paths social transformations in gender can take.

Imagined, Experienced, and Built Landscapes

The relationship between the built environment and social structures is complex. For example, the contradiction between the ideology of separate spheres and the reality of women in public is not a simple contradiction between the ideological and the real, but instead is a multifaceted interaction among ideology, experience, and the built environment. In order to think explicitly about the spatial dimension of each of these elements, I refer to them as the imagined, experienced, and built landscapes.[6] Separating out the built landscape, how it is experienced and how it is thought about, allows us to see the contradictions among the three landscapes more clearly. It is these contradictions that become the ground for women's everyday actions, as they negotiate the differences between the experiences made possible by a built landscape and the social norms for classed and gendered behavior. Imagined, experienced, and built landscapes not only provide a useful model for understanding women in space but also revise our understanding of the relationships among individual actors, ideology, and the built environment. We can better understand the nature of these three landscapes and how they interact by examining them in the specific case of downtown San Francisco.

The Imagined Landscape

The imagined landscape is the landscape as conceived of and understood by individuals within a group. While each individual may have a slightly different understanding of the landscape, I focus here on the shared aspects of these imaginings, particularly on the culturally dominant imaginings, those that have the most currency and the most influence on shaping built space. As described in turn-of-the-century travel books, the imagined landscape of downtown San Francisco contained two distinctly gendered and classed realms: a business district peopled by "bustling businessmen" and characterized by masculine efficiency, power, and modernity, and a shopping district frequented by "shopping matrons" and "the butterflies of leisure and of pleasure," a realm of feminine upper-class consumption, irrationality, and display. Both of these landscapes were served by a specialized and centralized network of public transportation converging on Market Street. Not only were these landscapes imagined as separate, specialized spaces, but also the built landscape largely reflected the imagined ones: shops along major streets, fronted with show windows; cellular offices on upstairs floors, served by a sober but magnificent entrance quite separate from the shops; and streetcars on specialized tracks in the center of the street.

Although women worked in offices and men in stores, these landscapes were imagined as gender-segregated spaces, with the gender served in each space predominating: the businessman in the office landscape and the female shopper in the stores. San Francisco guidebooks reinforced these gender assignments in a culturally co-ed language based on the ideology of separate spheres. Descriptions emphasized display, leisure, and whim for the feminized shopping landscape and production, hurry, and purposefulness for the masculine office landscape; the female "strolling shopper" was contrasted to the "hurrying businessman."[7] San Francisco's office landscape was usually described in primarily architectural and numerical terms, with enumerations of such facts as the number of offices and floors in each building and dollars in annual trade. The 1917 *Trips around San Francisco,* for example, extolled the modernity of San Francisco's "neat and clean" skyscrapers and listed prominent office buildings, including the height in feet for each, but said nothing of the people and activity within these impressive structures.[8] In contrast, accounts of San Francisco's shopping landscape, with detailed descriptions of "kaleidoscopic changes from one show window to the next," emphasized people and atmosphere over buildings and facts.[9] The feminine shopping downtown was imagined as a space of pure consumption, driven by sensual experience and emotion, the opposite of the productive, logical space of the masculine business downtown.

The Experienced Landscape

The experienced landscape is the built landscape as actual people used it in daily practice. Thus, the nature of this landscape is highly dependent on the social position of the person experiencing it. For example, Market Street, as described in the quotation above, provided divergent experiences for businessmen, for whom it was a space to move through; for "shopping matrons," for whom it was a space of consumption, leisure, and pleasure; and for the mixed, mostly working-class throng, for whom it was a space of vicarious consumption through window shopping. For middle-class shoppers, the experienced landscape of San Francisco's shopping district did not fit its imagined gender segregation. Women walked or took streetcars, which they shared with men, to get to the downtown shopping district. Once downtown, they walked from store to store along the sidewalks of that district, window-lined worlds of vicarious consumption that were frequented not only by women shoppers but also by men and women for whom the sidewalk was part of a landscape of office work. This experience of mixture on the street is a consequence of the built landscape of downtown San Francisco.

The Built Landscape

The built landscape is the built environment and its spaces; in the example of Market Street, it includes the pavement, sidewalks, streetcars, buildings, and store windows as well as the interior and exterior spaces they define. The built landscape is shaped by the imagined landscape and reflects the beliefs, practices, and social structure of the culture that produced it. In the case of downtown San Francisco, the standard building type maximized the landlord's profits by combining shops, which required street frontage, on the ground floor with several stories of offices above. Nonetheless, the female-gendered shopping space and the male-gendered office space were well segregated within these buildings, which generally had separate entrances for shops and offices and no communication between these two sections of the building. One of many examples of this separation is the Flood Building (Figure I.2), on the corner of Market and Powell Streets downtown. Each shop had its own entrance directly on the street, while the offices were accessed through a separate entrance on Market Street. This same separation between shop entrances and a single office entrance, often marked by an arch, can be seen in all the buildings along Market Street in the area of greatest overlap between the downtown shopping and business landscapes (Figure I.3). Even the Emporium department store had offices lining its facade, with selling spaces behind the offices. Thus, the built landscape of the downtown reflected the ideology of separation, at least at the level of spaces within a building.

While space was strictly gender-segregated within each building, the effect of this building type was to encourage an active mix of sexes. The sidewalk in front of these buildings, traveled both by men en route to offices and by women walking from store to store, functioned simultaneously as part of the primarily male-gendered imagined landscape of white-collar work and the primarily female-gendered imagined landscape of shopping and was experienced as a mixed-gender space. When the downtown shopping district and the downtown office district in 1911 are mapped (Figure I.4), we can see clearly that although they were concentrated in different areas—a triangular area roughly defined by Powell, Sutter, and Market Streets for the shopping district and by Sacramento, Battery, and Market Streets for the office district—a large area of overlap occurred, especially along Market Street. As Martyn Bowden's work on the historical geography of San Francisco's Central Business District shows, this mixing of shops and offices was also common earlier in the city's history.[10] Because downtown shops and offices share many of the same requirements, such as high accessibility by public transportation, a dense concentration of people and businesses, and proximity to banks, this overlapping of business and retail functions is in fact common in cities throughout the United States.[11] Photographs of the streets of San Francisco's downtown shopping district reveal a mixed crowd, with business-suited men and groups of women sharing the sidewalks (Figure I.5). Throughout the city, women and men negotiated the same public spaces of streets and public transportation, shopping districts, and places of amusement, although this sharing often conflicted with the imagined ideal gendering of these spaces.

Figure I.2. Flood Building, 1909. The ground-floor shops opened directly onto the street. The entrance to the upstairs offices is through the archway at the far right end of the facade. Courtesy of The Bancroft Library, University of California, Berkeley.

Figure I.3. South side of Market Street west from Phelan Building, 1909. From the left, the Pacific Building, the Commercial Building, and the Emporium. The pre-1906 mixture of smaller buildings between the Emporium and Fifth Street is being replaced by a single building. The Emporium department store had an imposing entrance at the middle of its facade, while the more modest office entries were at either side of the facade. Courtesy of The Bancroft Library, University of California, Berkeley.

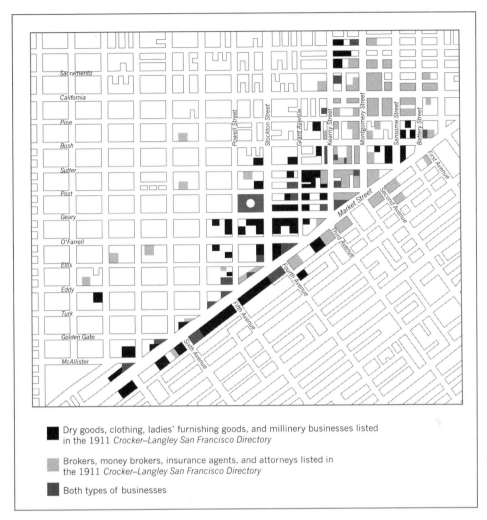

Dry goods, clothing, ladies' furnishing goods, and millinery businesses listed in the 1911 *Crocker–Langley San Francisco Directory*

Brokers, money brokers, insurance agents, and attorneys listed in the 1911 *Crocker–Langley San Francisco Directory*

Both types of businesses

Figure I.4. San Francisco's downtown shopping district and downtown office district, 1911. Union Square is designated with a white circle between Powell and Stockton Streets. The downtown shopping district centered around Union Square, Grant Avenue, and Market Street, while the office district was most concentrated along Montgomery and California Streets. Note the areas of overlap along Market, Grant, and Kearny Streets.

Buildings such as the hybrid shop–office buildings of San Francisco's downtown were created to try to bridge the conflict between the sorting of people by gender, race, and class and the practical requirements of modern commerce. In the built landscape, they are a trace of a clash between the imagined landscape of separation and the experienced landscape of mixture as well as an attempt to reconcile the imagined and the experienced. They both reflect imagined gender separation and shape an experience of mixture.

Figure I.5. Market Street, early 1900s. Men, women, and children shared the downtown sidewalks. Courtesy of San Francisco History Center, San Francisco Public Library.

Imagined, Experienced, and Built Gendered Landscapes

As the example of downtown San Francisco shows, the imagined and the experienced landscapes are particularly important to understanding gendered landscapes. How a built landscape is gendered is difficult to tell merely from looking at it. Gendered landscapes are often imagined landscapes, socially understood to be the space of one gender without necessarily being physically marked as such. This imagining can even supersede experience. For example, at the turn of the century department stores were imagined as entirely female-gendered spaces, to the extent that one department store owner referred to his store as an "Adamless Eden."[12] However, photographs of department store interiors show a number of male employees, including clerks and managers (Figure I.6). The strength of the imagination of this landscape as female makes the male workers culturally invisible.

Figure I.6. Interior of the City of Paris department store, 1910s. Department stores were imagined as female, but this photograph shows a male shopper and several male clerks. Courtesy of San Francisco History Center, San Francisco Public Library.

Gendered landscapes are also experienced landscapes. The presence or absence of women or of men can instantly gender a space. Thus, the same public hall when used for the Women's Congress is a radically different gendered landscape when used for a meeting of the Native Sons of the Golden West, although the built landscape stays largely unchanged. Similarly, the landscape of Market Street shifted gender through the course of the day. The quotation near the start of the Introduction suggests that Market Street was male before noon, female from noon to five, and mixed-gender from five on.

In the interactions among imagined, experienced, and built landscapes, there is space for understanding not only dominant practices but also practices that resist or subvert the dominant practices. This subversion resides not within just one of these three categories but rather within all three; change often takes place in the interactions among them. Because of the close ties among the three aspects of landscape, the imaginings, experiences, and spaces that do not fit in with hegemonic practices and conceptualizations resonate with one another. When any one of these aspects changes sufficiently that the contradictions between it and the others become severe, the others often are changed in response. As this book details, women negotiated the contradictions among imagined, built, and experienced landscapes in their everyday lives, making choices about what spaces to frequent and what to do there in reaction to imagined gendered landscapes. In addition, shopkeepers and others reacted to changes in imagined and experienced gendered landscapes, creating new business and architectural types to respond to women's desires and changes in the imagined landscape. The interaction of imagined, experienced, and built landscapes and the ways that each shapes the others are important to understanding how landscape genderings change and how gendered landscapes participate in social change.

Women in Public

In this book I use the lenses of imagined, experienced, and built landscapes to focus on the contradictions between a set of ideologies that privileged gender and class separation and the modern consumerist city, whose spaces and uses promoted gender, class, and ethnic mixture. The fissures between these imagined and experienced genderings of public space in the city played out in the everyday use of space by men and women. I concentrate primarily on the years between 1890 and 1915, because they constitute an eventful period in the transition from gender-segregated to mixed-gender public spaces in the downtown, as well as a period in which women's public roles expanded significantly. In addition, only beginning in about 1890 did downtown shopping become dominant in American cities, around the same time that downtown office, retail, and wholesale activities became specialized and separated.[13]

In 1890, at the beginning of this period, women were commonly in public, particularly in shopping landscapes, such as the "ladies' mile" in New York and lower Kearny Street in San Francisco. At this time the contradiction between women's presence in public and the ideology of separation was accommodated, although not entirely smoothly, by a wide range of women-only public spaces, including separate women's lounges and restaurants in hotels and department stores and women's windows at post offices and banks. In 1890, department stores of some variety were common in all American cities, women often attended matinees, and ladies' tearooms were a feature of both department stores and better hotels. All of these spaces served middle-class and elite women, shielding them from interactions with the lower classes as well as unknown men. By 1915, women also frequented cafeterias and movie theaters that served people of all classes, both women and men, and they walked the streets alone with greater freedom. Their experience of the city was much more mixed-gender and mixed-class, as well as much more extensive in its scope, than that of women a generation older. The expansion of commercial amusements in the turn-of-the-century city and their increasingly heterosocial nature corresponded with shifts in gender ideology, accommodating women in public.[14] There is, however, no unidirectional causation between women's changing everyday habits and the creation of new feminine and gender-neutral urban institutions such as the nickelodeon and the cafeteria; instead, women's public presence as workers and shoppers helped to shape these new spaces, and these new spaces in turn created new possibilities for women's everyday use of public space.

An important aspect of public space is that within it, in the words of Hannah Arendt, "everything that appears . . . can be seen and heard by everybody."[15] This made women's appearance within public space problematic, as men's gaze was felt to be both controlling and sexualized, threatening to women's self-possession and reputation.[16] For nineteenth-century middle-class women, to be seen in public carried the danger of being understood as conspicuous and therefore a "public woman," a term that tellingly denoted a prostitute. Women in public were a source of cultural anxiety because of their discordance with the dominant linkage of women and domesticity. This was particularly the case in the late nineteenth century, but women in public are, to an extent, still a source of collective anxiety today.[17]

This anxiety is a symptom of the tensions between the imagined landscape of gender and class separation and people's experiences of the built landscape, in which this separation was necessarily incomplete. Everyday experiences unearth these contradictions. Everyday life is where abstract cultural and ideological principles are enacted but also where they have to be reconciled with each other and with the requirements of ordinary life, often through built spaces and objects. But more important, everyday experiences can also contradict the imagined landscape. Henri Lefebvre writes of everyday life that it functions as "feedback" between "understanding and ideologies" and that it is "the battlefield where wars are waged between the sexes, generations, communities, ideologies . . . where antagonisms are bred that break out in the 'higher' spheres (institutions, superstructures)."[18] In short, the relationship between the practices of everyday life and the spaces in which they take place make visible the antagonisms inherent in any complex society and thus is crucial to understanding the engine of social change.

Diaries and Everyday Life in San Francisco

The everyday life of the past is surprisingly difficult to access, and the lives of the most ordinary people can sometimes be the most difficult to study. Upper-class women tended to write extensively, often kept copies of their letters and other papers, and sometimes made them available in archives. At the turn of the century, working-class women were carefully watched, and their actions were noted by journalists, sociologists, settlement workers, and other reformers. In comparison, middle-class lives were less readily recorded. Therefore, ordinary middle-class lives can be more difficult to access and have been less attended to by historians exploring the history of women in the city. In order to get at the everyday lives of middle-class women, I use a variety of sources, notably diaries, and especially the remarkable diary of Annie Haskell. Unlike memoirs, novels, and many other sources, diaries are not inherently narrative. Rather than telling a story that unfolds, diaries record the events of each day singly. For the conscientious diarist, every day requires an entry, no matter how dull, so daily rhythms of life are made evident in diaries as they are in no other source. Ordinary tasks are noted each day, creating a record of the repetition of quotidian activities such as shopping, ironing, and catching streetcars. Because diaries are not narrative, using them requires techniques that go beyond those we use for memoirs and other more narrative sources. To interpret diaries chronicling everyday San Francisco at the turn of the century, I not only read the diaries sequentially but also coded each entry for what it told of various everyday activities that engaged the public realm. The occasional descriptions of activities supply richness, providing a glimpse at emotions and the nature of experiences. The more typical lists of activities speak to us instead in the aggregate, for example, in what they can tell of the geography and frequency of encounters with particular public landscapes. Diaries are unique in what they can tell us about the real movement of people through the city. They tell us what places and experiences are linked within a day or a week; how women moved from one place to another; whether they traveled by foot, carriage, auto, or street-car; and even sometimes the routes they took. They are only one source and are joined in this study by a number of others, including newspapers, maps, photographs, existing buildings, trade journals, and guidebooks. Existing buildings from the period add significant insight into the nature of the built environment these women experienced.[19] Yet diaries alone can tell us about the repetitions of everyday life.

For this study, I have made use of three diaries of white, middle-class San Franciscans who wrote of their everyday experiences.[20] Two of the women whose diaries are important to this work were upper-middle-class, middle-aged, white women. The first of these, who detailed her social and business activities for 1905 and 1906 in her diary, is Ella Lees Leigh, the only surviving child of the former San Francisco chief of police Isaac Lees. Leigh was in her midforties at the time of her diary.[21] She was married to Ernest Leigh, a real estate and insurance agent, and had no children. Leigh was a wealthy woman and wrote in her diary both of her own large house in Alamo Square, which she owned, and of an apartment building she was having constructed next door.[22] She was active in society and was a founding member of the exclusive organization Daughters of California Pioneers.

The other upper-middle-class diarist, Mary Eugenia Pierce, was also in her midforties when she kept her 1915–17 diary, which described regular outings to San Francisco, particularly to the theater.[23] Pierce was single and lived with her parents in Berkeley, where they ran a residential hotel, Cloyne Court, described in a local paper as "the permanent home of many outstanding faculty members and retired professional men and women, and the local residence of world famous savants here on their sabbatical leaves or on lecture tours."[24] She assisted her parents in running the hotel and managed it from their deaths until it was turned into a dormitory in 1946. Pierce's mother was a well-known singer and the one-time musical director of Berkeley's Unitarian Church, and her sister Virginia was an opera singer. Concerts were held regularly at Cloyne Court, and all the family members attended concerts and other performances in San Francisco, Berkeley, and Oakland several times a week. Pierce's sister Lucy, who also never married, was an artist, and her brother, Elliott, was an industrialist. Like Ella Leigh, Mary Pierce was comfortably well off and had the leisure to spend time shopping and going to shows without being concerned about spending money.

In contrast, Annie Fader Haskell (Figure I.7) was often short of money and had little free time. Haskell, born in 1858 in Trinity Center, California, was a socialist, a suffragist, and the wife of a utopian socialist lawyer, Burnette Haskell, whom she married in 1882 and left in 1897 (although she remained married to him until his death in 1907). She was the mother of one son, Astaroth, known as Roth, born in 1886. Haskell kept a diary from 1876 until 1942, although for this study I have

Figure I.7. Annie Fader Haskell, 1880s. Astaroth Haskell Scrapbook, Haskell Family Papers. Courtesy of The Bancroft Library, University of California, Berkeley.

concentrated on the years from 1890 to 1915 and on the periods in her life when she resided in San Francisco.[25] Haskell was thirty-two in 1890, a mother of a young child, living in a rented house in which she kept boarders. She left her husband after the failure of the socialist utopian settlement Kaweah, of which he was a founder. At that time Burnette Haskell was broke, drank heavily, and was openly carrying on an affair with another woman, who was at times a boarder in their house. After leaving her husband, Haskell never had a home of her own, living instead in the Mission District of San Francisco with her sister Helen or later with her son, Roth, after he grew up and married. She was unable to find employment in San Francisco as a teacher or librarian because of her age and marital status and thus worked on and off as a teacher in small remote towns in far Northern California to support herself. Although she was well educated and her husband was a lawyer, Haskell was never well-to-do and at times complained because she could not afford to take a streetcar and had to walk instead.

Annie Haskell's diary is an unusually rich source. She wrote a page every day of her adult life, from 1876 until her death in 1942, and filled each page no matter how little of importance had happened that day. The extraordinary volume and detail of her entries provide an extensive picture of the activities and rhythms of everyday life, spanning the changes that occurred during her long lifetime. Haskell was also a good writer who carefully, if sardonically, described her life and experiences in detail. Her diary is also of particular interest because, although she was unusual in many ways, her economic position was relatively typical of ordinary middle-class women, and thus she provides important insight into nonelite experiences. Because most diaries that make it into archives are those of the elite or those chronicling unusual experiences, Annie Haskell's diary of ordinary life is comparatively rare, and its length and detail make it extraordinary.

These women had different access to financial, social, and cultural resources, but they all fit broadly within the category of the middle class and were all native-born white women.[26] Neither Ella Leigh nor Mary Pierce had discernible concerns about money; also, both enjoyed significant access to resources other than strictly monetary ones. Leigh had considerable social capital as a founding member of the Daughters of California Pioneers, and Pierce had social and cultural capital through her connections to the worlds of music and academia.[27] Leigh's and Pierce's access to financial resources put them in the upper middle class. In contrast, Annie Haskell, although highly educated, with a mother who was a published poet, a lawyer husband, and a sister who owned two houses, experienced significant financial constraints throughout her life and had only minimal social connections, largely in the world of socialist and suffragist politics. Her comparative lack of access to resources put her functionally in the lower middle class, although her education and interests did not solidly fit into that class culture. The contrasting positions of these women were also reflected in their access to spatial resources, as will be described in detail throughout the book. For example, although Pierce lived in Berkeley, she visited downtown San Francisco more often than Haskell did. Pierce moved easily throughout the Bay Area, with a sense of comfort wherever she went. In contrast, Haskell's life was lived primarily in her own neighborhood, and trips beyond it were often marked with discomfort and difficulty.

San Francisco and Its Downtown

This book looks at San Francisco not only because of its particularities but also because in many ways San Francisco was a typical large American city of the turn of the century. Like many cities, particularly in the West, it was largely created after 1850, used grid planning, and was significantly shaped by public transportation. San Francisco began as a small Mexican settlement and grew quickly after the discovery of gold in 1848. While early on San Francisco was disproportionately male and had a reputation as a lawless town, by the 1890s its white population was nearly 50 percent female, and it had a big city's sophistication, with museums, private clubs, and high-end theatrical entertainments.[28] In the late nineteenth and early twentieth centuries San Francisco was a thriving and expanding mercantile and manufacturing metropolis.[29] By the early 1890s, with a population of 298,997, it was the eighth largest city in the United States and the only city west of St. Louis to rank among the fifty largest U.S. cities.[30] In 1910, in the wake of the massive destruction of the 1906 earthquake and fire, San Francisco was still the eleventh largest city in the United States.[31] Until the 1920s, it was the most important city in the American West.

The city of San Francisco grew outward from a settlement clustered near San Francisco Bay in an area that became, by the turn of the century, its downtown (Figure I.8). This originally settled area is bisected by Market Street, leading from the Ferry Building (which connected San Francisco to the East Bay and the rest of the United States) southwest into the rest of city (Figure I.9). Two different grids extend from Market north and south. North of Market lie the financial and shopping districts, Chinatown, and, farther from Market, Nob Hill and North Beach. The area south of Market was mixed at the turn of the century, including warehouses and manufacturing, as well as a densely packed, largely working-class residential population.[32] As in other cities, neighborhoods had local main streets, typically transportation spines, which served their neighborhoods with a range of goods and services, including shops, banks, dentists, barbers, and meeting halls for local organizations (Figure I.10). In addition, in San Francisco two of these local main streets, Mission and Fillmore, grew to become district main streets,

Figure I.8. San Francisco, 1852, showing buildings. In 1852, San Francisco's buildings were concentrated in the area near the port, north of Market Street. The early city set up two main street grids: a smaller north–south grid north of Market Street and a larger northeast–southwest grid, parallel to Market Street, to its south. *U.S. Coast Guard Survey, City of San Francisco and Its Vicinity, 1852.* Courtesy of Historic Urban Plans, Inc., Ithaca, New York.

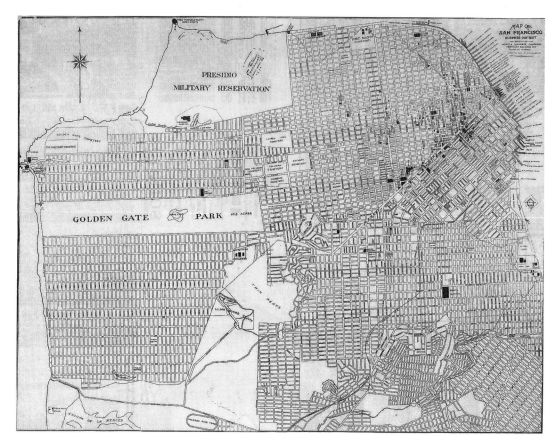

Figure I.9. San Francisco, 1904. By the early twentieth century, San Francisco had expanded significantly to the west and south of the original settlement near the port. J. B. Chadwick, *Map of San Francisco Business District,* 1904. Courtesy of the Earth Sciences and Map Library, University of California, Berkeley.

providing a wider range of goods and services in a more specialized space and serving as substitutes for Market Street immediately after the 1906 earthquake and fire.

Turn-of-the-century downtown San Francisco, like other modern downtowns, was a specialized space of shopping and commerce, with only hotel residences along Market Street. This is in marked contrast to American cities a century earlier, when both offices and shops were typically combined with the living quarters of those who worked in them. In San Francisco, the fire following the 1906 earthquake made this specialization more acute, because institutions such as museums, churches, and synagogues, as well as the owners of destroyed buildings that had included living spaces, found it easy to sell off their now-empty lots at a profit and move to new locations, accelerating the changes already underway in the downtown. This new specialized space was supported by a network of streetcars, cable

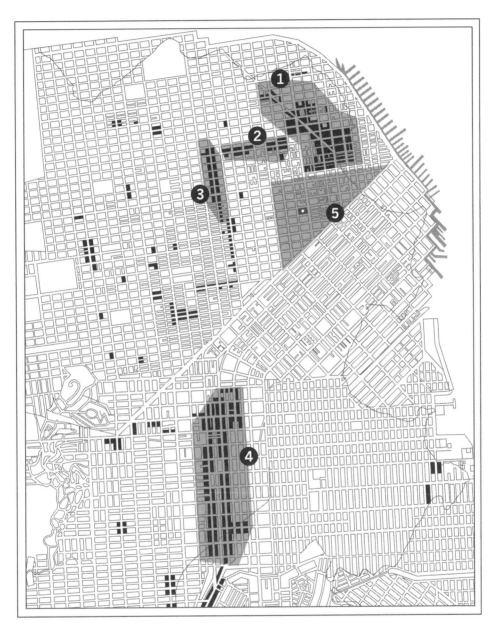

Figure I.10. Local and district main streets in retail districts, San Francisco, 1899. Small local main streets were spread throughout the city, while larger and more complex district main streets, particularly in the Mission District, served larger portions of the city. The retail districts are (1) Montgomery Avenue; (2) Broadway; (3) Polk Street; (4) Mission and Valencia Streets; and (5) the downtown.

cars, and ferries that made it possible for workers and shoppers who lived in primarily residential districts to move easily between their homes and downtown. This network was focused on Market Street, the spine of the streetcar network, with the ferry terminal at its base. The importance of Market Street and its focus on the ferry terminal also had consequences for the particular shape of San Francisco's downtown. While retail and commercial activity expanded southwest, from lower Kearny Street to Union Square, it has never migrated far from Market Street or the ferry terminal, unlike shopping districts in cities such as Chicago and New York, which have moved much farther from their original center because of changes in population and other forces.

Women in San Francisco's Urban Public Landscape

In this book I explore several overlapping urban landscapes and how they were imagined, experienced, and built. In each of the first four chapters I focus on the network of spaces that made up one type of gendered public landscape, noting where they were in the city, tracing how those spaces changed over time, exploring the ways material culture marked these sites as classed and gendered, and investigating how women negotiated them in their everyday lives. By looking both at the larger scale of the entire network of spaces that make up a landscape and at the smaller scale of individual buildings and their design details, I examine how gender was practiced and patterned in the city and how certain gendered practices were represented and reinforced through material culture. In the final chapter I revisit the gendered landscapes discussed in the previous chapters, showing how women's presence and power within public space had implications for their battle for political rights and for their place in the public sphere.

The most public space of all, and that most regularly encountered, is the street, which I discuss in chapter 1. In order to go out, whether to visit any other public place, to work, or to meet friends and relatives, women took to the streets. The streets and streetcars between their homes and their destinations were an important public landscape, the one in which women most frequently appeared. Streets and streetcars were a space of gender-based tension, as evidenced in the debates over appropriate street and streetcar behavior in turn-of-the-century etiquette books.

As the consumers for their households, women went out regularly on errands. The spaces of everyday shopping and appointments are explored in chapter 2. Analyzing shopping trips in diaries, I describe three main landscapes of shopping: local daily grocery shopping, short trips to neighborhood and district main streets, and expeditions to the department stores and specialty shops of downtown Market Street. Women's varied access to and use of these three shopping landscapes helped to construct their social positions and affected how they engaged with the city as a whole.

As women went out in public more often, they also ate in public more often. In chapter 3 I explore the expanding number and variety of institutions serving hungry women at the turn of the century. In the late nineteenth century most restaurants were male spaces, which women would visit only when escorted by men. Middle-class women could eat at all-female department store or hotel tearooms, and working-class women might have eaten at a lunchroom with ladies' tables or in the ladies' lounge of a saloon. In the early twentieth century, women increasingly ate out, patronizing a wider range of lunchrooms, tearooms, ice cream parlors, and cafeterias. I trace this change in the context of San Francisco, focusing on how the landscape of eating out connected with other gendered landscapes; which eating places women frequented when and with whom; and how the design of restaurants reflected their appropriateness as space for women.

The public spaces of the city also provided experiences of amusement and spectacle for women, the spaces explored in chapter 4. Unlike shopping, which was sometimes pursued with female companions but often pursued alone, going to amusements was usually done with others, typically with a man or as part of a mixed-sex group. However, over time women increasingly went to places of amusement without men, especially after the introduction of movie theaters. The spectacle of the theater was mirrored by the spectacle of the streets of the downtown, both on ordinary days, when men and women walked the streets at dusk to look at window displays, and on holidays, when the entire street became a space of spectacle for parades. I also explore how women participated in these parades, both as spectators and as actors, and how parades and celebrations recast the gendering of the spaces in which they took place.

The consequences of women's use of public space went beyond simply an increasing comfort and familiarity with that sphere, particularly the downtown. Women's everyday use of public space had consequences for their position in the public sphere and in politics. In chapter 5, in which I discuss the California woman suffrage campaigns of 1896 and 1911, I revisit the landscapes discussed in previous chapters in the context of the political use of public space. To demand a place in the public sphere, women reworked the uses and meanings of commercial public space, which they redefined as a site of political activity. In 1896, such public spaces were used cautiously by suffragists, but by 1911, suffragists aggressively redefined lunchrooms, stores, streets, streetcars, and theaters as political space. The political use of gendered public space shows the importance of gendered public landscapes to women's power to act, and the changes between the two campaigns highlight the enormous changes in the gendered public landscape—imagined, built, and experienced—from 1896 to 1911.

ONE

SIDEWALKS AND STREETCARS

Oh, I have no language to express myself about the cars. I waited in a pouring rain for a half hour for the Castro, and not one came. Then I took the Valencia, stood up and walked up the hill in the mud. Merry Xmas.
                                        —Annie Haskell, December 25, 1906

WHEN WOMEN LIKE ANNIE HASKELL went out in public, whether shopping, going to the theater, visiting, or for any other purpose, they took to the streets in order to get to their destinations. Streets, streetcars, and ferries made up a web of transportation that connected domestic spaces to one another and to other landscapes. The streets and the public transportation that ran on them were thus the most commonly encountered and inhabited public spaces for women. They were also the spaces in which women were most publicly visible. Even in the highly domestic and feminine world of visiting, most women (those without personal carriages) walked on the streets or took streetcars and, in San Francisco, ferries to get from their parlors to their friends' parlors. As expressed in Annie Haskell's diary entry, the experience of the transportation landscape was often frustrating, particularly for nonelite women, challenging their control over their time and their appearance in public, because transferring between and waiting for streetcars made it necessary for women to loiter on the streets and sometimes to get soaked in the rain.

Women's use of public transportation increased in the late nineteenth and early twentieth centuries for several reasons. As cities expanded and housing was increasingly segregated in neighborhoods with only a small number of shops and businesses, women were more likely to have to travel in order to do errands and to frequent amusements. In this period women's reasons for going out also increased. Shopping became a more central activity with the increase of ready-made goods and with the expansion of new forms of retailing, such as the department store. Commercial entertainments and restaurants became a larger part of the lives of all people, and particularly those of women. In addition, an ever-increasing number of women had to travel daily in order to go to work. In California, as in the rest of the United States, the number of women working increased steadily from the mid-nineteenth century into the early twentieth. In 1880, only 8 percent of women in California worked for money, while by 1910, 17 percent of California women worked.[1] Not only did an increasing number of women work, but also the work they did was increasingly likely to take them away from their immediate neighborhoods. The largest growth in women's jobs was in white-collar positions, particularly in clerical work but also in sales, the professions, and management. Service positions outside private households, such as waitressing and hotel work, also increased significantly.[2] Both white-collar and commercial service workplaces tended to be located downtown, so women commuted in increasing numbers, alongside the men they worked for.

However, the increasing presence of women on the streets and streetcars was often problematic, as it conflicted with powerful ideas about the masculinity of public spaces. In order to present themselves as respectable, middle-class women were required to maintain a bubble of privacy around them in public even as they joined the throngs on downtown streets and crowded streetcars. At times the built landscapes they encountered helped them with this social task, but more often it made the task more difficult. By examining the imagined, built, and experienced landscapes of transportation in San Francisco in this chapter, I explore how ideas about women on the streets and on public transportation, as well as in the other spaces they inhabited, changed from the late nineteenth century into the twentieth. I argue that for middle-class women, the experienced landscape was shaped by a number of improvised strategies they used to negotiate a built landscape in which their presence was imagined as unnatural.

Etiquette books reveal how attitudes toward women on the streets and on street-cars and their behavior there changed from the high Victorian era to the early twentieth century. As John Kasson argues in *Rudeness and Civility,* etiquette books are a rich source for recovering "changes in cultural practices, conduct, and consciousness" that attended urban transformations in the nineteenth century.[3] Etiquette books are, of course, conservative; they reflect upper-middle-class ideals rather than the ideals of a wider range of classes or the actions of the members of any class. However, looking at changes in descriptions of proper behavior in these books provides a sense of trends in behavior and attitudes that transcend the class dictating etiquette rules. When common behaviors changed significantly, the rules eventually had to react in some way in order to retain their credibility.[4] Etiquette books also give us clues about changes in behavior so ordinary, like taking streetcars, that they were only rarely discussed in diaries and other firsthand sources.

Imagining the Streets

For a polite woman in the late nineteenth century, the task of negotiating the street was nearly impossible. A woman on the street had to interact with her equals and be invisible to her inferiors. As detailed in 1882's *Our Deportment*, "The true lady walks the street, wrapped in a mantle of proper reserve, so impenetrable that insult and coarse familiarity shrink from her, while she, at the same time, carries with her a congenial atmosphere which attracts all, and puts all at their ease."[5] Her dress, which "must never be conspicuous," her mode of walking, her gaze, and every aspect of her behavior went into making her nearly invisible and separated from the social space around her. At the same time, she was required to be congenial and attractive, "recognizing acquaintances with a courteous bow and friends with words of greeting."[6] She had to be open to acquaintances but at the same time preoccupied, thereby "secure from any annoyance to which a person of less perfect breeding might be subjected."[7] Late-nineteenth-century advice to women about their behavior on the streets can be summed up by the admonition to act so as to "escape all observation."[8] A polite woman is "always unobtrusive, never talks loudly, or laughs boisterously, or does anything to attract the attention of the passers-by."[9] It was particularly important for her to talk quietly when out of doors and to control her body and use of space, never swinging her arms when walking and certainly never skipping, running, whistling, or yelling.[10]

Unobtrusive public dress and manners became markers of middle-class status, while working-class norms of self-presentation in public did not emphasize invisibility.[11] The distinction between visible working-class women and unobtrusive middle-class women served to reinforce the dichotomy of dangerous and endangered women, which Mary Ryan argues ruled the understanding of American women in public by 1880.[12] The visibility of working-class women marked them as potentially dangerous, especially because it attracted the gaze, which was associated with prostitutes, for whom being sexually attractive in public was an essential part of their trade. In contrast, the ideal invisibility of middle-class women, who were understood to be endangered by any contact with unknown men and dangerous women, both helped to distinguish them from poorer women and made them less attractive to the gazes of dangerous men. While for middle-class women the street was primarily a space moved through, and sociability occurred in large part within their own and others' homes, for working-class women the street was itself a major space of sociability. Their homes were often crowded, and the street provided young working-class women a freedom they could not find in a space ruled by their parents. Stylish clothing, worn on the streets and in other public places, was an important aspect of young working women's culture. Through clothing, working women could play with the signifiers of "ladyhood" and aristocratic culture and could mark their economic independence through their ability to buy their own finery.

Middle-class women's unassuming public presentation of self was part of the "sincere" fashion begun in the 1840s, in which the public self was to reflect the inner virtue of the domestically focused ideal woman.[13] This particularly American style included not only dressing and acting as unobtrusively as possible in public but also following fashion at a distance, rather than being up-to-date. Publications such as *Godey's Lady's Book* published English and French fashions well after they were shown in Europe, and in *The Age of Innocence*, middle-aged ladies complained of the changes since their youth in the 1840s, when "it was considered vulgar to dress in the newest fashions . . . the rule was to put away one's Paris dresses for two years."[14]

Not only were polite women advised to make themselves invisible to others' senses as much as possible, but they were also to restrain their own sensory engagement. Several etiquette books summed up this advice: "A lady walks quietly through the streets, seeing and hearing nothing that she ought not to see and hear."[15] Other books also addressed women's vision, advising women never to look behind themselves and to walk on the streets "neither looking to the right or to the left."[16] The admonition to restrain the gaze was combined with advice not to stop on the street. When men met with a woman of their acquaintance on the street, they were told to walk with her rather than stopping to speak. Women were advised not to "stop to chat with a friend in the middle of the sidewalk."[17] Elite commentators imagined that women were on the streets purely to get from one place to another. Any behavior that interrupted this purposive activity was problematic, especially as stopping would increase their public exposure. In addition, spending time on the street meant risking being mistaken for a working-class girl or, worse, a prostitute. Polite middle-class women were not meant to be seen participating in the public space of the street: they were to remain as invisible as possible, not to see or hear what went on around them on the street and not to stop and spend extra time in the street.

By the late nineteenth century, this fairly long-standing advice was increasingly challenged by modern merchandising methods, which depended on women seeing posters, billboards, advertisements, and store windows. This required women both to see the world around them and often to stop as well, in order to read the frequently wordy texts or to look carefully at window displays. At least one early etiquette book rejected this advertising culture, writing in 1879, "A lady who desires to pay strict regard to etiquette, will not stop to gaze in at the shop windows. It looks countrified. If she is alone, it looks as if she were waiting for someone; and if she is not alone, she is victimizing some one else, to satisfy her curiosity."[18] However, as window displays became an increasingly important aspect of merchandising, advice changed to meet practice. By 1891, Annie White's *Polite Society At Home and Abroad* reversed earlier advice. Although White wrote that women should look neither right nor left when walking and should "never hear a rude remark, or see an impertinent glance," she also admitted, "If anything in a store window attracts her notice she can stop and examine it with propriety, and then resume her walk."[19] Although the admonition not to look at other people remained, looking at shop windows, which explicitly courted the female gaze, became an acceptable behavior. Window shopping in fact was extremely common well before etiquette guides condoned it. It was a popular form of entertainment for a range of women, especially those who could not afford the goods they admired through the glass.[20]

What was written about women's behavior on the street also changed in other ways to reflect changing practices. Although etiquette books continued to suggest that women should dress and behave unobtrusively in public, the context in which they did so changed. Books written in the nineteenth century advised quiet clothing and behavior but gave no intimation that actual behavior might be otherwise. In contrast, later books gave the impression of holding up a dying practice. For example, in the 1901 *Book of Good Manners,* Mrs. Kingsland complained, "The old rule, 'Dress so as to pass unobserved,' seems to have changed to 'Dress so as to challenge admiration or attention,'" but argued that whatever the common practice was, "in the street elaborate dressing is always in bad taste."[21]

A shift in women's walking alone at night made it harder to distinguish between respectable women and prostitutes. Etiquette books from the 1890s and earlier advised a young woman that she "would not be conducting herself in a becoming manner, by walking alone" and that she should always arrange for an escort home from any evening activity.[22] The streets after dark were presumed to be, in part, a space of prostitution, and thus a woman who ventured out on the street alone after dark compromised her dignity.[23] Going out at night alone also courted physical and class danger, because in doing so a woman exposed herself to "indignity at the hands of a rougher class."[24] This fear of the lower classes, and immigrants in particular, marks the statement, "In New York, with its large foreign population, many ladies do not like to go out in the evening without an escort."[25] However, women in many cities were increasingly going out in the evening unescorted. As noted in a 1911 guide, women were taking the streetcars alone at night:

> How great would be the surprise of a foreigner of distinction if he should happen to catch a glimpse of the interior of a Boston trolley-car, at that time in the evening when the performances at the theatres and concert halls have just come to an end! If you should tell him that those groups of ladies without any attendant cavalier belonged to "Boston's best," and that the friendly trolley-car would carry them safe and unmolested almost to their very doors, he would scarce believe the testimony of his ears![26]

In spite of the potential dangers of the night, this guide also observed, "The use of electric lights in our cities is making women less timid. Where the streets are brilliantly lit and well-policed, there is little danger of annoyance."[27] Street lighting alone is insufficient for explaining a change; gaslights had lit the streets for many years before the advent of electric light and were championed for making streets safe as early as the seventeenth century.[28] But the language used in this description, of timidity and annoyance, rather than indignity and bodily harm, marks a shift in which the streets at night were imagined as rightfully a space of women.

In spite of the real shifts in etiquette pertaining to street behavior, for both middle-class and working-class women, the streets remained, and remain to this day, an often problematic space, where women's respectability and control of their own bodies is potentially menaced, particularly after dark. However, those changes that have occurred are significant. In particular, the changes in street behavior and norms in the etiquette books I have surveyed include a number of shifts in which street behavior moved toward working-class norms, redefining them as modern and middle-class. In dressing in noticeable rather than drab clothing, spending time on the street looking at windows and signs, and walking on the streets at night without a male escort, the respectable women described in the etiquette books claimed the streets as a space of their own, to enjoy and use without fear. In this they followed the lead of working-class women, who, as we've seen, used the street as a primary space of sociability.[29]

Imagining Men and Women on Streetcars

While the streets were a pure public space, open to and used by all, streetcars were imagined as somewhat more complex. Unlike streets, streetcars were small, enclosed spaces. This difference made questions of streetcar etiquette more problematic, because people were forced to be in close proximity to strangers much more than they were on the streets. One could even consider the interior of a streetcar to be like a very small, public parlor. In addition, streetcars were commercially run, and all those who rode on them paid for the privilege, in contrast to the street, which was accessible to all and publicly owned. This complicated the understanding of the rules of behavior governing streetcars, as they were not precisely those of the street, or of the parlor, or yet of other publicly accessible commercial spaces, such as theaters. The difficulty in determining what sort of space streetcars were and what rules should apply fueled highly fraught discussions of whether men should give up their seats to women. Nineteenth-century etiquette books agreed that the rule that men should cede their seats to women was absolute. However, the discussion of this rule shifted in significant ways from the 1880s through the 1920s. In the 1870s and 1880s etiquette writers focused on men's behavior in this exchange, emphasizing the necessity of giving a seat to women on streetcars and the advisability for "a gentleman of genuine breeding" to do the same on railway cars. Over time the burden of etiquette shifted from the man, who was obliged to give up a seat, to the woman, who had to behave politely and gratefully if she wished to have a seat. Later manuals included increasingly lengthy descriptions of the poor manners of American women, who were "too prone to take this altogether optional courtesy on the part of men as a matter of course, deserving no thanks at their hands, or to look upon its omission as an infringement of their rights."[30] Several early-twentieth-century etiquette books argued that the extreme rudeness of women who were given seats in streetcars led to the decrease in the practice of men giving their seats to women.[31] Although not explicitly stating that men were not obliged to give up a seat to women, etiquette experts gave men a good excuse for not doing so. The 1922 parody *Perfect Behavior* summed up this discourse on streetcar behavior in its mock advice to a woman streetcar traveler:

> She should enter the car. At the opposite end of the car there will undoubtedly be three or four vacant seats; instead of taking one of these she should stand in front of some young man and glare at him until he gets up and gives her his place.
>
> It is not customary in American cities for ladies to thank gentlemen who provide them with seats.[32]

In this quotation, women's impoliteness in demanding a seat is the focus of censure; men are merely hapless victims.

Another significant shift was in the reasoning behind giving up seats on streetcars. In earlier handbooks, men were instructed to give a seat to a woman because to do otherwise would be ungentlemanly. No further explanation was deemed necessary; a woman's status as a woman was sufficient reason for her to be given a seat, given the parlorlike space of the streetcar and women's imagined endangered nature in public. Later etiquette manuals provided a reason why a man should give a seat to a woman, arguing, "Unless a man is very tired indeed he is better able to stand in a car than a woman and he knows it."[33] Once the ability to stand became a gauge of appropriate behavior, the question of giving up streetcar seats shifted from a question purely of gender to one that also admitted age, infirmity, and tiredness, which sometimes overturned the earlier gender rules. Rather than discussing the etiquette of giving up seats for women, guides such as the 1913 *Putnam's Handbook of Etiquette* spoke of a man "resigning his seat to a woman, an invalid, or an elderly member of his own sex."[34] With this shift to need rather than gender as the basis for a claim on seats, not only were men required to give up seats in favor of others, but so also were women. For example, the 1905 manual *Everyday Etiquette* argued that a young woman should resign her seat in favor of a woman with a baby in her arms, an elderly woman, or an elderly or infirm man.[35] Just as with men, this practice should cross class boundaries, as in the 1901 advice book *To Girls: A Budget of Letters,* which describes the nobility of a healthy young woman who gave her seat to "a working-woman with her arms full of bundles."[36] This episode was used to emphasize that true good American manners meant treating those of a lower class position well, not using etiquette to emphasize class lines.

The discussion of comparative need gave men an excuse for not giving up a seat to a well-rested, upper-middle-class woman. As early as 1891, in *Polite Society At Home and Abroad,* the "moot question whether it is the duty of a gentleman to rise in a street car and offer his seat to a lady" was discussed in terms of relative tiredness as much as gender, arguing, "It might be asserted that a man is weary after a hard day's work in office or store."[37] Margaret Sangster, in the 1904 *Good Manners for All Occasions,* added to this discussion the idea that a man had a right to a seat because he had paid for it.[38] In this argument, streetcars had moved from being like a parlor, where a man should serve a woman, or the street, where he should defer to her, and were instead seen as more parallel to commercial public spaces like theaters, where consumer rights were paramount, and no man would be expected to give up his seat to anyone else.

The shifting ideals of streetcar seat behavior and the fraught discussion of the issue are evidence of changing imagined relationships between men and women in public space. The primary causes for changes in etiquette, as acknowledged in the etiquette books themselves, were women's increasing use of streetcars and women's expanding roles in the workforce, which combined to normalize women's presence on streetcars. As discussed in the Introduction, the downtown shifted gender throughout the day; therefore, women who rode streetcars as shoppers often rode at different hours from those of commuters, making streetcars a feminine space in the middle of the day. In the morning commute hours the population was more masculine, although in the evening it may well have been mixed. Early on, some midday streetcars along San Francisco's Sutter Street, leading from an upper-middle-class residential area to the downtown shopping district, were even designated as "shoppers' specials" and were populated entirely by women.[39]

However, as an increasing number of women worked at a range of clerical jobs in downtown offices and at shop-clerk jobs in downtown shops, they became "constant riders at the busy hours, and thus [came] into direct competition with men," causing men not to cede their seats, as W. C. Green commented in the 1904 *A Dictionary of Etiquette.*[40] Margaret Sangster argued that the changes in women's status resulting from their increasing presence in the workforce were the most important determination of streetcar behavior. She declared that men had ceased to offer seats to ladies in large part because of "the increasing independence of women who compete with men on equal terms in every industrial field, and who, in becoming equals and competitors, have ceased to be superiors."[41] The changing gender order of workplaces and public transportation led to men's becoming increasingly accustomed to sharing space with women outside the home. As Marshall Everett wrote in *The Etiquette of Today* in 1902, "Men are now seldom free from the presence of women, no matter what their vocation. The sexes work side by side in the counting room, the editorial room, the printing office, the studio, the hotel, the restaurant, the university, and the forum."[42] In these rationalized spaces of work, old systems of gendered conduct could quickly become obsolete. Customs that involved men's deferring to women were particularly poorly suited to the business world, because women were usually in positions that were subordinate to men. Treating a woman with deference was largely incompatible with maintaining one's superior status and ordering her to do work. Despite Margaret Sangster's assertion that women were changing from men's superiors to their equals, women were in fact serving as their subordinates. After being served by women in the office or shop all day, men might not choose to defer to the same women by offering them seats on the streetcars on the way home. Gender alone would not necessarily give working women greater rights to a seat in the eyes of men, who were their social superiors and who were accustomed to being served by women both at home and in the office. Thus increasingly, class became more important than gender in dictating the practical application of seat-giving etiquette.

These changes in streetcar etiquette are a sign of changes in women's practices and in women's social roles. As more and more women took streetcars at all hours of the day, whether for shopping, visiting, or work, they became ordinary riders, on an equal social footing with the men who rode the streetcars. The contradictions between an ideology that saw women as endangered, frail, and only rarely in public and the reality of large numbers of women riding the streetcars every day and working with and for men in offices and shops led to this ongoing debate over men ceding streetcar seats to women. As practices changed, so did ideology, so that women were no longer seen as inherently frail, at least while on streetcars, and the right to a seat became embodied in need rather than purely in gender. Both on the streets and in streetcars, changes in experience helped to lead to changes in ideology. As respectable women walked on the streets at night and respectable men kept their seats on streetcars, the imagined landscape shifted to accommodate experience. However, women in public have remained problematic, and neither the question of women on the street at night nor that of giving up seats on public transportation has been entirely resolved, even in the present day. In turn-of-the-century San Francisco, women who used the streets and streetcars and wished to be respectable found that the built landscape of the streets and public transportation at times facilitated, but more often frustrated, attempts to follow the spatial practices imagined in etiquette books.

The Design of Streetcars and Ferries

Streetcars were initially designed to express middle-class ideals but also often made it difficult for women to practice the reserve required by those norms. Early streetcars, as well as ferries, were designed for attractiveness. Decorative metalwork and carefully painted exteriors complemented simple wooden seats on streetcars and cable cars (Figure 1.1), while on ferries shipshape exteriors were complemented by simple but elegant interiors, often of polished teak and other woods (Figure 1.2). In his history of streetcars, *The Time of the Trolley*, William Middleton writes that streetcar decoration, both interior and exterior, was "often lavish in the extreme," with the exterior involving at a minimum two weeks in the paint shop. Interiors used multiple hardwoods and occasionally colored glass and hand-painted designs. In 1892, one author argued for streetcar decoration: "Not only should a reasonable amount of decoration be provided in cars which are patronized wholly by a cultivated class of people, but in all cars, for by this means the comforts and solaces of fine art will be brought to a large number of lives and hearts that cannot afford to provide them in their own homes."[43] Thus streetcars, while used by all, were built and decorated initially according to middle-class norms, with the ideal of making everyone in them conform to the ideals of the middle class. Similarly, the ferries, while serving as regular public transportation, referred to the refined, upper-class space of ocean liners through their highly decorative interiors and parlor spaces. A few specialized streetcars also took on the trappings of a parlor. In San Francisco, a streetcar used to transport schoolchildren on school trips was furnished with plush-upholstered wicker chairs, a carpeted floor, and window drapes (Figure 1.3). Similarly, funeral cars included a section for mourners, with upholstered furniture, carpeted floor, and drapes.[44]

Over time streetcar design became less elaborate, as evidenced by the relatively spartan "pay-as-you-enter" streetcars (Figure 1.4). This shift toward less decoration corresponded in part to the sorting out of classes, as the rich increasingly could use personal automobiles to get around, leaving streetcars to a less affluent range of people, but was also in keeping with general stylistic changes that favored simple lines. More than the level and style of decoration changed with these new

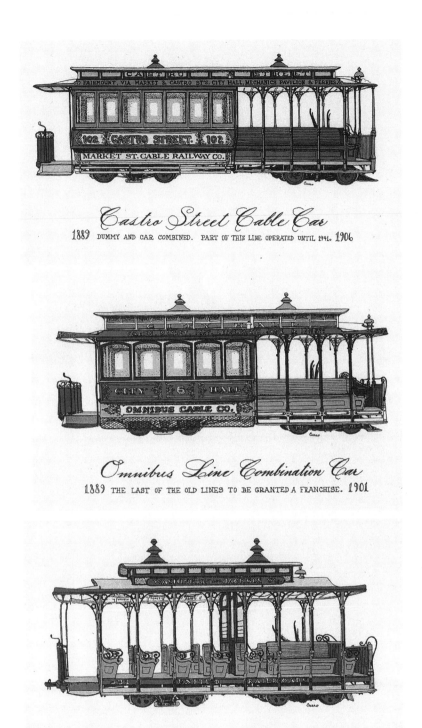

Castro Street Cable Car

1889 DUMMY AND CAR COMBINED. PART OF THIS LINE OPERATED UNTIL 1941. 1906

Omnibus Line Combination Car

1889 THE LAST OF THE OLD LINES TO BE GRANTED A FRANCHISE. 1901

Powell Street Open Car

1902 POPULAR FOR THE SUNDAY TRIP TO GOLDEN GATE PARK. 1906

Figure 1.1. San Francisco cable cars, 1889–1906. In comparison with later streetcars, these cable cars, sporting elaborate ironwork, decorative clerestory roofs, and bright paint, were highly decorative. Note the extent to which the seats are open to the outside, displaying the riders to pedestrians. From the collection of Evelyn Curro; courtesy of the Cable Car Museum, San Francisco.

Figure 1.2. Ferry interiors. Ferries were decorated in a refined manner, with carpets, carved wooden details, and stained-glass windows. Top image courtesy of The Bancroft Library, University of California, Berkeley; bottom image courtesy of the San Francisco Maritime National Historical Park.

streetcars, however. The new cars provided less service as well. Riders previously could enter the streetcar from multiple points, and a conductor would come to them for payment. Now riders paid the driver as they entered at one designated point. In addition, new seating patterns changed the experience of riders and their relationship both to other riders in the car and to the city outside. Most older cars had large portions of the vehicle open to the out-of-doors, blurring the boundary between the interior and the exterior of the car (see Figure 1.1). On many of these cars, riders faced away from one another, toward the street outside. For women passengers, this design was a boon to avoiding contact with strangers but was problematic in that it made them visible in public, a situation that was taboo. The 1911 pay-as-you-enter cars were enclosed, ridding female passengers of the burden of visibility to those on the street but also depriving male passengers of a chance to smoke on the cars, which they decried bitterly.[45] Even more significant, the new cars replaced rows of seating with long benches facing each other across the center of the car (Figure 1.5). This design provided more space for standing passengers but made the task of avoiding both physical and eye contact with other

Figure 1.3. "San Francisco" school streetcar (first used 1904). This special streetcar was decorated in the manner of a parlor, with carpeted floors, plush seats, movable chairs, and window drapes. From Smallwood, *The White Front Cars of San Francisco*, 256.

riders more difficult. Helen Dare, a columnist for the *San Francisco Chronicle* (hereafter the *Chronicle*), described the experience of the new streetcars in 1911:

> The cars are arranged, with one long seat down each side, the length of the car—for the
> men to sit on; and the space between the seats, the length of the car, into which the women
> are packed. . . . The men all sit with their legs crossed, one foot on the floor extending into
> the aisle. . . . Women so fill the space designed for them that there is a woman on each side
> of every man's extended foot. With this convenient and methodical arrangement it is
> possible for the seated men passengers to easily and economically . . . get a [shoe] shine.[46]

The physical closeness that allowed the shoes of seated passengers to rub against
the legs of standing passengers made no allowances for women to maintain physical reserve on streetcars, especially if men took all the seats, as Dare claimed. The
shift to this design suggests that the concern for shielding women in public, through
such mechanisms as "shoppers' special" streetcars and women's windows at banks
and other businesses, had become archaic by 1911.[47]

The new bench seats also made it more difficult for passengers to avoid eye
contact, as they were no longer facing forward or outward, but inward, toward
one another. Advertisers exploited the desire of passengers, especially women passengers, to avoid looking at the people seated across from them and used the space
above the windows as a canvas (Figure 1.6). This space well above the heads of
other seated passengers was easily examined without the danger of looking directly
at another passenger. In these new cars, riders had to work harder at creating a
social distance between themselves and other passengers. The physical intimacy
of being in an enclosed space, facing other passengers, required that women work
harder at seeming unapproachable.

The Built Network of Transportation in San Francisco

The lines that these streetcars traveled and the streets of San Francisco that they
served were structured around the needs of efficient transportation much more
than the social desires of respectable women, although the design of streetcars
and improvements to streets and sidewalks responded in part to desires for clean,
orderly space for polite women. Local improvement societies, particularly the Merchants' Association of San Francisco, made many improvements to the streets,
including street cleaning, street sprinkling, street paving, electric lighting, sidewalk
paving, and the creation of pedestrian islands at the busiest downtown streetcar
stops.[48] While these made the streets more pleasant, they did not mitigate the
problems of crowding on the sidewalks, especially on Market Street. The intensi-
fication of business on and around Market Street and the centrality of that street

Figure 1.4. PAYE streetcar, 1911. This pay-as-you-enter car was significantly more enclosed and more simply styled than earlier cars. From Smallwood, *The White Front Cars of San Francisco*, 105.

to the public transportation system not only led to a great number of people on the street but also increased their social variety. Although the sidewalks of the downtown were relatively wide, they were narrowed by street-widening projects aimed at improving the circulation of vehicles, which exacerbated the problem of maintaining physical as well as social distance between pedestrians.[49]

The structure of public transportation in San Francisco was organized primarily around the needs of male and female workers, and to a lesser extent female shoppers, who traveled to and from the downtown. The spine of San Francisco's transportation is and was Market Street, where the city's first streetcar ran (Figure 1.7). At the end of Market Street, streetcars and pedestrians met at the Ferry Building, from which ferries ran to points along the East, North, and South Bay, from where people could travel to the rest of the United States by train (Figure 1.8). These ferries, run by several railroad and streetcar companies, provided a means for East and North Bay residents to work in, shop in, or visit the city and for San Franciscans to frequent the East Bay and the North Bay.[50] In keeping with the history of the city's development, which expanded outward from the area near the foot of Market Street, streetcar service was densest in the central part of the city both north and south of Market Street, as can be seen in Figure 1.9, which shows the public transportation system in 1913. Parallel lines down Mission, Valencia, Howard, and Folsom Streets served to connect the Mission District, centered on

Figure 1.5. PAYE streetcar interior, 1911. Unlike earlier cars, which were furnished primarily with front-facing two-person seats, the pay-as-you-enter cars made strangers share space on one long bench and offered more space for standing straphangers. From Smallwood, *The White Front Cars of San Francisco,* 471.

the historic Mission Dolores, to Market Street and the downtown. The residential area north of Market was also well connected to the downtown. Several lines extended out from the core of the city to the Western Addition and then farther out to excursion destinations, including the Cliff House and Sutro Baths, Golden Gate Park, and the Chutes amusement park to the west and Ingleside Race Track to the south. As the population of the city expanded westward into the Richmond and Sunset Districts, streetcar service expanded with the population. With the Panama–Pacific International Exposition in 1915, intensive connections were also created to its site in the north of the city between the Presidio and Fort Mason.

In the nineteenth century, multiple competing companies ran public transportation in the city, using a combination of cable cars, electric cars, horsecars,

In every city and town of this country we tell the story of *HEINZ QUALITY* through the *STREET CARS* as well as through various other advertising mediums.

It will be to your advantage *ALWAYS* to have a good assortment of *HEINZ PRODUCTS* in your store to meet the steady, increasing demand created by our advertising.

A good *HEINZ* display means quick, steady sales.

H. J. HEINZ COMPANY
PITTSBURGH, PA.

(3)

Figure 1.6. Heinz advertisement, 1913. This advertisement, directed to grocers, shows the typical placement of streetcar advertising above the windows. As the dotted line representing the streetcar rider's gaze shows, this style of advertising helped to minimize eye contact among riders. This advertisement also indicates that Heinz saw women as regular riders of streetcars. From *The Modern Grocer*, May 3, 1913: 8.

Figure 1.7. Market Street as seen from Ferry Building, 1905. Market Street was the spine of San Francisco's transportation system, and several lines of streetcars ran on it. Courtesy of San Francisco History Center, San Francisco Public Library.

and steam railway. Some lines even combined multiple technologies, such as the Sutter Street Line, which in 1897 began as a horsecar from the ferries to Sutter and Sansome and continued from there as a cable car on Sutter.[51] Consolidation of companies in 1893 and 1902 left the United Railroads of San Francisco controlling 229 miles of track, with only three small competitors remaining.[52] These consolidations did not strongly affect the location of routes, only the ability to transfer easily between them. Not until 1944, under enormous competition from automobiles, were competing streetcar and bus lines combined into one municipal system.[53]

Experiencing the Streets and Streetcars of San Francisco

For women shoppers who wanted to go downtown, the streetcars were ideal; for women visiting or working across town, however, they were often problematic.

Figure 1.8. Ferry Building, 1915. The Ferry Building, built in 1898, sits at the end of Market Street. On the plaza in front of it was a large streetcar turnaround, where ferry riders from across the bay made connections to city transportation. Courtesy of San Francisco History Center, San Francisco Public Library.

The web of connections created by the streetcar systems of San Francisco tied residential neighborhoods to Market Street and the downtown but only rarely connected neighborhoods without going by way of Market Street.[54] This was a built landscape based on the idea that streetcars were used primarily to travel from home to work or to go shopping. In addition to the problem of having to go to Market Street en route to another neighborhood, a crosstown trip before the extensive consolidation of 1902 often required taking streetcars run by different companies, and thus paying a fare twice. The process of taking multiple streetcars and transferring from one to the next also required women to stand around on the sidewalk, of necessity breaking the etiquette rules that women should not loiter on the streets.

Streetcars, ferries, and other forms of public transportation were open to and used by men and women of all classes and races. Very few people had private carriages or automobiles that they used on a regular basis, and although hired vehicles

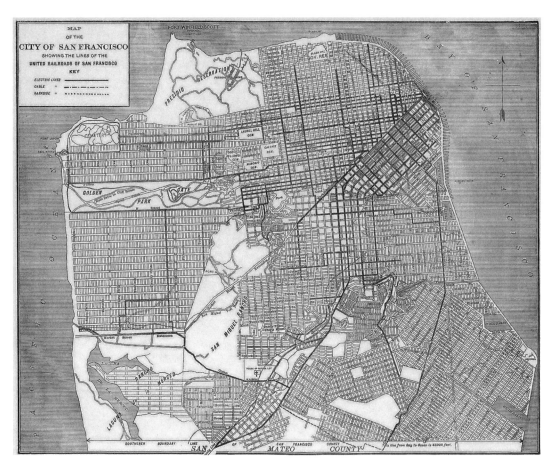

Figure 1.9. Public transportation system, 1913. Several lines crisscrossed the downtown and connected it to areas to the north and west, while other lines connected the industrial area south of Market Street and the Mission District. As the city grew, service expanded, with new lines extending into the Richmond and Sunset Districts, north and south of Golden Gate Park. Areas that had been served for some time, such as the Mission District and the area north of Market Street, experienced increasing density. "Map of the City Showing Lines of the United Railways of San Francisco," from *McGraw Electric Railway Manual: The Red Book of American Electric Railway Investments* (New York: McGraw Publishing Company, Inc., 1913). Courtesy of the University of Texas Libraries, The University of Texas at Austin.

were available, they were used only rarely. Carriages were hired for the ceremonial occasion of funerals, but Annie Haskell mentioned riding in a hack without such an occasion only once, when her estranged husband insisted on their taking one home from the park because the streetcars were "so crowded."[55] The much richer Mary Eugenie Pierce once mentioned taking her sister home in a taxi but otherwise took public transportation or, occasionally, was given a ride to Oakland by friends with automobiles.[56] Streetcars transported people to work, to visit friends, to shop, to downtown amusements, and on excursions to sites such as

Sutro Gardens and Sutro Baths, Ocean Beach, Golden Gate Park, the 1894 Mid-winter Fair and the 1915 Panama–Pacific International Exposition. Streetcar fares were relatively low, five cents (about one dollar in current value), and thus afford-able by a wide range of the population.[57]

However, women with limited means often walked when possible, rather than ride the streetcar, in order to save money. Young working women often had little money for themselves, as the money they earned usually went entirely into the family budget.[58] Kathy Peiss writes of how young working women in New York would save money for movies or other luxuries by walking to and from work and pocketing their carfare. She quotes an investigator who wrote, "A carfare saved by walking to work is a carfare earned for a trip to a dance hall."[59] Although Annie Haskell had more control of her household money than the young working women studied by Peiss, she also often walked to save money. She regularly walked long distances to visit family members or to do errands downtown, even though she had easy access to several streetcar lines that served the Mission District, where she most often lived. After an outing in 1909 to see the annual police inspection and to do some shopping, for which she walked downtown and back from Twenty-first Street, a trip of nearly three miles each way, she wrote that she came home "tired and faint from hunger," adding, "I don't think it is a good way to exhaust one's self to save a few nickels, but I suppose it is the only way to acquire wealth."[60] On a few other occasions, Haskell compromised, saving just one nickel by walk-ing one direction and riding back.[61] At several times in her life, Haskell did not have enough disposable income to take streetcars. Sometimes she walked, but on other occasions the lack of a nickel for carfare meant forgoing activities, as on April 17, 1897, when she wrote in her diary: "The Women's Congress begins next Sunday and even if I were willing to go with shabby gloves and a shocking bad hat and the same dress I have worn for two years, and go without lunch and all that, *still* I can't go for lack of carfare!"[62] That same year, she also complained of missing celebrations such as Memorial Day and the Fourth of July because she couldn't afford carfare.[63]

When taking streetcars, frugality could also make for a longer and more com-plicated ride. Annie Haskell mentions taking a circuitous route to "save two car-fares" by not transferring between different companies.[64] Taking the streetcars to get across town could also be onerous if one's route did not center on Market Street. Haskell regularly complained of the wait and unpleasantness of transfer-ring from one line to another, writing one day in 1916 that she "took five cars and had to wait for every one."[65] Transfers were also an issue; she complained that it was difficult to visit her sister Kate: "It takes quite a little strength and time to walk, and it is too short to ride considering the transfer, and extra distance to walk."[66] These long rides were presumably made even more uncomfortable by the lack of public restroom facilities in San Francisco. While after 1903 women and men could avail themselves of San Francisco's only public restrooms at Union Square, and women who felt comfortable going into more elite spaces could also use toilets in downtown hotels and department stores, when they traveled beyond the downtown women had no bathroom facilities available to them.[67]

Although men and women from all walks of life took streetcars, the experience of the built landscape of streetcars varied depending on the rider's means. For men and women with money, streetcars could be taken without regard for cost; for poorer people, streetcars were still accessible, but the decision to take one was not automatic, and complicated, time-consuming trips that might be more easily taken by automobile or a more direct, but also more expensive, route made the experience of the streetcar somewhat less pleasant. In addition, the actual streetcars experienced by men and women of different stations varied depending on the lines they rode. Lines south of Market Street, which served a more working-class population, regularly had older and less well-appointed cars assigned to them, while the newest and most luxurious cars were assigned to lines serving the financial district, Nob Hill, and other wealthy neighborhoods.[68] Crowding was also a problem on the more heavily used working-class lines. Haskell often complained about having to stand on the streetcars, as in this entry from 1907: "We took a car for Roth's. Stood up all the way too. As they were all upside down we did not want to stay long. And again waited long for a car, two did not stop at all, & we stood up all the way home again. I shall be glad to get away from the street cars if nothing else. The service is worse than diabolic."[69]

Ferries also provided convenient and inexpensive (usually a nickel) transportation for riders of all class positions.[70] Unlike streetcars, which could be circumvented by walking or riding in a private or hired vehicle, ferries were the only reasonable option for going to or from San Francisco from the north and east in the era before the construction of the Golden Gate Bridge to the North Bay in 1937 and the Bay Bridge to Oakland in 1939. Ferries, however, were more commodious than streetcars and provided a range of other services, including restaurants and newsstands. In addition, on the ferries, as in the Ferry Building, some separate spaces were provided for women in the form of a women's parlor (on the ferries) and a women's waiting room (in the Ferry Building). These spaces provided polite, middle-class space for travelers on their relatively brief trip across the bay and their even briefer stay in the Ferry Building.[71] The experience of riding a ferry could be ordinary and unremarkable for upper-middle-class riders like Mary Pierce, who took one several times a week to visit San Francisco, or for regular commuters. For others, like Annie Haskell, the trip could provoke a dream of ship travel and an opportunity to "enjoy the water and the ships" and how "the sun glittered on the waves."[72] For elite women, the comfort of the ferry ride was taken for granted; for less affluent women ordinarily frustrated by a streetcar system that served them poorly, the ferry was a respite as well as a glance at the luxuries of a life they could not afford to live.

Negotiating the Streets

Women in San Francisco walked the streets and took public transportation on a daily basis to go visiting, shopping, or to work. This shaped the experienced landscape of these public spaces, making men increasingly accustomed to women's presence in public. Changes in the built landscape of sidewalks and streetcars by the 1910s reflected the normality of women's use of them, as narrower, more crowded sidewalks and packed streetcars with lengthwise benches made it increasingly difficult for women to maintain a physical and social distance from those around them. As middle-class women walked the streets of the city and increasingly rode the streetcars at the same hours as men, they also became freer in their use of the streets, dressing and speaking more loudly, walking without an escort, and treating the streets as a space of sociability as well as transportation, following the lead of working-class women and shifting the norms of appropriate behavior. The imagined landscape shifted to include women of all classes as appropriate inhabitants of public space. Norms of behavior toward women also shifted; they were treated with less deference now that they had become more common figures on the streets and streetcars and working in shops and offices for men.

Women shared many of the same streets and streetcars, where their gender, not their class, was central to how they were treated. However, class affected how women were able to negotiate these spaces and their inconveniences. Elite women were able to use their financial power to avoid some of the pitfalls of the crowded transportation landscape, often taking private automobiles rather than streetcars and thereby also avoiding some of the most crowded streets. When they did take public transportation, they rode on the lines with the most luxurious cars, as well as on the well-appointed ferries, where they could travel in the women's parlor. Their trips could be planned solely on the basis of convenience; they could avoid the circuitous routes and multiple transfers that plagued the travels of women who needed to avoid the double fare involved in switching from one streetcar company to another. Middle-class women without private automobiles and poorer women who sometimes could not afford even a nickel for carfare were less lucky; they could not avoid standing on crowded cars or waiting on the street, potential victims of weather and of impolite men. In the next chapter I will delve more fully into how class mediated women's gendered experiences of San Francisco, by focusing on the landscapes of shopping.

TWO

ERRANDS

Met Helen at 18th & Castro and we went down town. She had some errands to do, and I trailed around in her wake. Then went to the Owl, to show them my rubber gloves. After much time and argument they offered me another pair at half price. I said I wouldn't do it, so they gave me another pair. Then I left Helen and rushed to Hale's, where Kate was waiting for me. She had a turban she had made for me—with much pains and I wore that. We lunched at the Tivoli Café, then went to the Penn. Ins. where she arranged to have the policy made over to me—after her.

—Annie Haskell, August 24, 1914

IN THIS DIARY ENTRY Annie Haskell describes the rounds of errands she made on one ordinary day. The desire to exchange a pair of rubber gloves and an appointment at an insurance agency became the basis for a trip (probably on public transportation), a meal out, and visits to a number of other stores. For Annie, as for other women at the turn of the century, the most common reason to go out in public was to run errands, especially errands that involved shopping. The daily job of managing a household, which included feeding, clothing, and looking after the health of all the members of a family, required shopping for food and clothing, going to banks and other offices to conduct household-related business, and visiting doctors and dentists, both alone and with other family members. In addition, women were responsible for maintaining and expressing their family's status in an increasingly anonymous world, something they accomplished primarily through consumption, as Thorstein Veblen noted as early as 1899.[1] Errands created a regular public presence for women in a web of interlocking landscapes that spread across most of the city. These landscapes combined the streets and public transportation discussed in chapter 1 with the interior spaces of stores, quasi-public spaces that were accessible to the public in general but were controlled by shopkeepers, constraining both women's access to them and their behavior within them.

Different sorts of errands, the women who did them, and the landscapes in which they took place were imagined quite distinctly. In this chapter I examine how three major landscapes of errands—downtown shopping districts, grocery stores, and local main streets—were imagined, built, and experienced, focusing on the tensions between the imagined and built landscapes. Women used their experiences of these landscapes to negotiate the discrepancies between how shopping was imagined and the spaces in which it took place. These experiences, however, were radically different for women of different class positions, as were their relationships to the imagined and built landscapes. In part, these three different landscapes each served a different class of women. Equally important, women of different class positions also had divergent experiences of many of the same landscapes, particularly the downtown shopping landscape. The private control over spaces of shopping meant that only upper-class women could experience them as if they were fully public. Ultimately, these varied experiences helped to construct and reinforce class differences that fostered different relationships between each class of women and the city.

The Department Store and the Downtown Shopping Landscape

In the turn-of-the-century city the department store emerged as a major venue for the newly feminized activity of shopping. A particularly modern space, the department store was a central agent of change, helping to create modern consumer culture and its focus on spectacle, as well as functioning as a location for the rationalization of selling as an industry.[2] More important, the department store focused on women as consumers, making women an important new presence in the city.[3] Through its use of display windows, it also helped to create the possibility of a female flaneur. The flaneur, seen by many theorists as the quintessential modern urban figure, roamed the city, observing people and activities and deriving pleasure from the crowd, without being noticed.[4] While acting the role of the flaneur has been understood as a male prerogative, recent scholars have argued that women were able to become female flaneurs by walking the city alone, observing, in the role of a shopper.[5] As we have seen in chapter 1, women's presence as window shoppers helped to change the norms of sidewalk etiquette, allowing them to stop politely on the streets and to be seen looking, both activities that mid-nineteenth-century etiquette guides deplored. Department stores, then, helped to make a form of flanerie possible for women and are deeply implicated in the gendered use of the public space of the street.

Imagining the Downtown Shopping Landscape

The department store functioned as an anchor for a downtown shopping landscape that was imagined by its boosters as female, white, and upper- and middle-class. The owners and managers of department stores focused on affluent shoppers who followed middle-class standards of respectability. The norms of etiquette understood these women to be potentially endangered by the mixed street outside the store, so department stores functioned like self-contained cities, offering a sanitized version of the urban environment. For example, in 1910 San Francisco's Emporium provided

> a parlor with papers, periodicals and writing materials; a children's nursery; an emergency hospital, with trained nurse in attendance; a Post Office Station; a Western Union telegraph office; a theater-ticket office; a manicuring and a hair-dressing parlor and a barber shop; public telephones; a lunch room; an information bureau; [and] always some free exhibition in the art rooms.[6]

This range of goods and services all provided under one roof theoretically made it possible for women shoppers to do all their downtown errands without ever stepping foot between one store and another.

Managers saw department store shoppers as emotional beings, easily overwhelmed by a desire for goods, stimulated both by the elaborate spectacles of commodities staged within the store itself and also by the suggestions of saleswomen. The marketing strategy of the department store was not so much to sell necessities as to sell desires. These desires were created most elaborately within the space of the department store, but the department store in turn anchored a shopping district that was also imagined by its turn-of-the-century boosters as an entirely feminine space of fantasy and consumption. Lower Kearny Street, the center of San Francisco's shopping district from the 1870s through the 1890s and a major shopping street until the 1906 earthquake, was described in a guidebook put out by the California Promotion Committee in 1903:

> Kearny Street is the highway for shopping, and hosts of fair ladies trip its stony pavements, looking with absorbed attention at window displays of silks and laces, coats and curtains, or casting glances at the latest walking exponent of fads and fashions. Some are lured by the fragrant aroma or tempting window exhibition into the sanctuary of ices and candies; others succumb to the florist, and thus money circulates by the caprice of feminine fancy.[7]

The women in this quotation are not rational shoppers, shopping for necessities, but rich women of leisure, whose shopping is motivated entirely by desire. Notably, these women are sensory creatures, attracted not only by the visual beauty of goods but more strongly through other, less rational senses, such as smell. These women's assumed emotional irrationality and love for beauty, advertisers and retailers believed, made them susceptible to wooing by commodities.[8] Goods could seduce them, and the selling techniques within department stores aimed to do precisely that. They stimulated women's desires through visual display, as well as through music, light displays, food, and other aspects of spectacle (Figure 2.1). The smell of food, perfume, and flowers, the sound of music, and the feel of sumptuous materials, which were available to the shoppers in the department stores of this time in a way that was not the case in their predecessors, seduced women

Figure 2.1. Decorated store interior. This interior display, made with more than a thousand handkerchiefs and moving electric lights, emphasizes the importance of creating a fairyland within a department store in order to transport shoppers into a sense of being within a dream. From *The Art of Decorating Show Windows and Interiors*.

through all of their senses.[9] A 1901 study of women's shoplifting argued that the dreamworld of the department store overstimulated women: "Temptation is so strong, surging desire so powerful, so impervious, so irresistible that the act is accomplished before reason has time to plead its cause."[10]

To maintain female respectability in a space in which shoppers so openly gave in to desire, department stores were imagined as entirely feminine spaces, peopled not only by female shoppers but also by female workers. Descriptions of department stores, such as the following, from 1910, made male owners, managers, buyers, and clerks invisible:

> Buying and selling, serving and being served—women. On every floor, in every aisle, at every counter, women. . . . Behind most of the counters on all the floors . . . women. At every cashier's desk, at the wrappers' desks, running back and forth with parcels and change, short-skirted women. Filling the aisles, passing and repassing, a constantly arriving and departing throng of shoppers, women. Simply a moving, seeking, hurrying mass of femininity, in the midst of which an occasional man shopper, man clerk, and man supervisor, looks lost and out of place.[11]

Although men owned and managed most stores, because of the carefully maintained femininity of the space, department stores were seen as safe and respectable places for young women to work as well as for richer women to shop. These department store workers were typically white and native born but were largely working class, without the education of clerical workers. Their class background was a problem for store managers, who wanted to create a sophisticated, refined environment for shoppers. In order to bridge the difference between the reality of their workforce and the imagined seamlessly polite, elite nature of the department store, most department stores ran the equivalent of finishing schools for saleswomen by the early twentieth century, teaching them genteel manners and introducing them to the social expectations of their middle- and upper-class clientele.[12] This was essential to their credibility as authoritative experts in their interactions with shoppers, an authority essential for increasing sales through suggestive selling.

However, the need for saleswomen to be authoritative often conflicted with the need to be deferential to middle-class shoppers, who were offended by any suggestion that they were the social equals of working-class shopgirls. Dress codes were one expression of this conflict. Elaborately dressed-up saleswomen could be read either as expressing working-class culture or as attempting to compete with shoppers. Dress codes that required dark, plain clothing imposed refined good taste and simultaneously clarified the hierarchy between shopper and saleswoman.[13] In short, department stores were imagined as spectacular upper-class spaces, peopled exclusively by women, notably affluent, respectable women for whom shopping was primarily about pleasure and the expression of desire, relatively unmediated by logic. These stores were imagined to be quite separate from the city around them, elite islands untouched by the din and grit of the major thoroughfares nearby.

The Built Landscape of Downtown Shopping

The architecture of department stores reinforced these imaginings, through spectacular interiors and inward-focused design. For example, the Emporium's impressive 1896 atrium mimicked the streets outside with its height and architectural details, while providing light and a grand space for the interior of the store (Figure 2.2), reinforcing the idea that the department store could stand in for the downtown as a whole. After the earthquake and fire, the rebuilt City of Paris department store outdid the Emporium with its finely detailed atrium, topped with a stained-glass ceiling. These atria, a feature of department stores throughout the United States and Europe, combined with displays, decorations, and often live music to create spectacular spaces meant to keep shoppers in the store and off the street.

However, while department stores were imagined as islands of consumption, in reality they were elements of a more complex landscape, for which they served as an anchor. They were surrounded by smaller stores and were experienced both within their interior space and through windows that looked from those interiors out onto the heterogeneous space of the sidewalk.[14] The specialized downtown shopping district was the home of not only department stores but also a high concentration of shops selling dry goods, clothing, household goods, stationery, furniture, and a range of luxury goods, as well as banks, hotels, and theaters. Shopping districts throughout the world were located centrally, in a place easily accessible to a large portion of the populace. Thus the built landscape of downtown shopping contradicted the imagined landscape, as it included much more varied shops—including those catering to men—and served a clientele from a wider range of class positions.

In San Francisco the downtown shopping district was located along Market Street and to its north, an area that was particularly well served by public transportation. As the city grew, the businesses that made up this shopping district followed, migrating west, from lower Montgomery Street to lower Kearny Street, beginning in the 1870s, and continuing to spread west toward Union Square.[15] After the 1906 earthquake, the downtown shopping district moved farther west, on and just to the east of Union Square (Figure 2.3), where it has remained. A number of the businesses that made up this shopping district, including the department stores the Emporium, Hale's, Pragers, and Roos Bros., were located along Market Street west of Fourth Street. The remainder of the trade was in the area between Kearny and Powell Streets and Sutter and Market Streets. Grant Avenue housed several large stores, including the White House (Figure 2.4), Davis Schonwasser

Figure 2.2. Atrium of the Emporium department store. The columns and arches defining the space of the atrium mimic the architecture of building exteriors, creating a sort of sheltered exterior space, with a restaurant and bandstand in the center, raised above the main selling floor. Courtesy of San Francisco History Center, San Francisco Public Library.

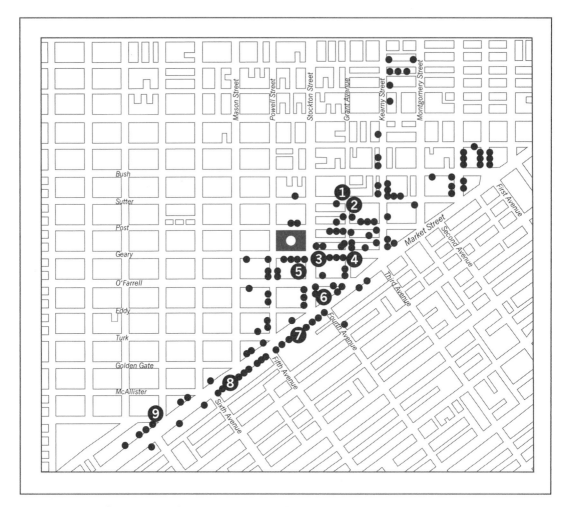

Figure 2.3. San Francisco shopping district, 1911. The downtown shopping district was mostly concentrated in a triangle bounded by Mason, Bush, and Market Streets and also extended west along Market to City Hall. The unlabeled smaller dots on this map represent the dry goods, clothing, ladies' furnishing goods, and millinery businesses listed in the 1911 *Crocker–Langley San Francisco Directory.* The large dots with numbers represent the following department stores: (1) Davis Schonwasser; (2) the White House; (3) the City of Paris; (4) I. Magnin; (5) Newman and Levinson; (6) Roos Bros.; (7) the Emporium; (8) Hale's; and (9) Pragers.

and Company, I. Magnin, and the "Tiffany's of the West," Shreve & Co. Other major dry goods and department stores included the City of Paris, just off Union Square, and the Lace House at the corner of Stockton and O'Farrell. These large stores carrying diverse merchandise were surrounded by smaller, more specialized shops.

In postearthquake San Francisco the area north of Market Street served a more upper-class clientele than the stores on Market. *Care-Free San Francisco,* a 1912 guidebook, contrasted this "heart of the shopping district" to Market Street:

Figure 2.4. The White House department store, 1909. Located on the southeast corner of Sutter and Grant, this building, with its ground-floor facade of show windows and its grand entrance on Sutter, was occupied entirely by the White House. Courtesy of The Bancroft Library, University of California, Berkeley.

> Not so many afoot here as on Market Street. The patronesses alight from gas or electric-driven cars of every expensive, exclusive style and make. Here fashion reigns, and furs are ermine and mink. Your Market Street maiden will wear white serge at Christmas if she fancies it becoming, her admirer sport his straw in March and only abandon it in November because the football season has commenced and vaguely he fancies it incongruous. Not so on Post Street or Grant Avenue. The Boston bull wears an uncomfy but swagger suit of knitted wool matched to harmonize with his mistress's toilette and the lining of her limousine.[16]

This quotation exaggerates, of course. Most shoppers did not come downtown in private cars in 1912, and the Emporium, on Market Street, was described in 1902 as "the largest, and by far the grandest, department store in the world."[17] In 1912 it was still the largest department store in San Francisco, if not in the world, and was highly praised for its services, the quality of its goods, and its excellent restaurant.[18]

Although the atmosphere on Market and that north of it were certainly distinct, these shopping areas were not mutually exclusive.

Only a small number of the buildings within the downtown were stand-alone department stores, occupying all of the stories of a building, as the White House did. Most downtown shops occupied only the ground floor of downtown buildings, and offices filled the floors above. The space of women's downtown shopping was not primarily the enclosed space of department stores but rather the space of the sidewalk, which carried them from shop to shop. Together, the show windows of department stores, large dry goods emporiums, and smaller stores created a spectacular space of window shopping along the sidewalks of the postearthquake downtown. Window shopping was important and accommodated both in the pre-earthquake downtown (Figure 2.5) and in its rebuilt form. Department store owners took advantage of the necessity of rebuilding after the earthquake and fire to create more spectacular buildings with interiors as well as show windows that would impress potential shoppers. The design of show windows acknowledged the importance of the sidewalk by making the line between the inside of the shop and the sidewalk ambiguous (Figure 2.6). Show windows were visually, and often physically, separated from the interior of the store. Books and articles on window decorating, as well as contemporary photographs of window displays, show the nearly universal use of a background to screen the window from the store, allowing the

KEARNY STREET—WEST SIDE—FROM POST TO SUTTER ST.

Figure 2.5. West side of Kearny Street between Post and Sutter Streets, 1895. Lower Kearny Street was the center of the downtown shopping district before the earthquake and fire of 1906. Note the concentration of dry goods and clothing businesses and the large number of plate-glass show windows. Several businesses on Kearny moved toward Grant Avenue and Union Square after 1906, including the White House, Roos Bros., and Newman and Levinson. From *1895 Illustrated Directory of San Francisco*, 30.

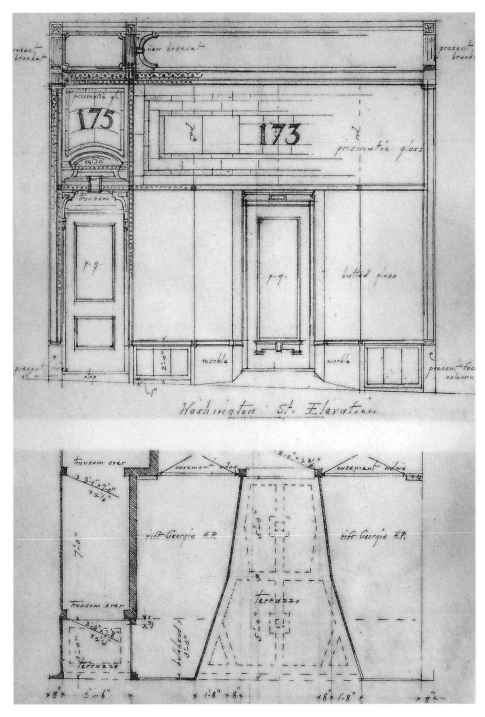

Figure 2.6. Plan and view of storefront, 1907. Entrances to early-twentieth-century stores were typically recessed, so that the door lined up with the rear of the window display space. In the bottom diagram, note the casement windows at the back of the window display space, separating that space from the interior of the shop. From Walters, "Modern Store Fronts," plate 33.

window to function as an autonomous space. In contrast to this solid background, the glass that separated the window from the sidewalk was made as invisible and immaterial as possible. In order for displays to appeal directly to potential customers and draw them into the store, the display space in the window had to appear as if it shared the sidewalk with viewers. Multiple articles and words of advice in trade journals, as well as advertisements for prefabricated shop fronts and window fixtures, emphasized the importance of windows for attracting customers. More than one advertisement showed window glass pierced by giant hands reaching out to grab customers on the sidewalk (Figure 2.7).[19]

The downtown shopping district was not only a space of shops, however. Ordinary errands also brought women downtown. Most banks were clustered in the downtown district, and Annie Haskell, who banked at the Hibernia Bank, often went down to Market Street to deposit or withdraw money. Other errands might bring women to insurance agents, brokers, or lawyers, all of whom clustered in downtown offices, including those above the shops on Market Street. Haskell mentioned going downtown several times to visit a photographer's studio. Many dentists' offices were also located downtown. Several were located along Kearny before the earthquake and fire, as well as along Market, in the Phelan Building, and throughout the downtown shopping district. Mary Pierce, although an upper-class resident of Berkeley, traveled to downtown San Francisco in 1915 and 1916 to visit a dentist on Post Street, in the heart of the shopping district, rather than patronizing an East Bay dentist.[20] Before 1900, Haskell also traveled downtown

Figure 2.7. Butler Brothers advertisement, 1911. Several advertisements, including this one for Butler Brothers, showed hands going through windows to pull customers off the street. From *The Modern Grocer*, 1911.

regularly to have her teeth examined by Dr. Lundberg and Dr. Treadwell, pioneer female dentists.[21] Restaurants, hotels, and theaters were also in and around this downtown district and were commonly visited by women in combination with shopping expeditions. Thus, the built landscape of downtown shopping was complex and mixed, with an architectural focus both on the interiors of large stores and on the shop windows as a space of display.

Experiencing the Downtown Shopping Landscape

Women's experiences of the downtown shopping landscape mediated between the imagined ideal of a purely feminine interior space of upper- and middle-class pleasurable consumption and the built reality of a street-focused district that combined large and small stores, bringing in female shoppers from a range of class positions, who shared the sidewalk with men. The extent to which a woman's experience approximated the ideal was greatly influenced by her class position, as well as by the frequency and type of her encounters with the downtown shopping landscape. As women shoppers, shop assistants, and office workers came to know the streetcar conductors, shopkeepers, and downtown workers they encountered regularly, they made the downtown into a familiar space, one in which they were known and which they knew intimately. They engaged in a process of domestication of public space that is described in *The Practice of Everyday Life* as "the progressive privatization of public space" that is the "result of everyday use."[22] In so doing, they gained both a comfort with the space and an authority to act within it, although the nature and extent of their comfort and authority were dependent on their role. Women who visited the downtown only rarely and were typically of a lower class position than those who were imagined to be its denizens did not have the same comfort and authority there as those for whom it was a familiar space.

For upper- and upper-middle-class women, the downtown shopping district was the most commonly experienced shopping landscape. Even Berkeley resident Mary Pierce visited downtown San Francisco much more often than downtown Oakland for her shopping and never mentioned shopping anywhere other than these two downtowns. Downtown functioned as a main street for rich women, and they commonly visited its restaurants and theaters, used its hotels and restaurants for club meetings and socials, and rested and wrote letters in downtown hotel parlors. Upper-class women felt comfortable downtown. Part of this comfort was created by the ability to pay full price for items without concern. Unlike Annie Haskell, both Ella Lees Leigh and Mary Pierce never mentioned the high cost of items, looking for bargains, or attending sales.

For upper-class women, the downtown landscape was a place in which women were served at their leisure, as they were by servants in their homes. A 1904 etiquette

book, giving advice to women shoppers, makes explicit the parallel between servants in the home and workers in downtown shops: "Domestics appreciate the
people who always remember their names, who take pains to inquire for them,
and who treat them as human beings. This is equally true of saleswomen."[23] Upper-
class women's domestication of the downtown was also evident in the range of
services of which they took advantage. Shopping trips taken by Ella Lees Leigh
and Mary Pierce often included time spent in the parlors of the Palace Hotel writing letters, in hotel and downtown restaurants eating meals, and visiting theaters.
In comparison, Annie Haskell very rarely ate downtown, and her shopping trips
were seldom combined with pleasure, although when they were, she visited nickelodeons rather than major theaters. Upper-class women also visited the downtown more often than middle- and working-class women, for whom downtown
shopping trips supplemented more regular trips to grocery stores and local and
district main streets. In contrast, the downtown shopping district was sometimes
the only shopping landscape experienced by upper-class women. In her 1903 diary,
for example, Ella Lees Leigh never once mentioned shopping anywhere but downtown. Elite women did not visit the nearest local main street but instead visited
the downtown shopping district for all their shopping needs. Thus, the downtown
shopping district was more familiar to richer women. Indeed, all of the services
and spaces of the downtown shopping district and the associated hotel and theater district were readily available to upper-class women because of their ability to
pay. The downtown was a space that provided not only goods but also the equivalent of a parlor and dining room at their convenience, staffed by salespeople and
waiters who knew them, much as their servants at home did.

For upper-class women the boundaries of the shopping district in the postearthquake city were different from those for middle-class and working-class women.
Mary Pierce's experience of the downtown closely matches this 1912 definition:

> The heart of the shopping district proper, where prices are not so much a matter of
> consideration, lies north of Market Street in a district bounded by Powell and Kearny
> streets, Sutter and Market. There are stores not bettered by any in the New World, few
> in the Old. All the heart feminine, or masculine, can desire of raiment or decoration, of
> furnishings for self or home, is centered here, imported from afar or near, the choice of
> the world's choicest.[24]

Pierce's shopping trips were focused on the area north of Market, especially along
Sutter, Grant, Post, and Stockton (Figure 2.8). She regularly visited Gump's,
Sloan's, the City of Paris, and the White House and never mentioned visiting
any Market Street stores except the Emporium, which she visited once for lunch.
By remaining purely within this elite district, upper-class women diminished
their contact with shoppers and spaces that contradicted the ideal of refined, elite

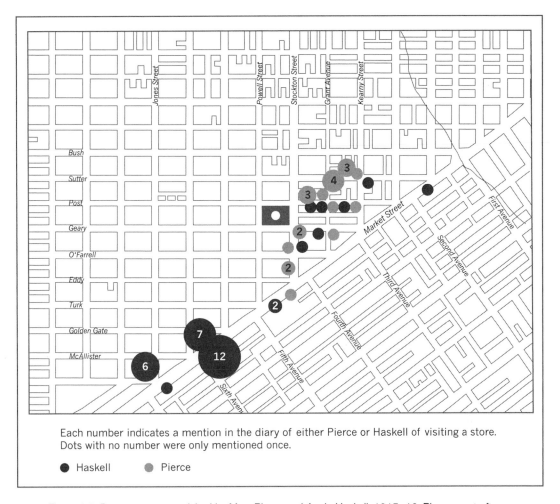

Each number indicates a mention in the diary of either Pierce or Haskell of visiting a store.
Dots with no number were only mentioned once.

● Haskell   ● Pierce

Figure 2.8. Downtown stores visited by Mary Pierce and Annie Haskell, 1915–16. Pierce most often shopped at the White House, at the corner of Grant and Sutter; Sloan's, on Sutter near Kearny; and Gump's, on Post between Stockton and Grant. She never frequented the discount stores farther west on Market, and she crossed to the south side of Market only once, to visit the Emporium. Annie Haskell most often shopped at Hale's, on Market Street between Fifth and Sixth; Owl Drug, across Market Street from Hale's; and Pragers, at Jones and Market. She visited stores in the high-end area around Grant and Stockton, but much less frequently.

downtown shopping. Those upper-class women who were driven downtown in cars or carriages were further able to insulate themselves from the messier aspects of the built landscape.

The downtown landscape experienced by middle- and lower-middle-class women was not identical with that of upper-class women, although they overlapped. Annie Haskell's trips downtown after the earthquake were usually centered on the western part of the district, along Market Street (see Figure 2.8). She particularly frequented the department stores Pragers, at the corner of Jones and Market

(Figure 2.9), and Hale's, on Market between Fifth and Sixth, and the Owl Drug Co., which had several branches on Market, although she most likely visited the branch immediately adjacent to Hale's. However, her experience of the downtown was not confined to this area. She also made forays into the more upper-class shopping area, visiting shops on Post, Kearny, O'Farrell, and Stockton Streets. Both she and the upper-class Mary Pierce mention visiting the Emporium department store and the Sherman, Clay & Co. music store.

While upper-class and upper-middle-class women treated saleswomen as the equivalent of their servants, for middle-class and lower-middle-class women the salespeople were closer to their equals. For example, Annie Haskell's son, Roth, was a clerk at Pragers, and Ruth Hutchinson, a young woman from Haskell's hometown who lived with Haskell in 1910 and 1911, worked at I. Magnin in the 1910s.[25] Ruth was a typical department-store employee, a young American-born white woman from a rural area who came to the city to work. Like many new city

The Store of Staple Merchandise at Popular Prices

Figure 2.9. Pragers, a discount department store, was located at the corner of Market and Jones Streets, at Market, far west of the high-end stores centered around Union Square and Grant Avenue. From *San Francisco Bulletin*, August 21, 1911, 16.

dwellers, she began by living with family friends and eventually moved into a flat that she shared with two other young women who worked with her at I. Magnin. Because department stores had to project refinement, their managers carefully chose employees who could appear middle-class and who spoke good English without an accent.[26] These employees could easily be the sisters, children, or cousins of middle-class shoppers.

Not only was the attitude of shoppers toward salespeople different for upper-class and other women, but so was the attitude of salespeople toward shoppers. Because their dress and style marked them as rich, upper-class women were relatively sure of being treated well by sales staff. This was not always the case for other women, as was attested to by the following advice on manners to saleswomen:

> A saleswoman must show good manners in waiting on her customers. She must not discriminate between customers on account of their dress. She must be as polite to the woman who spends five cents as to her who spends five dollars.
>
> To snub a customer or to show crossness or irritability to a customer who does not buy, and to exchange covert glances of amusement with fellow-clerks if a customer is at all eccentric, are all breaches of etiquette that are inexcusable.[27]

Except when the saleswomen were paragons of politeness, having less money to spend meant getting less service, regardless of this advice. For middle-class American-born women, less service was probably the only discomfort, while poorer and foreign-born women were more likely to be the victims of the mocking sales staff described above. Presumably, many of the forms of eccentricity that rude salespeople mocked were markers of ethnicity, such as accents, an imperfect command of English, and ethnically marked clothing styles. Being mocked or looked down on by sales staff made the downtown shopping landscape a potentially uncomfortable one, especially for immigrant women.

However, working-class and immigrant women were not entirely unwelcome as shoppers downtown. American department stores were founded on the democratic practice of serving a range of women, not just the rich, such that an 1854 etiquette book advised richer women, "Testify no impatience if a servant girl, making a sixpenny purchase, is served before you—which she certainly will be, if her entrance has preceded yours."[28] In San Francisco, the likelihood of finding a servant girl making a purchase varied from store to store. Although the fancier parts of the shopping district north of Market catered strictly to the upper end of the class spectrum, the Emporium and Hale's did occasionally advertise in foreign-language papers, such as *La Voce del Popolo*, *L'Italia*, *Bien* (a Danish paper), and the *California Demokrat*. The last, a German paper, also carried advertisements for the White House, D. Samuel's Lace House, and other fancier stores, many of which were owned and run by German speakers. However, although the Emporium advertised daily in the major English-language papers, it did advertise much more rarely in foreign-language papers, typically for sales (Figure 2.10).

One way that the Emporium managed to serve both the upper-class shoppers of San Francisco and bargain-hunting and immigrant shoppers was by opening a "basement sales room" in 1911, which it referred to as a separate store, stating, "The reason for this new store is that The Emporium desires to serve *all* the people of *San Francisco* and therefore opens a store where the less expensive lines of merchandise will be sold at prices the lowest in San Francisco, in assortments the best."[29] Other discount downtown stores also welcomed working-class shoppers. These stores included Pragers on Market Street, a "popular price store" whose advertised purpose was to "supply the needs of that great body of people who must buy carefully and economically," and the Owl Drug Co., "cut rate druggists," with four downtown branches, one at Sixteenth and Mission, and one on Fillmore

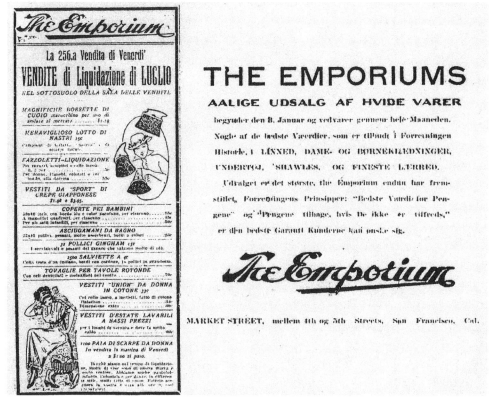

Figure 2.10. Advertisements for the Emporium from *La Voce del Popolo* and *Bien*. Advertisements in San Francisco's foreign-language papers demonstrate that the Emporium marketed itself to immigrant women. These foreign-language advertisements ran more rarely than English advertisements in the three major papers and were more likely to relate to sales, such as the liquidation sale in the Italian advertisement. From *La Voce del Popolo*, July 7, 1916, 2; and *Bien*, January 7, 1910, 4.

Street (Figure 2.11).[30] Pragers also actively courted immigrant shoppers, as evidenced by its advertisements in foreign-language newspapers (Figure 2.12).

Both middle-class and working-class women often went downtown in response to advertised sales, in contrast with upper-class women. Annie Haskell often writes of "rushing off down town" and "doing the early bird act" to make it to advertised downtown sales when the stores first opened.[31] Going to sales was a more frustrating and hectic experience than ordinary shopping. Haskell wrote in annoyance of one outing: "Went out with Helen over to Livingston's to a sale. There was a crowd and the doors were locked. We waited until another installment were let in, and being excluded left in disgust and went down town."[32] Another unsuccessful trip to a sale combined unpleasant crowds and a rude salesperson:

> I went down town to see some wonderful bargains at the Emporium, and my experience there goes a long way to help me get cured of trying to get something for nothing. I got among a bunch of clawing women, with a pair of 48 ct shoes in my hand. I waited till a clerk came to ask about them, when he took them saying it was a pair he just laid down. I told him it was a funny way to do business and left. After this when I want anything I am going to get it and pay for it. I am sick of junk and junk methods.[33]

Even when the crush of "poor, miserable, pushing, struggling women" was not overwhelming, the goods were often disappointing, making the trip a waste of time and carfare.[34] Of one frustrating trip, Haskell wrote, "I walked down to Hale's to look at some advertised hats which I wouldn't wear to a dog fight."[35] After another fruitless trip, she complained, "I got soaking wet for nothing."[36]

Figure 2.11. This stylized image of the Owl Drug Co. as the "civic center" of the drug business expresses its dominance of the business, cemented by its four downtown branches (778 Market, in the Phelan Building; 976 Market, opposite Hale's department store; 710 Market, opposite the Call Building; and Post and Grant) as well as its branches on the two major district shopping streets, at Sixteenth and Mission and at Fillmore and Geary. From *San Francisco Bulletin*, August 10, 1911, 4.

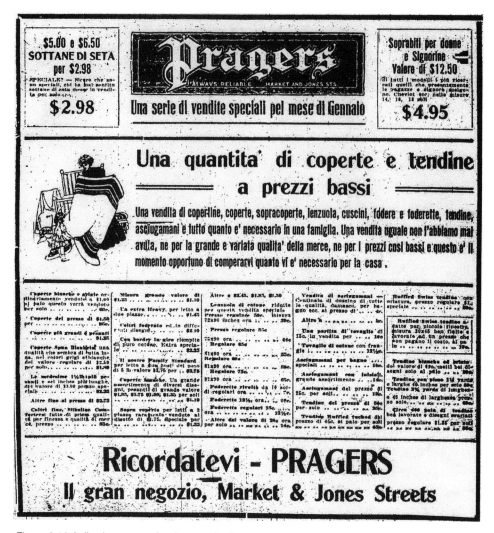

Figure 2.12. Italian-language advertisement for Pragers. This "popular price store" advertised to immigrants in foreign-language papers. From *L'Italia*, 1911.

Bargain hunting, a necessary task for a woman with a limited income, also made for exhausting shopping trips. Annie Haskell often described shopping as a process of "hunting," a term that implies hard work, in contrast to "browsing," "looking," or even merely "shopping."[37] The need to find good prices added anxiety to the shopping process, and finding goods later at a better price could cause frustration and anger. Haskell complained, "I saw a suit exactly like mine in the same place for $12.50, so that I am five dollars sore, in such a short time, a reduction like that is absurd."[38] Buying goods on sale could also cause anxiety when shoppers bought things that were not strictly necessary because of the good price. Often, Haskell had to rationalize her purchases to herself. After spending five dollars on hair tonic at Owl Drug downtown, she wrote, "A fearful extravagance, but as I could get six bottles for five dollars, and also use a $1.00 coupon that I had why, I indulged in the expenditure."[39]

The other problem with buying goods at bargain prices was that they were not always satisfactory. On sale, Annie Haskell bought neckware that was "too nice to be worn every day," a "lovely well made suit, but a little out of style," a good dress that did not quite fit, a corduroy suit that was not what she wanted, and a dress at Pragers about which she wrote, "I thought I could manage with, goblin blue and I can just barely stand it."[40] Purchases such as these combined the thrill of finding a bargain with the disappointment of wearing ill-fitting and ill-suited clothing. A further frustration for women of limited means was, of course, not being able to afford the goods they wanted or needed or having to pay more than they could really afford in order to get necessary items. Haskell often worried about spending more than she felt comfortable with.[41] She also complained about not being able to afford items she desired. On June 2, 1909, after looking at an electrophone for her mostly deaf best friend, who could not manage the cost of thirty-five dollars, she also "looked through some binocular glasses," writing, "They are wonderful. I could never see at a distance before. They were forty-five and I must go without."[42]

The spectacular aspects of the downtown shopping district, while focused primarily on seducing elite shoppers, could also make downtown stores function as a source of amusement accessible to a range of women. The Emporium regularly presented free concerts on Tuesday, Thursday, and Saturday nights and was "only open for business on Saturday nights, but . . . thrown open Tuesday and Thursday nights for promenade only." This music was presented in the main rotunda, which was lit with over ten thousand lights at night to add to its already spectacular appearance, making it "a veritable fairy palace."[43] The Emporium was a particular spectacle when it first opened in 1896 and was visited by a wide range of women and men. Annie Haskell went to see it with her best friend, Rose, a dressmaker. She wrote in her diary:

> We went over to the Emporium and saw it and heard the music and had some ice cream. It is beautifully decorated and lighted with electric lights. There was an immense crowd of people there. I don't know how it will turn out as a financial venture, it is run on a new plan for San Francisco—a great department store—with everything in it imaginable.[44]

Entertainment was also available in music stores, such as Sherman, Clay & Co., which Haskell visited with her sister just to hear free concerts.[45] These interior amusements were probably mostly available to upper- and middle-class women, who looked more like potential shoppers, rather than to working-class and immigrant women.

In contrast, store windows provided a diversion open to all. Because the space on the streets was fully public, not policed by saleswomen and floorwalkers, it was more open to women, and men, from a range of classes. The 1912 guide *Care-Free San Francisco* described a wide variety of people of "a dozen tongues, a dozen grades of color . . . upper, lower, and half world" who partook of the pleasure of window shopping.[46] An evening's or afternoon's entertainment for Annie Haskell and her friends could easily include "gadding up and down looking in the windows."[47] The "fine new stores" of the postearthquake downtown were also objects Haskell went to see independently of the activity of shopping.[48] For working women, the streets of the downtown at night, after working hours and after the shops were closed, provided free entertainment without the presence of upper-class women, who might disdain them.

In negotiating the discrepancies between how the downtown shopping landscape was imagined and how it was built, women's experiences led them in contrasting ways. For upper-class women, their experiences allowed them to paper over many of the contradictions between the reality of a mixed downtown and the fantasy of an all-female, elite space of spectacular consumption. While rich women inevitably did experience some of the mixture inherent to the downtown, by concentrating their visits in the most exclusive shopping area, often avoiding public transportation, and spending freely so that they were treated with respect in shops, restaurants, and theaters, they were able to minimize experiences that would interrupt the ideal of a comfortable, elite, feminine downtown. For middle-class women, achieving the imagined ideal was much more difficult. Because they had some ability to pay and to dress appropriately, they were able to enjoy many of the benefits of the services provided by department stores, making use of their parlors to write letters, for example, and attending free concerts. These moments of leisure and pleasure, however, were interrupted by the reality of shopping for bargains, both in the big department stores, which were less accommodating to sale shoppers, and in discount stores, which focused more on prices and less on creating a spectacular dreamworld. In addition, taking public transportation and walking among shops exposed middle-class women to the mixture of the streets, contradicting the imagined nature of the downtown shopping district as feminine and upper-middle-class. For working-class women, this fantasy was even less accessible. Depending on their ability to pass as a department store shopper, they might experience only the basement of the department store, where they could not see the elaborately decorated light-filled atrium, hear the live music, or smell the treats in the tearoom. For many working-class women, the spectacle of downtown shopping was something to be experienced only vicariously, through the show windows that spoke to the mixed, public streets.

Shopping on Local and District Main Streets

On the shopping spectrum's next scale down from the downtown district were several district and local main streets. Each of these main streets, typically a transportation spine, served its neighborhood with a wide range of goods and services. Lawyers, dentists, barbers, and other professionals; restaurants and theaters; services such as laundries and shoe repair shops; and shops selling a variety of food stuffs (including butchers, bakers, confectioners, and some grocers), dry goods (clothing, trimmings, fabric, shoes, hats), furniture, drugs, cigars, and other goods were located on district and local main streets.

Imagining the Local Main Street

The local main street functioned as the imagined heart of a neighborhood. Not only did it provide most of the necessities of life, but also its shops reflected the character of the population surrounding it, providing ethnic foods, for example. A sense of community was also formed in the lodge halls, many associated with ethnic societies, that often graced district and local main streets. Churches and synagogues serving the neighborhood were also typically located within a block of a main street. Although such neighborhoods were part of the larger city of San Francisco, they also functioned in some ways like smaller towns, with the main street serving much as a small-town main street does. The centrality of the main street to the neighborhood is noticeable in the tendency to name neighborhoods after the main street, such as the Castro and the Haight. The idea that each neighborhood functioned as a self-contained entity, with the main street at its heart, is expressed in Charles Caldwell Dobie's 1933 description of the Mission District:

> It is, perhaps, the most self-contained of any of the village centers that make up the city and county of San Francisco. Mission Street, its main thoroughfare, is crowded with shops, fraternal halls, movie palaces, and undertaking parlors. Indicating that people may live and die within its borders without reference to the rest of the town. The majority of its citizens find everything needful without straying from its confines and there are those who boast that they rarely set foot on other soil.[49]

Notably, Dobie refers to residents of the Mission District as its "citizens," implying a political independence from the city as well as a functional one.

For the most part the shops on district and local main streets, usually smaller than those downtown, sold everyday goods rather than the big-ticket or high-style items that would require a trip downtown. Equally important, the clientele of main street shops typically was much more local, so shoppers and shopkeepers were more likely to know one another and to share traits, such as class position and ethnicity. This means that the relationships between shoppers and those working in shops had a certain intimacy, attested to by the Castro Street hardware man's once giving Annie Haskell a nickel for carfare so that she could go to a friend's funeral.[50] While downtown shoppers were imagined to be upper- and middle-class women, shopping for pleasure, those on local main streets were less elite, and this colored the kinds of shopping they might have done. Although local main streets certainly sold items that were not necessities and also used elements of spectacle in whimsical window displays, shopkeepers selling to main-street shoppers understood that their desires were reigned in by practicalities.

The Built Landscape of Local and District Main Streets

There were several different scales of urban main streets. The largest, district main streets nearly duplicated the goods and services available downtown, although with fewer high-class and specialty items and a narrower range of merchandise. Mission was the major district main street in turn-of-the-century San Francisco (see Figure I.10). Mission was occasionally visited by people outside the immediate neighborhood, especially in the years directly following the earthquake, when the downtown was destroyed and Mission and Fillmore served temporarily to replace it. For two years after the 1906 earthquake, Mission and Fillmore shared the celebration of New Year's Eve, traditionally held on Market Street, and in 1909 they shared the celebration with Market.[51] Before the earthquake, Fillmore Street "was a thread of notion shops and small retail meat markets and fly-specked grocery stores. Suddenly, with the centers of town shifted, it changed overnight into a shopping district which swarmed and bustled even if it did not bear the mark of exclusiveness."[52] In contrast, Mission Street was a major shopping street even before the earthquake and fire. It served as the core and transportation spine of the Mission District, a neighborhood of working-class and middle-class families, both native-born and immigrant (particularly Irish and Hispanic, but also Swedish, Italian, and other nationalities). Although it boasted no major department stores, Mission Street did have large dry goods and notion shops, such as Lippman Bros., as well as numerous smaller shops. Postearthquake Mission Street was also like the downtown because it was an entertainment district, with one major theater, the Wigwam, and several nickelodeons.[53] In addition, in 1911 the only three banks outside the downtown business district were all located in the Mission District along Sixteenth Street on or near Mission Street.[54] Mission could and did serve as a smaller-scale version of the downtown for many San Franciscans.

Local main streets, smaller and more numerous than district main streets, were Castro Street, Twenty-fourth Street both west of Mission and in Noe Valley, Montgomery (now Columbus) Avenue, Broadway, and Sixteenth, Polk, and Haight

Streets, among others. They provided a smaller range of goods and services. Some local main streets primarily served a single ethnic community; for example, Montgomery served Italians, and Castro and upper Market served northern European immigrants, especially Scandinavian and German skilled workers. Because these streets principally served an immediate neighborhood, they reflected that neighborhood's makeup. Shops were run in a variety of languages and sold ethnic foods and other goods that reflected the local clientele. For this reason, a local main street would have been the most comfortable space for immigrant women who did not speak English well and would have had difficulty negotiating English-only establishments.

The building types that made up district and local main streets were mixed and shared elements with both the types of buildings found downtown and grocery store buildings, being intermediate between the scales of those two. District main streets were lined with buildings that housed mostly shops or restaurants on the first floor and a variety of establishments above (Figure 2.13). Unlike the tall buildings of the downtown, these buildings were rarely over four stories high

Figure 2.13. Mission Street, 1930s. This photograph shows the primacy of commercial activity on a district main street in comparison with local main streets. Courtesy of San Francisco History Center, San Francisco Public Library.

and were more typically two or three stories. In some buildings the upper stories housed offices, but upstairs space was also used for dance, meeting, and lodge halls; hotels and rooming houses; small-scale manufacturing; and sometimes flats. On the ground floor, district main streets such as Mission were lined entirely by businesses, including theaters, pool halls, saloons, and a wide range of shops (Figure 2.14). Although the upper stories sometimes housed residences, the sidewalks of Mission Street were solidly lined with commercial establishments from Sixteenth Street to Twenty-fourth Street. On the smaller, local main streets, buildings typically combined shops downstairs with flats above, essentially duplicating the grocery store building type along an entire block (Figure 2.15). Buildings here were two or three stories. On district main streets, shops created a nearly continuous facade along the sidewalk, whereas on local main streets shops were often interspersed with dwellings (Figure 2.16). On local main streets, the dwellings upstairs often had a stronger presence than the shop tucked underneath, whereas on district main streets, the shop commanded the sidewalk.

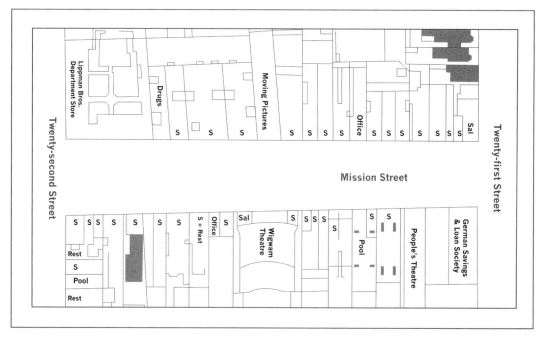

Figure 2.14. Mission Street between Twenty-first and Twenty-second Streets. Residences are shaded gray; no residences were directly on Mission Street on this block or on the block to the east, although a few flats were fitted behind businesses, and the back of each block was largely residential. The businesses on Mission included a large number of shops (marked with S), saloons (Sal), pool halls (Pool), restaurants (Rest), a small department store (Lippman Bros., on Mission and Twenty-second), a large theater (the the Wigwam), and smaller motion picture theaters. Based on 1914 Sanborn Fire Insurance Map.

Figure 2.15. Castro Street, c. 1900–1910. On this local main street, shops were mixed with residences, both at the ground floor (as at near right) and in many buildings with shops below and flats above. Courtesy of San Francisco History Center, San Francisco Public Library.

As they did with the downtown, errands besides shopping brought women into the area of local main streets. Trips to the dentist often brought patients to major main streets such as Mission as well as downtown. After 1900, Annie Haskell, who had a great deal of trouble with her teeth, regularly visited dentists on Mission, Sixteenth, and Castro.[55] She was also a faithful patron of the Mission branch library, which was located on Mission Street before the fire and on Sixteenth near Mission afterward. These and the establishments of other service providers, such as lawyers, hairdressers, and the Christian Science practitioners that Haskell consulted, clustered on or near local main streets, making it easy for service-related errands to be combined with shopping trips and making services convenient to public transportation.[56] Local main streets thus often functioned as a version of the downtown in miniature, with shops, services, restaurants, and theaters, but served a more local and less elite clientele.

Experiencing Local Main Streets

Local main streets were the main shopping locale for working-class and immigrant women, because the shops on these streets were more likely to carry less

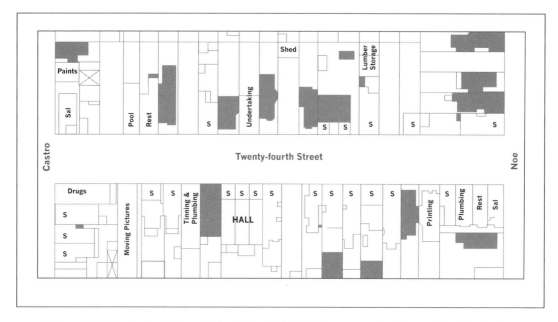

Figure 2.16. Twenty-fourth Street in Noe Valley, 1914. Residences are shaded gray along this local main street for the Noe Valley neighborhood. This street contained a mixture of residences, shops (marked with S), and other commercial activities, such as moving picture theaters, restaurants (Rest), saloons (Sal), pool halls (Pool), meeting halls (HALL), and an undertaker's parlor. This block held the highest concentration of businesses in this neighborhood, although the north side of the street was still about one-third residential. Based on 1914 Sanborn Fire Insurance Map.

expensive goods. For immigrant women, shops on a local main street might have clerks who spoke their languages, as well as familiar goods from their home countries. For example, in *Bring Along Laughter*, Milla Zenovich Logan's memoir of growing up Serbian in San Francisco, Logan's grandmother conducted her errands on Polk Street and in North Beach in Serbian, for the only English she knew was "Pliss-Kondoktor-stop-ona-nex-corneesh."[57] Local main streets also served poorer women, who were not welcome in most downtown stores because they clearly could not afford to shop there. The local main street was central to the lives of working-class and immigrant women both for practical purposes and as a center of social life, where women could gossip in line at the butcher's and observe the behavior of their neighbors and where teenage girls like Milla Logan and her friends could dress up and "go strolling."[58] Both *Bring Along Laughter* and *Mama's Bank Account*, Kathryn Forbes's (née Anderson) tale of growing up Swedish in San Francisco, illustrate the centrality of the local main street to immigrant life in San Francisco, Polk Street for the Serbian Logan and Mission Street for the Swedish Forbes. Neither author mentions going to downtown shops, but both describe the shops and street life of their local main street.[59] Thus, for these immigrant women, the local main street functioned as it was imagined to, as the center of an enclosed neighborhood, quite separate from the larger city of San Francisco.

In contrast, the more middle-class, native-born Annie Haskell shopped downtown as much as on local main streets. She moved to Army Street in 1890, and after leaving her husband in 1897, she stayed with her sister Helen on Sixteenth Street, in Berkeley, and at 3679 Twenty-first Street and, after her son, Roth, was married, also with him at 5702 Mission Street and then at 4419 Twenty-third Street. Therefore, her primary local main street after 1897 was Mission Street and its tributaries, Sixteenth, Eighteenth, Twenty-fourth, and Valencia Streets. More rarely, she also visited Castro, Noe, and, in the years immediately after the earthquake, Fillmore. The smaller local main streets (all those except for Mission, Sixteenth, and Fillmore) she visited primarily for items such as meat and groceries.[60] On Sixteenth, she bought foodstuffs and visited a jeweler, a milliner, and a shoe store, where she bought shoes for Roth when he was young.[61] In comparison, both Mission Street and the postearthquake Fillmore Street functioned more like the downtown shopping district. Haskell even wrote once of walking on Mission just to gaze into the store windows.[62] Compared with the expeditions taken downtown, trips to Mission Street, which was nearer her home and had services such as grocery stores and a public library, were often brief and combined multiple tasks. Mission Street was also a convenient location to pick up a few staples on the way into or out of the neighborhood. But local and district main streets could not provide all the goods and services necessary for the lives of middle-class shoppers. So, for women like Haskell, they functioned as a space of movement between the neighborhood and the downtown or other parts of the larger city, in addition to functioning as the center of a neighborhood.

Local main streets were imagined to allow a neighborhood to function like a self-enclosed town. Furthermore, they expressed the nature of that neighborhood, particularly its ethnic makeup, but also its class position, typically working and lower middle class. The experience of working-class and immigrant women often supported this imagining, as they typically did most of their shopping within their neighborhoods and when possible patronized stores run in their native languages. However, the complexity of the ethnic makeup of some neighborhoods was also evident in the shops next door to those they most often patronized, in the Italian shops near the Serbian ones and in the Mexican and German stores near the Swedish shops. Upper-class women's lack of engagement with local main streets also reinforced their dominant image. For upper-class women San Francisco was their neighborhood, as far as shopping was concerned. Middle-class women's experiences of local and district main streets, in contrast, interrupt the idea that local main streets are purely part of self-sufficient neighborhoods and connect the local main streets to the downtown and the city as a whole. For middle-class women, local main streets were part of their daily life, experienced every time they took public transportation out of the neighborhood, as well as when visited to get ordinary necessities and to do basic errands. But the everyday goods and services of the local main street, while useful, were not sufficient. For these women the local main street was not the center of their lives but just one element of it.

The Everyday Landscape of Grocery Stores

At the most local and small-scale end of the shopping spectrum, grocery stores were imagined as a familiar, almost domestic space, in which neighborly men and, increasingly, women served local working- and lower-middle-class women. Before the invention of refrigeration, perishable foodstuffs such as vegetables, dairy products, and meat needed to be purchased fresh on a daily basis when they were not produced at home. Although many households had small gardens or kept a few animals, the space available in the backyards of city lots was far from sufficient for producing enough to sustain a family. The necessity of daily shopping meant that the relationships forged between a grocer and his shoppers were potentially very familiar. As groceries were ubiquitous within most neighborhoods, to compete, a good grocer had to make the woman shopper feel comfortable in his store. The grocer acted as an adviser, helping the shopper make good choices and providing her with recipes for new or seasonal products. Unlike department store purchases, grocery purchases were understood by grocers as motivated by logic, so rather than seduce the shopper through spectacle, the grocer needed to convince her that his goods were of a high quality and priced fairly and would fit into her everyday life. The grocer also needed to be clean and trustworthy, because he chose and handled most of the food for the shopper. Whereas in department stores shoppers could touch most of the merchandise themselves, in grocery stores the grocer or a clerk would typically fetch, weigh, and package items requested by a shopper. This did shift somewhat with the expansion of sales of prepackaged brand-name goods, which did not need specialized weighing and packaging and which advertised themselves through their packaging, but until the 1920s self-service grocery stores were not common in San Francisco.[63]

In keeping with the domesticity and local focus of grocery stores, women increasingly became involved in running them around the turn of the century. As early as 1890, eighty-seven of the grocers in San Francisco, or about 7 percent, were women. This number grew steadily, until by 1911, 149 of San Francisco grocery stores, or about 12 percent of total stores, were listed in city directories under women's names. In addition to the women-run grocery stores, a great many stores were run by women and men together or by women in their husbands' names.

Because groceries were often family businesses, women were active in them. Running a grocery store was also a common occupation for widows, who made up 40 percent of the female grocers in the city in 1911, and for other independent women (29 percent of female grocers in 1911).[64] Beginning in about 1908, several articles in San Francisco's grocery journal, the *Retail Grocers' Advocate,* refer to female grocers. Women were discussed as clerks; as grocers' wives, who both worked in stores and managed them; and as grocers themselves; notably one 1908 article stated that women ran one-third of the grocery stores in Los Angeles.[65] The articles in the *Retail Grocers' Advocate* conceded that women were "very pleasant and ever willing and ready to wait on a customer."[66] In some cases, they even suggested that a woman's gender offered her advantages in her job performance: "A . . . young lady . . . can explain the different processes of cooking different articles better than some men. She can dress a silent salesman or a showcase neater and keep the store more clean and tidy and can also put new ideas into the boys' heads about window dressing. She also adds a cheerfulness to a store that no one man can."[67]

However, this embrace of women as grocery workers was limited. One article argued, "One of them is plenty, generally, as where two or three are gathered together there is too much talking and laughing among themselves."[68] Women who ran a grocery store were even more problematic, according to George Place, who argued in 1908 that women were insufficiently businesslike: "They are unprogressive and seldom ever expand or improve conditions around them to facilitate in doing business. They know nothing about the manufacture of goods. . . . When it comes to competition they seem to lack energetic efforts. . . . They are poor promoters unless through the advice and foresight of some man."[69] This resistance to women shopkeepers may also have been a cause for the founding of the all-male secret society of grocers, the Gobblers, in the first decade of the twentieth century, as women grocers became more numerous.

This resistance to women grocers points to a conflict in how grocery stores were imagined. In the journals, grocery stores were professional spaces, with science and order on their side, and their appeal was to shoppers drawn by quality and value, not by personal ties with the grocer. The grocer in the journals was male and professionalized, not female and domestic. The journal-promoted ideal of the grocery store as a progressive, businesslike, scientifically organized, middle-class space conflicts with the domesticity and familiarity of the grocery store that prevailed in popular imagination.

The number of women running grocery stores points to the domesticated status of this business, a status that created a wedge for women to participate in a commercial public space not only as consumers or even employees but also as bosses. Grocery stores were associated with home and family and, thus, were comparatively acceptable for women to run. Middle-class reformers might not have considered running a grocery store a respectable trade because of the historical link between groceries and the sale of liquor, but the women who ran them were largely working-class, and running a grocery store made it possible to make money while staying near home. For women grocers, the store was particularly likely to be a domestic business; fully 90 percent of them lived at the same address as their store, compared with 58 percent of grocers overall.[70] Even for stores run by men who did not live above or behind the store, their location in an otherwise residential neighborhood, typically on the first floor of a building with apartments above, made grocery stores the most domestic of shops.

The Built Landscape of Grocery Stores

Grocery stores were the most numerous and the most widely distributed stores in turn-of-the-century San Francisco. The 1911 *Crocker–Langley Directory of San Francisco* included approximately 1,255 grocers, 335 fruit and vegetable merchants, 250 bakeries, and 380 butchers, but many fewer typical downtown shopping establishments; only 153 dry goods retailers and 161 retail clothing shops were listed. A similar relationship between the number of grocery-related stores as opposed to clothing and dry goods stores is shown in the 1890 directory, which listed only 116 dry goods establishments and about 1,200 grocers. Grocery stores were distributed broadly throughout the city rather than concentrated in particular neighborhoods or along certain streets. More specialized food businesses, such as butchers and bakers, were also spread throughout the city but tended to cluster along local main streets.

Some grocery stores were on local main streets, but the majority were located within residential areas. They were typically located on a corner lot on a block on which the other buildings were residences, whether flats or single-family houses (Figure 2.17).[71] The building type for grocery stores was typically a shop on the first floor with flats or apartments above (Figure 2.18). Often, the family running the grocery store would live in an apartment above the store, and advertisements for grocery businesses for sale often mentioned the living quarters as well as the store. Approximately 52 percent of grocers in 1890 and 58 percent in 1911 lived at the same address as their businesses.[72] Many of the remaining grocers lived within a block of their businesses and often immediately next door. This pattern of living above or near the store and of most grocery stores being independently owned small businesses remained essentially the same from the 1890s through the 1910s.

The stores themselves were similar in design to other small stores, whether on local main streets or downtown. The store space was usually a single rectangular room, filled with neatly organized rows of goods. Display windows flanked a

Figure 2.17. Block defined by Diamond, Castro, Twenty-third, and Elizabeth Streets, 1915. This block in the Noe Valley neighborhood is basically residential, with modest one- and two-bedroom houses and flats. It had two corner groceries (marked with S) in 1915. At 649 Diamond (the corner of Diamond and Elizabeth Streets), Paul and Frances Matulich ran a grocery store and lived at the same address, probably in the dwelling behind the store. F. G. Enderle ran the grocery at 601 Diamond, at the corner of Diamond and Twenty-third Streets, and lived four blocks away. Based on 1915 Sanborn Fire Insurance Map.

central doorway on the front wall or at the corner for a corner store. Evidence from trade journals for grocers suggests that display windows were seldom separated from the store with backdrops, as we've seen was typical of other store windows. Instead window space was treated simply as a continuation of the store interior, not a space of elaborate display.[73] Grocers' display areas often extended beyond the store onto the sidewalk, which was furnished with stands holding fruits and vegetables (Figure 2.19). Thus, for grocers, the store ended not at the window but on the sidewalk. This contrasted with downtown stores, which usually stayed within the boundaries of the store window and treated the window as a display space separate from the interior of the store. While department stores created a distinction between the feminine space of their interiors and the mixed space of the sidewalk, mediated by their windows, grocery stores flowed easily onto the sidewalk, for the sidewalk and the grocery store were both equally part of the domesticated space of the residential neighborhood. Just as residents might sit on their stoop, extending their domestic space onto the street, fruits and vegetables displayed in front of the store extended the shop onto the street.

Like the windows of grocery stores, which were more practical than spectacular,

Figure 2.18. Corner grocery, Twenty-third and Hoffman Streets. Like most corner groceries, this one combines a ground-floor corner shop with flats above. This was the closest grocery to Roth Haskell's home at 4419 Twenty-third Street, where Annie Haskell often stayed.

Figure 2.19. Cleland's Grocery, Des Moines, Iowa, 1913. Grocery stores in the early twentieth century typically used the sidewalk in front of the store as a display area. From *The Modern Grocer,* August 2, 1913, 8.

the interiors also reflected a conceptualization of women shoppers as rational housewives who desired the best for their families at the best price. The design of fixtures and the display of food focused on keeping goods clean and fresh and presenting them as such. Boxed and canned food was lined up on shelves or in precise pyramidal displays, fruits and vegetables were neatly arranged in bins, and sanitary closed cases showed other foodstuffs, such as dried fruits, nuts, and flour. Although goods were displayed attractively in grocery stores, the overall impression was not one of excess or spectacle, as in the department store, but rather one of order (Figure 2.20). Goods were kept clean, carefully sorted, and arranged in an orderly fashion. Cleanliness was important because it implied that the goods were pure. Order also expressed the modernity of the store, presenting it as a scientifically managed space, in which goods were organized by general category and specific type, just as biologists categorized plants and animals by genus and species. The clean and orderly store was ideal, and the sort of spectacular display that was necessary in department stores was rare in grocery stores, where honesty was prized over flash.

Figure 2.20. This grocery store display, published as a model in the *Modern Grocer,* typifies the ideal arrangement of the grocery store interior. All the goods are laid out very neatly, within cabinets, on shelves, and in decorative pyramids on the top shelves. The interior conveys the idea of abundance, but an orderly, hygienic abundance. From *The Modern Grocer,* November 25, 1911, 14.

Experiencing the Landscape of Groceries

Groceries were, of necessity, a part of every woman's life. However, the landscape of groceries and the methods by which women obtained them for their households were radically different for women according to their class status. Upper-class women for the most part did not frequent grocery stores, unlike most working-class and middle-class women, who went shopping for groceries at small local grocery stores and butcher shops on a daily basis. The diaries of the upper-class Ella Lees Leigh and Mary Eugenia Pierce never once mention groceries. For those in the upper classes, groceries were more likely to be delivered, minimizing the need to go to shops, and, should grocery stores need visiting, servants could take care of it. In *920 O'Farrell Street,* a memoir of an upper-middle-class Jewish girlhood in

San Francisco in the 1880s, Harriet Lane Levy describes the life of her kitchen and Maggie Doyle, the Irish cook:[74]

> Twice a day the tradesman or his emissary knocked at the kitchen door. In the morning he took the order, in the afternoon he delivered it. The grocer, the baker, the steam laundry-man, the fish man, the chicken man, the butcher boy, came twice a day proffering a salty bit of conversation or a flashing glance of fire.[74]

The one San Francisco grocery store likely to be visited by upper-class women was Goldberg, Bowen & Company, which, unlike other grocery stores, was not located within a residential neighborhood or on a local main street near one but was located instead within the downtown shopping landscape. Its main store was at 232 Sutter, across the street from the White House department store (Figure 2.21). It carried a wide range of luxury goods. Goldberg, Bowen & Company would deliver groceries free of charge within a fifty-mile radius, taking orders in person or by phone, and for those outside the Bay Area, it would ship groceries by parcel post and Wells Fargo.[75] Goldberg, Bowen & Company's catalog and magazine, *Master Grocer,* emphasized both the centrality of deliveries to their business and the high class of their goods and clientele: "All purchases are delivered regularly, three times a day . . . year in and year out to a refined, cultured and intellectual class of people, who appreciate good groceries and good service."[76] This was a grocery store run like a department store, a place you could browse in and buy goods that were delivered to your home. The goods in this store also marked it as the department store of grocery stores, a place where big-ticket, high-quality goods were sold, rather than ordinary goods. In many other cities, department stores included a high-end grocery department, and most cities had at least one fancy downtown grocery store similar to Goldberg, Bowen & Company.[77]

For middle-class women without servants, as for poorer women, grocery shopping was an everyday errand but one rarely written about. Even Annie Haskell's detailed diary only occasionally mentions getting groceries, although her cash accounts, for those years when she kept them, show that she regularly bought groceries.[78] For example, her cash account for 1916 implies that she bought groceries thirty-one times between May 23 and September 3. However, only six of these trips register in her diary, and only twice did she explicitly mention buying groceries. The other entries only mention "packing a load of eatables" to her sister Kate.[79] Generally, buying groceries is so ordinary that it merits at most an aside such as "got lots of stuff for dinner" or "loaded ourselves up with fruits and vegetables."[80] Shopping for groceries barely registered as a shopping activity, and Haskell primarily mentioned groceries only in the context of doing "the burro act," "struggling up the hill" to carry them home.[81] A typical entry reads, "I had to get some things to eat so I went down, walked down to Mr. H. and got the things

Figure 2.21. Goldberg, Bowen & Company was a high-end downtown grocery store, with its main store located on Sutter Street across from the White House department store. This building, which is decorated with terra cotta details of fruits and vegetables, was built for the company in 1909 and was occupied exclusively by the company. From Goldberg, Bowen & Company 1925 catalog, 3. Courtesy of The Bancroft Library, University of California, Berkeley.

coming back. Nearly killed myself carrying them up this awful hill."[82] Often, Haskell combined buying groceries with running other errands. A trip to the library or to pick something up on Mission Street often ended with picking up some "eatables" and lugging them up the hill, with help whenever she could persuade her son or another member of the household to carry some of them for her.

Similarly, working-class women shopped for groceries for their families at local stores, and those who worked as kitchen servants did the shopping for their employers as well. Although grocers and other tradespeople made regular rounds of deliveries in some working-class and immigrant neighborhoods, deliveries were supplemented by trips to the grocer's, butcher's, and baker's.[83] For example, *Bring Along Laughter* is peppered with references to trips out for groceries and to the butcher's. As a girl, Logan was often sent out on these errands, but her mother, grandmother, and aunts are also described going to the butcher's for roasting meat and to North Beach for salami and cheese.[84] The domesticity and highly local nature of grocery stores made it feasible to send a child on grocery errands, because they were going to a place where they were known, and the grocer, as a neighbor, could be trusted to treat a child well. Being well known at local stores could be helpful for those who were sometimes short of cash, for credit was often available from the corner grocer.[85]

Working-class women—married, widowed, and single—often ran grocery stores. Among the married women grocers listed in both the 1890 and 1911 directories, nearly all were married to working men, listed in the directories as laborers, longshoremen, bricklayers, tanners, and soapmakers. Grocery stores functioned as a domesticated workplace for working-class women, a workplace they could control, unlike factories or shops where they might have worked as shopgirls when they were younger. A commercial space, the grocery store was also an extension of the home of the shopkeeper, who typically lived behind or above the shop. Grocery stores could become a comfortable female space for working-class women, one controlled by and serving women who spoke the same language and lived in the same neighborhood.

Working-class women's experiences of the grocery landscape, both as shoppers and as shopkeepers, reinforced an idea of grocery stores as an extension of domestic space, an intensely local world dependent on personal relationships. For shopkeepers, the fuzzy boundary between the home and the store, in addition to their use of the sidewalk as a space for display, reinforced this image of grocery stores as an integral element of the residential landscape, a more public part of a domestic world, like a front stoop. For middle-class women, groceries might have been delivered, often by a grocer's boy, making the grocer's role more that of a servant than of an equal. Even though middle-class women shopped in grocery stores routinely enough to make their local landscape so ordinary as to be unremarked upon, the class differences between themselves and the shopkeepers probably affected their experience. These middle-class shoppers are the focus of articles in grocery store journals, which suggest appealing to shoppers through modernity rather than familiarity.

Shopping and Place-Based Identity

Through their daily rounds of errands, women in different social and class positions constructed radically different relationships to the spaces of the city. Class, as much as gender, shaped both experiences of the shopping landscape and its built form. Upper-class women, for whom the downtown was a familiar space, created an identity for themselves as residents of the city of San Francisco. The downtown was a space in which they were served, as they were in their homes, and it, not their immediate neighborhoods, provided them with services and a public life. Their frequenting of the downtown created a strong relationship to the city as a whole, as well as to the networks of national and international connections embodied in imported and fashionable goods. These women understood the city, and even the entire Bay Area, as a single entity, attested to by the largely downtown San Francisco–based public life of Mary Pierce, a Berkeley resident.

Working-class women, especially those who were immigrants or nonwhite, were tied most strongly to their immediate localities. They were residents of the Mission District or of North Beach and, more narrowly, of their immediate few blocks, the area served by their grocer. The grocery stores and main-street shops they frequented created a strong tie both to their neighborhoods and to their homelands, through language and food, reinforcing an ethnic definition of spaces within the city. If they themselves were employed, they might also have experienced other neighborhoods through work, but their residential neighborhood was the one in which they were served and made most comfortable. Unlike the downtown shopping district, which tended to create the fiction of one united San Francisco, local main streets defined the smaller districts, such as the Mission District and the Western Addition, out of which the city as a whole was composed. Their strong local ties tended to create an understanding of the city as a collection of fragments and an identity tied less to the city as a whole than to the district within which they lived and shopped.

Native-born middle-class and lower-middle-class women like Annie Haskell had the most complex and layered relationship to the city. Their experience, more than that of other categories of women, touched on all of these three landscapes; they shopped regularly for groceries, did errands on local main streets, and went on shopping expeditions downtown. Like upper-class women, they experienced the downtown regularly, although not as a space that they felt existed *for* them in the way it did for richer women. They also had strong ties to their neighborhood created by shopping at local grocery stores and on a local main street, but the main street did not function as the center of their shopping world. Their identity was tied simultaneously to the city and to a neighborhood, making their relationship to the spaces of the city the most complex.

Women's experiences of shopping landscapes reinforced their class-based relationships to the city as a whole as well as their roles within the city and these landscapes. Through their experiences, women negotiated the gaps between the imagined and built landscapes of the downtown shopping district, grocery stores within residential districts, and local main streets. Those women with the most mobility and the most money were able to shape their experiences, especially downtown, to fit imagined ideals more closely, while others regularly experienced conflicts between those ideals and built reality. These conflicts were most striking for white, native-born, middle-class women, who frequented both the downtown and the local main street but whose experiences conflicted with the imagined nature of each of these. In the downtown, middle-class women's experiences juxtaposed spectacular department stores and more ordinary shops, and the pleasure of shopping was interrupted by the inability to pay. On the local main street, middle-class women often found the goods insufficient for their needs, contradicting the idea of the neighborhood as a self-sufficient entity. It was when women frequented a space designed for them—local main streets and grocery stores for working-class women and the downtown for elite women—that their experiences and the imagined landscape harmonized most closely.

Examining shopping beyond the narrow focus of department stores and upper-class patrons shows that the importance of shopping goes well beyond women's role as consumers of spectacle in a newly spectacular downtown. The everyday practices of shopping, the paths trodden every day in search of food and other necessities, were important elements in the creation of the classed identities of city dwellers and of women's identities as citizens of the city. Class, as much as gender, constructed the landscapes of errands. Everyday shopping also constructed a relationship to the city within which other practices can be understood. In the next chapter, we will turn to eating in public, a practice that took place along those same streets where errands were run and was shaped not only by class and gender but also by ethnicity.

THREE
DINING OUT

We have a room at Mrs. Ballou's—a back room. It runs very small after our big rooms. But it is comfortable and there is a big back porch where the baby can play. I expect this will be a trial for him. We shall of course eat at restaurants.
—Annie Haskell, August 31, 1890

FROM THE LATE NINETEENTH CENTURY to the early twentieth, dining out became increasingly common for women of all class positions. As women's roles in the workforce expanded, and as they increasingly went out to shop and for amusement as well as to work, a growing number of institutions served meals away from home to women. For women, eating out was problematic, however. In the late nineteenth century, restaurants were a space primarily for men and for escorted women. Eating in public was considered risqué for unescorted upper- and middle-class women except in a small range of establishments that catered to a female clientele and provided a highly policed and chaste environment. Poorer women like Annie Haskell often ate at restaurants out of necessity, as when they lived in lodgings without cooking facilities, but even in the family restaurants they patronized they needed to guard against contact with strange men.[1]

By the second decade of the twentieth century, the number of places where women of all classes could eat politely in public had expanded enormously. For the elite women, female-gendered tearooms moved beyond the bounds of the hotel and the department store, providing public places to eat throughout the downtown. Tables for ladies in lunchrooms and the newly invented cafeteria served working women and shoppers alike in modern spaces free from liquor and the tradition of masculine patronage.[2] Establishments aimed at women of varied class positions used a variety of tactics to guard women's respectability, from borrowing from the domestic sphere in the case of hotel dining rooms and family restaurants to creating new feminine spaces in downtown tearooms and providing new gender-neutral restaurant forms such as the cafeteria.

In this chapter I explore the eating establishments patronized by women of all classes and the ways that they were transformed in response to women's desires for acceptable places to eat out. I begin with recently invented institutions in the late nineteenth century: tearooms, confectioners, and ladies' dining rooms in hotels, establishments created to serve elite women dining alone. These establishments used two strategies beyond gender segregation to establish themselves as polite feminine spaces: association with the domestic sphere in the case of the ladies' dining room, and the creation of a new feminine type of restaurant in the case of the tearoom. Ordinary middle-class and working-class women and families were served instead by a wide range of mixed-gender restaurants, including the cafeteria, a twentieth-century gender-neutral invention. Family restaurants followed the model of association with the domestic sphere, and cafeterias used novelty and their relationship with modernity to mark themselves as ungendered, so that they became respectable spaces for women to dine, particularly for lunch. While poorer women searched for respectable restaurants, elite women used the power of their class to patronize the mixed-gender realm of eating for entertainment and thrills in downtown cafés and bohemian restaurants, where the thrill resided in playing with a lack of respectability. Each type of eating establishment and the motives that drew women there created distinctly classed and gendered experiences of public space, ranging from the genteel and protected experience of eating a light meal with other women in a tearoom to the slightly dangerous experience of drinking and dining with a male escort in a bohemian restaurant. The geography of restaurants reinforced the differences among women, with elite women patronizing downtown tearooms and spectacular cafés and poorer women going to homey family restaurants on their local or district main streets.

Imagining Feminine Refreshment: Tearooms and Hotels

In the nineteenth century, restaurants were primarily spaces for men, in part because they were spaces of drinking as well as eating. The masculinity of restaurants was marked not only by the fact that they served alcohol but also by their design, which often made use of dark wood and leather, and by the male waiters serving the food. Booths that could be closed off with curtains provided space for sexual impropriety, further marking most restaurants as inappropriate for respectable middle-class women. So strong were the masculine connotations of the "restaurant" that establishments serving women dining alone took on a number of other names: ladies' dining rooms, tearooms, lunchrooms, cafeterias, bakeries, and confectioners.

A woman eating alone in public left herself open to being taken for a prostitute, and as late as 1904, in the respectable spaces of hotel dining rooms, ladies were advised, "A lady should never go alone to the supper table after ten o'clock. If she returns from an entertainment at a late hour, and has no escort to supper, she should have that meal sent to her room."[3] The ideal solution to this quandary was for women to eat in an establishment that served only women. Dining rooms in major hotels, especially the ladies' dining room or the hotel tearoom, were the first to provide a space that women, particularly elite and middle-class women, could patronize alone without compromising their respectability. The ladies' dining room used its association with domestic space to suggest that it provided a sort of bubble of such space that served to protect women in public. Both its name and its role in the daily lives of women who lived in or visited the hotel marked it as a grander, more public version of the domestic dining room.

The hotel tearoom and its counterpart, the department store tearoom, similarly provided a female-only space, safely enclosed within a larger, policed, respectable upper-class institution. Because high-end hotels and department stores served primarily a white, American-born, well-to-do clientele, the women likely to eat in either of these spaces were upper-class themselves, a situation that was ensured both by the prices and by the policing function of the hotel lobby and its concierge and the department store selling floor with its salespeople, managers, and floorwalkers. While a ladies' dining room or tearoom in a hotel was part of a polite institution, the department store tearoom was located in a female-gendered institution. Many San Francisco department stores included tearooms; the most celebrated of these was in the Emporium, opened in 1896. These tearooms were safely ensconced on an upstairs floor within the feminine enclosure of the department store.

The tearoom, unlike the hotel dining room, was not directly modeled on a domestic space.[4] Instead, the gender of the tearoom was marked through its association with both tea the drink, which was a decidedly female and elite beverage that was often presented as the opposite of liquor, and tea the meal, which included a light snack eaten in the afternoon, when men and lower-class women worked.[5] As they were open only during the day, tearooms' hours of operation helped to mark both their association with elite shoppers and their difference from masculine restaurants. The food served in the tearoom, "dainty sandwiches and salads, and . . . desserts that have a little flavor of the home-made about them," reinforced its femininity.[6] It offered light meals, served by a waitress wearing a "nifty little apron instead of one of the all-enveloping variety," with "a mincing manner that indicates refinement."[7] The small dishes at tearooms expressed the refined femininity of delicate women with contained appetites, whose tendency to eat sparingly expressed their distance from the crass and bodily. The presentation of food also indicated feminine refinement through its frills. "The meat dishes are garnished with a bit of parsley or a lettuce leaf and the desserts rest upon small plates that are 'underlined' with doilies; the china is dainty, the napkins have a bit of individuality about them; the ices and sherbets are finished with a luscious cherry."[8] According to a manual on tearoom management, they were "altogether feminine in their aspect and appeal, being equipped with fragile furnishings and decorations and serving small quantities of dainty food. Men avoided them as entirely inappropriate and unsatisfactory for masculine needs."[9] The femininity of the tearoom was seen as almost oppressive by some later observers, such as R. N. Elliott, who wrote a manual on the management of tearooms and cafeterias in 1935. Elliott argued for making tearooms more hospitable to men than they had been in the past:

> The original tea room was almost impenetrably limited in its appeal to women and in its scope to the furnishing of afternoon tea. . . . The tea room was in the nature of a hermetically sealed lodge of some secret society of women which, moreover, held little appeal for men whether they could have successfully invaded its precincts or not.[10]

Over time, as the potential for profits in feeding the female shopping public became apparent and as San Francisco's shopping district expanded into a district "scarcely to be matched elsewhere in this country outside of New York and Chicago," tearooms expanded beyond the bounds of the department store and the hotel, spreading throughout the downtown shopping district.[11] Some of the establishments providing tea and light meals to a feminine public classified themselves as confectioners or bakeries rather than restaurants, underlining their separation from the masculine world of freestanding restaurants and their connection to frivolous sweets.[12]

The Built Landscape of Feminine Refreshment

Respectable feminine places for elite women to eat were marked as distinct from masculine restaurants through location and decoration. They were typically screened from the street and other masculine space not only by their location within polite institutions, such as department stores and hotels, but also by their location within buildings. For example, in the 1890s the Palace Hotel, then one of the grandest hotels in San Francisco, opened a grillroom that catered specifically to women diners, to supplement its restaurant, bar, and Gentlemen's Grill-Room, which was "a most popular resort for merchants and business-men and their guests."[13]

The Ladies' Grill-Room . . . is entered from the west end of the Palace Block on Market Street, through an arched Roman vestibule and promenade, built expressly for this purpose. Potted palms line the wide passage, which opens on a roomy landing, and you are at the entrance of a most beautiful room, tasteful and chaste in decoration, and choice in every particular of furnishing. The walls are of highly polished native woods. Here one may feast according to necessity, desire, or the depth of the purse.[14]

The promenade veiled the ladies' grillroom from the street and the rest of the hotel, its gendering marked through its use of palms. Palms, and plants in general, were often used to mark feminine dining spaces in hotels, as were delicate furniture and light colors.[15] Similarly, tearooms in department stores were usually located on an upper floor, far from the bustle of the street, and were often decorated with a garden theme.

As tearooms became freestanding businesses, they nonetheless kept their somewhat distant relationship to the mixed sidewalks of the city. Donovan writes of the tearoom, "It is seldom located upon the ground floor but hides itself away upon the upper floor of an office building and is easily accessible only to the initiated."[16] This echoed the placement of department store tearooms on upper floors. With an upstairs location, the tearoom could remain a polite space, accessible from the street, as was necessary if it was to serve shopping women, but not part of either the show and bustle of retail activity or the class and gender mixture of the sidewalk. It was also a cheaper space to lease, which may have helped to keep meal prices reasonable. Similarly, female-only lunchrooms for working women, such as the Ogontz and Ursula lunch clubs in Chicago or the Mid-day Lunch Room for Women in San Francisco, located in a working-class area south of Market Street in the 1910s, were often on upper floors and sometimes were enclosed within the feminine space of a settlement house.[17]

By 1912, women in San Francisco could choose from many tearooms. Helen Throop Purdy, in *San Francisco As It Was, As It Is, and How to See It,* suggested "innumerable pleasant places, some luxurious, some plainer—all good" for "ladies unattended," including the Golden Pheasant, the Pig 'n' Whistle, Swain's, the Women's Exchange, the Emporium restaurant, the Tea Cup, and the Bon Ami.[18] An earlier guide, Charles Keeler's 1903 *San Francisco and Thereabouts,* mentions only two: "Swain's is the oldest and best known of the bakery restaurants, while the ladies caught out shopping generally drop into the Women's Exchange, where all is dainty and appetizing."[19] Some of these feminine haunts were remarkably discreet. For example, the Tea Cup was not listed in the *Crocker–Langley San Francisco Directory,* and the Women's Exchange was listed only in the alphabetical listing of residents and businesses. Presumably women who ate at these tearooms would be introduced to them through acquaintances, thus assuring that the clientele remained appropriate. All of the places mentioned by Purdy and Keeler were safely ensconced within the upper-class shopping district, along Post, Geary, and O'Farrell Streets within three blocks of Market Street (Figure 3.1). The dainty and feminine design of the tearoom interior carried over from its earlier incarnation in the department store and hotel, marking it as a feminine space.

The decoration of the tearoom, as well as its food, expressed refinement and femininity. For example, the Laurel Court Tea Room at the Fairmont Hotel (Figure 3.2) was a light and airy space, conspicuous by its spaciousness and its greenery. Simple Ionic columns were made of a rich, veined marble, and the glass ceiling

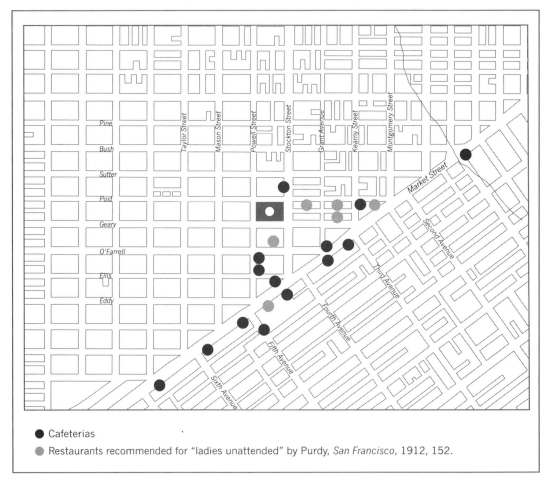

● Cafeterias
● Restaurants recommended for "ladies unattended" by Purdy, *San Francisco*, 1912, 152.

Figure 3.1. Downtown establishments appropriate for women dining alone, 1910s. The restaurants recommended by Helen Throop Purdy for "ladies unattended" in 1912 are located firmly within the elite shopping district and in the Emporium, the most prominent San Francisco department store. Cafeterias in 1911 and 1915 were most common along Market Street, especially on its south side, although they were also spread throughout the downtown (and not, for the most part, in other areas of the city), reflecting their status as restaurants that served workers and shoppers of all classes. The locations of cafeterias are taken from San Francisco directories from 1911 and 1915.

Figure 3.2. Laurel Court Tea Room, c. 1910s. This high-end tearoom in the Fairmont Hotel had a garden theme. It was a light and airy space with plants, a significant contrast to male eating establishments decorated with dark wood and leather.

featured floral stained-glass flourishes. Trees in pots, hanging plants, filigree cast-iron railings, and a liberal use of trellis patterning on the walls and ceiling made this tearoom into a fantasy of a manicured garden. This lightness and the floral motifs stand in strong contrast to masculine spaces such as the Gentlemen's Grill-Room and Bar in the Palace Hotel and to Schroeder's Restaurant on Front Street, which did not serve women lunch until 1970. These, like other masculine spaces, were furnished in dark woods and other dark materials and were lit more dimly.[20] For example, the barroom at the Palace Hotel was "finished a third of its height in brownish-red Egyptian marble," while the bar itself, which was the length of the room, had an African onyx front.[21]

Experiencing Feminized Dining

Hotel dining rooms, department store lunchrooms, and tearooms functioned in large part as a convenience for well-to-do women. These spaces provided a comfortable way for these women to take care of refreshing and refueling themselves.

Visits to freestanding tearooms and department store lunchrooms, primarily for lunch, were usually mentioned as just one part of a full day of shopping in the diary of Mary Pierce. Lunch out was also combined with meetings, outings to the 1915 Panama–Pacific International Exposition, and sometimes a movie or matinee.[22] Both hotel restaurants and tearooms, therefore, were located primarily downtown, in the area frequented for shopping by well-to-do women.

Hotel restaurants served both people staying in the hotel and the general populace. As a commercial restaurant as well as a dining room for hotel guests, especially those on the American plan, which combined lodging and meals, a hotel restaurant was not strictly a public space but combined aspects of the domestic (a home away from home for guests and a home for permanent residents) with those of a commercial space. This domestication of the hotel was part of what made it an appropriate space for women, especially when female hotel guests and families were of necessity among the diners. Hotels were also appropriated by women's associations, as well as by associations made up largely of men, for banquets and other special events. In these cases, the public space of the hotel was remade into a private space of a club, but women's experience with the hotel as an extension of the club helped to make the space familiar and safe.

For both Ella Lees Leigh, writing in 1903, and Mary Pierce, writing in 1915–16, hotels were a favorite and regular place to eat meals. Leigh went to the California Hotel for dinner with her husband and other friends and relatives on three Sundays in January. These visits were outings, made not out of convenience because they were in the neighborhood but for the purpose of eating out. However, she writes about these outings very matter-of-factly, stating simply, "Went to the California Hotel for dinner," implying that this was an ordinary occurrence, not worth a lengthy comment.[23] Pierce regularly went to hotels for meals. Rather than patronizing only one hotel, she regularly visited the Hotel Oakland, the Palace, the Clift, and especially the St. Francis, as well as the Bellevue, where her sister lived. The single Miss Pierce, then in her early forties, ate in hotels most often with female friends and relatives, although she also dined out a few times with a male escort.[24] The St. Francis, located on Union Square next to the downtown shopping district, was a space of her club activity as well, as she and her mother also went to meals there for organizations such as the Laurel Hill Club and the Friends of Art.[25] Downtown hotels were, for this upper-class woman, a comfortable space that she could visit for lunch, dinner, or tea and whose parlor she could use to rest and write letters.

Hotels were not a common place to eat for less well-to-do women such as Annie Haskell. In her diary from 1890 to 1917, Haskell only twice mentioned partaking of refreshment at a hotel. Once in 1903 she ate dinner with family members at the Golden West Hotel, a respectable but not grand hotel on Ellis Street.[26] Her one visit to a grand hotel for refreshments was a special event. On September 9, 1910, after riding in a tally-ho (a small horse-drawn carriage) with fellow Native Daughters of the Golden West in "the greatest parade ever in San Francisco," she and her sister Helen, who had also been in the parade, celebrated by driving to the St. Francis, where they had ice cream and lemonade but did not eat a full meal.[27]

Department store tearooms, like hotel tearooms, were patronized by well-to-do women more than by women of modest means. However, just as Mary Pierce and Annie Haskell dined at hotels of different ranks, so did they patronize department store tearooms of different ranks. While Pierce took tea at Gump's, an exclusive store selling exotic imports, Haskell ate at the restaurant in Hale's, a discount department store.[28] Both of them dined at the Emporium, which was in keeping with the Emporium's status as a store that served a wide range of classes. Because the prices in tearooms were on the higher end, they were patronized primarily by women of leisure.[29] As well as going to the Emporium, Gump's, and the St. Francis for tea, Mary Pierce frequented other tearooms, including the English Tea Room in Berkeley and the Tea Cup, the Pig 'n' Whistle, and Foster and O'Rear's in San Francisco.[30] In contrast, tearooms were not part of Haskell's circuit, and the only time she mentioned having tea in a commercial establishment was on a visit to the 1915 Panama–Pacific International Exposition.[31]

Women in Mixed-Gender Restaurants

While single-sex tearooms and ladies' dining rooms served elite women and ensured their respectability when they ate alone, they were by no means the full extent of dining options for women dining unescorted. Working-class and lower-middle-class women needed less expensive and more filling food. For this they could patronize respectable mixed-gender restaurants, including family restaurants in their neighborhoods, reform lunchrooms for working women, and, by the 1910s, cafeterias downtown. In these institutions, particularly the cafeteria, they could eat alone or with other women without endangering their reputation. Elite women also patronized mixed-gender restaurants, including the same cafeterias and family restaurants frequented by poorer women. However, when elite women went to family restaurants, always escorted, they did so as an experience in slumming, to gain a thrill from exposure to foods and behavior, including drinking alcohol, that they found exotic. Elite women also ate and drank at downtown cafés, which made eating out more fun by pairing it with floor shows and elaborate mixed drinks but which initially also provided a separate ladies' dining room for the unescorted.[32]

Imagining Respectable Dining for the Ordinary Woman

For working-class and lower-middle-class women in the nineteenth century, the general landscape of respectable places to eat alone was thin. San Francisco, famous for its good cheap restaurants, boasted a great many restaurants serving a working-class clientele.[33] The 1897 *Doxey's Guide to San Francisco* declared, "There is probably no spot on the civilized globe where one may eat so well at such small cost as San Francisco. Even the penny coffee-shops of large English towns are outdone by some of the cheap coffee-saloons of San Francisco."[34] However, many of the sources of cheap meals were exclusively masculine haunts, such as the many middle-priced saloons that were popular spots for a cheap meal, providing a free lunch for their customers with the purchase of a beer. These saloons advertised prominently in foreign-language newspapers such as *Bien* and *La Voce del Popolo*. One of the city's guidebooks of the day describes these saloons:

> Great hot roasts are brought in and kept on a steam table. Big soup tureens come in emitting steamy odors to tempt even a jaded appetite. Salads and sauces, ragouts, stews and pies are furnished forth, until that sideboard looks like the banquet table of some fine old feudal baron about to entertain his knights. Servants in clean, white aprons take their places, alert for orders. Busy men come in by the dozens for a quick luncheon. If they wish, they are accommodated at small tables with white napery of good quality. If not wishing to sit down, they stand about the extensive sideboard. Then they are served with soup, roast, salad, stew, or whatever they wish, that is on the day's bill of fare—and all that is asked in payment is that they will buy a drink for the customary price of 12½ cents.[35]

This smorgasbord of hearty food, however, was not accessible to most women, and it stands in sharp contrast to the dainty sandwiches and carefully controlled portions provided at ladies' tearooms. As Roy Rosenzweig has argued, saloons were "'essentially a male refuge' pervaded by an 'aura of freewheeling masculinity,'" which made many women uncomfortable and marked women who entered as potential prostitutes.[36] Some saloons provided a separate room, accessed by a ladies' entrance, to serve working-class women and families. In *The Long Day*, a 1905 chronicle of the life of a working girl in New York, Dorothy Richardson describes going into a saloon for a lunch of beer and soup with a group of other working women. As they entered, each of the "workmen drinking beer and smoking . . . jumped up, and grabbing his glass, went out into the bar-room" leaving the dining room to the women. Although these working women did not have access to the all-you-can-eat bonanza of the free-lunch saloons, they were able to get a good hot meal for only five cents, more cheaply than at a "more godly and respectable dairy-lunch room."[37] However, saloons were problematic for respectable women, no matter how affordable the meal. In his 1907 novel *The Heart Line*, Gelett Burgess wrote that entering even "the most respectable saloon in the city where women were permitted," in which "the whole rear of the establishment was given over to a magnificently fitted-up department devoted to such women as were willing to be seen there," was perilous to a woman's reputation.[38] In this one San Francisco saloon, fictionally called "the Hospital," "one might go and still retain a certain relic of good-repute, if one went with a man—there were married women enough who did, and reckless girls too, who took the risk; but it was on the frontier of vice, where amateur and professional met."[39] The danger of a woman's being taken as either a professional or an amateur of vice kept saloons and their free lunches out of bounds for most women, and none of the women whose diaries and memoirs I have read mentioned visiting saloons. Even in *The Heart Line*, which tells of bohemians, fakirs, and the fast side of society, the only female character who goes into a saloon, a former vaudeville performer, kills herself almost immediately afterward.

Other eating establishments, such as the "hash houses" that Frances Donovan claimed in *The Woman Who Waits* made up three-quarters of the restaurants in Chicago, served inexpensive food to a primarily, though not exclusively, male clientele. Hash houses, which served "only short orders and 'plate dinners' (meat, potatoes, and one vegetable all on one plate) . . . at top speed," usually accompanied by a cup of coffee, provided inexpensive meals to working men and a few women.[40] The cheapest places typically served a stew that was short on meat, while slightly better hash houses served three ten-cent courses, including meat, for twenty-five cents.[41] Donovan wrote,

> [Hash houses] do most of their business at the lunch counters, but invariably they have
> a sign on the window outside which reads, "Tables for Ladies." These tables are, however,
> few in number and the ladies who frequent the hash houses are fewer still, even with
> the most liberal interpretation of the term. The hash house depends for patronage upon
> men customers.[42]

Both hash houses and saloons were imagined as male spaces, and women who ate in them were seen as compromising their virtue, if they had any left to compromise.

Family restaurants, serving a largely middle-class and lower-middle-class clientele of families, as well as single women and men, provided a less masculine alternative for nonelite women. The use of the word *family* in referring to these restaurants does not mean that their primary clientele was families but rather marked them as a space that enjoyed the sort of respectability that would make families welcome. In addition, the word *family* expresses an ideal of hominess and suggests that some of these restaurants may have been family businesses. Like the hotel dining rooms serving elite women, family restaurants aligned themselves with the domestic to be appropriate for women. Family restaurants, as well as the hash houses one rung below them, were often run by immigrants. In her memoir

Bring Along Laughter, Milla Logan wrote, "When two Greeks got together they always started a restaurant . . . [and] when seven Slavonians get together, first thing they do is start a restaurant."[43] Her grandmother predicted, "If gentleman is a Greek, name of restaurant will be Classic Grill. If it is a Slavonian, name will be Acme Grill. Sign on window will say, 'Booths for Ladies.'"[44] The listings of restaurants in San Francisco directories reflect the presence of many immigrant owners, including Greeks, other eastern Europeans, Scandinavians, Germans, and Italians. According to Frances Donovan, family restaurants, which she calls cafés, were neither as low-class as the hash houses with their lunch counters nor as high-class as the tearooms with their frills. She elaborates, "The café serves three meals a day and it serves them at tables, not at a lunch counter. It aims to give substantial food at these meals and at a reasonable price, but it does not attempt to provide the dainties either in food or appointments that are set forth by the tea room."[45] According to Donovan, the clientele of these restaurants ran the gamut of lower-middle-class types, including the respectable and the risqué, the American-born and the immigrant:

> The patrons of these cafés are vaudeville artists, chorus girls, actors and actresses in the legitimate drama, office men, brokers, shop girls, telephone girls, waitresses with their lovers, chauffeurs, railroad conductors with their wives, mothers and daughters from "down State" who are in town to do a little shopping, farmers . . . who are seeing the city, greasy Italians with their greasy wives and still greasier babies; in fact, a truly cosmopolitan crowd.[46]

Most family restaurants probably served a narrower clientele, the people who lived in the same neighborhood as the restaurant and often shared an ethnicity with the owner. The clientele would have included single people, both male and female, for they often lived in rooming houses that did not provide them with a place to cook. In addition to ethnic restaurants, primarily serving a specific immigrant population, ordinary middle-class and lower-middle-class restaurants included American restaurants, serving a general population, and some mixed restaurants, which combined an ethnic specialty with common American fare.

In the second decade of the twentieth century, these inexpensive domestic restaurants were joined by a new sort of establishment, the cafeteria. Cafeterias served meals efficiently and more cheaply by cutting out the waitress. Instead patrons, usually armed with trays, joined a sort of assembly line, choosing dishes from an array of choices. Rather than serving themselves, as men did at cheap buffets and in saloons offering a free lunch, patrons were served by workers who assembled plates of hot food to order from steam tables and who also arranged cold plates in advance. After assembling their desired meal, patrons paid a cashier and carried their food to a table or to a chair with a sidearm table to eat. Because of the speed with which they could serve meals, cafeterias became a popular option downtown, where employees often had a short and closely timed break for lunch. Cutting back on service also made meals less expensive, an important plus for people making do on a small income, and thus especially for working girls, whose income was significantly lower than that of young men.[47] In *The Long Day,* the "dairy restaurants" that Richardson describes as the primary eating places serving working women were cafeterias: "Everybody acts as his own waiter, buying checks for whatever he wants from the cashier and presenting them at a long counter piled up with eatables."[48] Cafeterias were somewhat less common in San Francisco than in other cities because of the power of the waiters' and waitresses' unions, but by the 1910s San Francisco boasted a number of cafeterias.[49]

The popular image of cafeterias was of a mixed-gender and mixed-class space, but one in which women predominated.[50] Cafeterias were seen as appropriate for women for several reasons. As a type they had feminine associations because of their history, which began with lunch clubs run for working women by middle-class reformers.[51] In addition, many individual cafeterias began their lives as feminized bakeries or confectioners that served light lunches and were later reborn as cafeterias or dairy lunches.[52] Because the cafeteria was an altogether new invention, scientific and efficient, it became a safe and appropriate place for women to eat. Cafeterias did not serve liquor and were free of the masculine associations of the restaurant.

The Built Landscape of Mixed-Gender Dining

The location of mixed-gender restaurants reflected their presumed clientele. Hash houses, such as Transfer Quick Lunch, Market Street Quick Lunch, and Golden Gate Coffee Parlor, all of which advertised in *Bien,* a Danish paper, were typically located in tiny storefronts or basements in rooming-house districts and industrial areas, areas most likely to be peopled primarily by men, although several were also situated along the mixed-gender Market Street.[53] Family restaurants were tightly tied to local and district main streets, especially those that served familiar ethnic food to immigrant populations. The advertisements in foreign-language newspapers give a sense of where different groups of people might have eaten. For example, in *La Voce del Popolo,* all of the advertised restaurants served Italian food, and the majority were located along Broadway and nearby streets in the area of North Beach, settled by Italians. In contrast, most of the bars and saloons advertised did not have Italian names, and some, such as the Bank Exchange, also advertised in several other foreign-language newspapers. This implies that male drinking establishments patronized by Italians often had a mixed clientele, united by their gender and class, but the restaurants that might have been patronized by families, including women, were more exclusively Italian and closer to home. The restaurants advertised in the Danish paper *Bien* were mostly run by Scandinavians (just as Italian restaurants served the Italian population), and many of these were clustered around Market and Church, although their locations were more varied than those of Italian restaurants. Many of these restaurants, however, also served a general population, which is evident from their English names, such as the Busy Bee and Pacific Restaurant, and from their advertised specials, including "ham and eggs *og* franks and beans."

While family restaurants were tied to main streets, cafeterias, like tearooms, clustered downtown. Although women from all walks of life frequented cafeterias, these eateries focused on a mass market of both genders. Their location within San Francisco reflects their popular but feminized audience. While tearooms clustered around the elite shopping district downtown, the largest concentration of cafeterias was along Market Street, particularly between Third and Seventh (see Figure 3.1). Market Street shops on the whole served a less elite audience, particularly south of Fifth Street, and these cafeterias were highly accessible to those less elite shoppers, as well as to women working in downtown shops and offices. The lack of any cafeterias beyond the downtown reflects the association of cafeterias with women shoppers and white-collar female workers.

Interior design, even more than location, expressed the expected clientele of restaurants. A very particular language of interior design, using dark materials and masculine symbols such as beer steins, trophy heads, and hunting paraphernalia, was used to mark primarily masculine spaces. The "tasteful and chaste" decor of the Palace Hotel's Ladies' Grill Room may be understood in part as a deliberate contrast with the entirely unchaste decoration of saloons and many male-oriented restaurants.[54] For example, in saloons, every space was "embellished within an inch of its life," and "it was a rare ceiling that was not strewn with plaster nymphs and satyrs in bas-relief."[55] The sexuality implied by the nymphs and satyrs was further heightened by paintings of nude women. Cavorting nymphs, satyrs, and historical and contemporary nudes marked saloons as spaces of sexuality and male desire, inappropriate for respectable women. The one exception was when high-end saloons functioned for some elite women as a place to visit for a thrill, much like the downtown cafés and bohemian restaurants discussed later in this chapter.[56] Dark wood, leather, and sports, hunting, and drinking paraphernalia also marked saloons as masculine space, just as dark wood, leather, and dark stone marked the more upscale hotel bars.

Cafeterias also marked their distinction from masculine spaces and their respectability through their decor. They were furnished with small tables covered with perfectly white tablecloths, which allowed diners to eat privately. Lightweight bentwood chairs were easy for women customers to move, added to the clean, light-filled appearance, and had no upholstery to collect dirt and odors. Tiled floors often added a hygienic touch, in combination with brass rails and the stainless steel and glass of the steam table, as well as the clean white aprons worn by the women and men serving food (Figure 3.3).[57] This modern design was largely gender neutral, because it dispensed with the decorative touches of feminine spaces and the dark materials of masculine spaces. However, the association of light colors with feminine space is sufficiently strong that one can argue a more feminine than masculine reading of the white interiors of cafeterias.[58] More important, the design of cafeterias was hygienic. A major selling point for the cafeteria was the opportunity to see one's food before eating it, thus assuring oneself of its quality.[59] At the turn of the century, the unhealthy circumstances in which a variety of goods, from clothing to cigars, were made and the danger of contamination through goods made in germ-filled workrooms were of great concern. This concern extended to the unseen kitchen and its "sneezy back-room kitchen help," replaced in the cafeteria by clean, visible steam tables and servers.[60] Some cafeterias also used design to convey a sense of refinement and class, much as tearooms did, although in a less gendered manner than tearooms. For example, the Boos Brothers cafeteria at 725 Market Street, which Annie Haskell patronized, featured panoramic

Figure 3.3. Colby Cafeteria, c. 1910s. This is a typical cafeteria of the 1910s, with lightweight bentwood chairs and small tables covered with white tablecloths. A brass rail separated the dining area from the line of patrons carrying trays, and a tiled floor emphasized cleanliness. The decoration was usually restrained, highlighting hygiene and forgoing frills.

paintings of historical California scenes on its walls, using art and a didactic desire for "presenting to the mind of the patron historical facts" to elevate its status above that of other inexpensive places to eat a quick meal.[61]

Spaces that were appropriate for women, however else they were furnished, provided individual tables. Frances Donovan, in her 1920 exposé of restaurants, argued that the counter and the table drew a physical distinction between establishments appropriate for women and families and establishments that catered primarily to men. A counter, reminiscent of a bar, marked a male-gendered space, and those eating establishments that respectable women frequented in the period never had a counter, although this changed later.[62] For example, ladies' dining rooms in saloons were furnished with little round tables at which women sat, unlike the main room of the saloon, which was furnished with a bar along which male patrons stood. Similarly, in the hash house, although the ladies were few, tables were reserved for them. This suggests the importance of some modicum of privacy to ensure that women were not accosted by strange men or assumed to be available to the ministrations of strange men. One step up in respectability, cafeterias emphasized their small tables in postcards, even though their mode of service was what made them interesting.

The awkwardness of not having a private table is clear in the advice given to women travelers who found themselves dining at a public table in a hotel, shared by several hotel guests in a homey but potentially problematic manner. The 1904 etiquette book *Good Manners for All Occasions: A Practical Manual* admonishes women to abjure "any bold or boisterous deportment," to "converse in a low, quiet tone," and to "wear the most modest and least conspicuous dress appropriate to the hour of the day."[63] In other words, a woman should be as invisible and inaudible as possible. At a shared table, she is advised to be extremely reserved: "If a lady accepts any civility from a gentleman at the same table, such as placing butter, sugar, or water nearer to her plate, she must thank him; but by no means start a conversation with him."[64] Eating at a counter could put a woman in the same situation of having to speak to a strange man, either to ask him to pass the salt or to thank him for such a courtesy, but without the insulating setting of the hotel. Private tables created, in contrast, a boundary between the women eating at the table and the others around them. At a private table, one was not in the ambiguous position of sitting next to a stranger but rather safely turned one's back on strangers.

The booth, found in several of the cozier establishments, served a purpose similar to the private table. It created an intimate and private space within the public space of the tearoom or café, especially when curtained. The intimacy of the booth made its meanings potentially fluid, however. Just as it protected women from other diners, it also shielded them from the policing gaze of waiters. A booth in a comfortably feminized and upper-class space could provide privacy for women, but a booth in a restaurant that served liquor was potentially problematic. The same fluidity was attached to the back room of a saloon, which originally was understood as a space frequented by prostitutes, but by the 1910s was used by respectable working women and in some cases was barred to all unaccompanied men or women, serving only respectable couples and families.[65]

Experiencing the Landscape of Ordinary Mixed-Gender Dining

For most nonelite women, eating out was not a very common occurrence. With the exception of working people who lived in rooming houses and hotels and had to take their meals in public, working-class and lower-middle-class women went to restaurants more rarely than rich women. They were more likely to bring food along to their workplace or while out for other reasons or to go home for lunch. For example, most of the working girls Richardson described ate sandwiches and pickles brought from home, a solution that fit their short lunch breaks as well as their thin wallets. Annie Haskell was similarly more likely to bring food than to eat out. For example, after visiting the 1915 Panama–Pacific International Exposition on May 21, she complained, "We had to walk a long way back to get lunch, that is a mistake. We shall have to manage better next time, maybe take lunch or something."[66] Four days later, when she visited the exposition again, she "took lunch and had no coffee."[67] In contrast, Mary Pierce brought a lunch only for the closing ceremonies and often bought one or more meals at the exposition's many restaurants.[68] For upper-class women, restaurants were a familiar and often-visited territory, and packing a lunch or breaking up a day's activity by going home for lunch was unnecessary. Upper-class women were much more likely to eat more than one meal out in a single day, but Haskell never once mentioned eating more than one meal a day in public, except when she was living in a rooming house.

Not all nonelite women had the option of bringing their own food, however. As the 1900 De Witt guide to San Francisco observed, "A very large portion of the population lives in hotels or hired rooms, and eats at the restaurants. This fact is very noticeable, and can be best seen in the evening, between five and seven, when the day's work is done."[69] For two months during 1890, Annie Haskell found herself in this situation when she, her husband, and her small child moved into a rooming house and ate at restaurants.[70] The restaurants she mentioned by name during this period were Campi's, at 531 Clay Street, and the Royal, on Mission Street. Campi's was described by Helen Throop Purdy twenty-two years later as "a well-known Italian place of long-standing renown for good dinners, many of whose patrons have been with it for a generation."[71] These restaurants, and the many others Haskell does not mention by name, were ordinary family restaurants.

Annie Haskell also ate at cafeterias often, beginning in 1912.[72] Although she patronized cafeterias, she did not enjoy them, and in 1915 she complained about a visit to a cafeteria at the Panama–Pacific International Exposition: "Had a time getting lunch at the cafeteria—no more. They are too slow and too dear and I loathe cafeterias anyway."[73] Downtown, cafeteria visits were part of shopping trips, a way to get an affordable meal, not worth mentioning except to complain about the price. Haskell's complaints notwithstanding, they swiftly became a regular part of her downtown excursions. Mary Pierce also mentioned having lunch at "some cafeteria" downtown with her sister-in-law.[74] Cafeterias were an acceptable part of Pierce's upper-middle-class female world by 1915, although she and Haskell may have visited different cafeterias, given the different areas downtown in which each woman did most of her shopping.

The Imagined Landscape of Dining as Entertainment

Mostly women ate out for convenience or necessity, getting lunch or light refreshments to restore their energies on a shopping excursion or to fuel themselves for an afternoon of hard work. But elite women in particular ate out as a form of entertainment also, either by itself or in combination with other activities, especially going to the theater or the movies. Hotel dining rooms were often used in this way, as a place for a meal before going to the theater, as part of an automobile outing, or sometimes just for a nice meal as an evening's or day's activity.[75] However, excursions to hotel restaurants more closely paralleled having a meal or tea at someone's house: they were an upscale version of home entertaining—elegant, refined, and delicious, but not exciting. An alternative was provided by two types of eating establishments that could in themselves provide a night's entertainment for an elite woman and her escort. One of these types, found in every major American city, was the downtown café, which provided live entertainment and a spectacular setting to go with a meal. Several downtown cafés served both women alone during the day and mixed-gender parties after the theater. These cafés combined good food, drinks, elaborate architecture, and musical performances to create an entertaining atmosphere. Among the most famous were the Techau Tavern, the Tait-Zinkand, and the Portola-Louvre, all located near Market and Powell Streets, tucked between the center of the upper-class shopping district and the theaters along Geary Street.[76] Downtown cafés were especially popular spots for a late supper after the theater. The other type, particularly important to San Francisco's mystique, was the bohemian or ethnic restaurant. Exotic ethnic restaurants, particularly Chinese and Japanese, provided the illusion of having taken a world tour. Bohemian restaurants provided a glimpse at a more risqué and literary life, a safe experience of the wilder side of life, just as tours of Chinatown and its opium dens provided a glimpse at the exotic and dissipated life of Chinese drug addicts. While downtown cafés existed purely as spaces of pleasure for the elite classes, ethnic and bohemian restaurants had different meanings for different users. For the elite they provided diversion through the thrill of slumming, but for the members of the ethnic communities served by many of these restaurants, they were more likely to function as an ordinary family restaurant.

The decorations, the other patrons, and the spectacles and performances that were often part of the experience of a meal, coffee, or a drink at a downtown café or bohemian restaurant made these establishments entertaining, interesting, and sometimes slightly dangerous—and therefore exciting. Because of the mixed company at downtown cafés and bohemian restaurants—a company with a mix of genders and, at bohemian and ethnic restaurants, of classes and ethnicities as well—women visited these establishments with male escorts, whether as a couple or in a group. Along with the exotic atmosphere, bohemian and ethnic restaurants and downtown cafés—unlike other female-appropriate restaurants—typically served alcohol as well as food, providing an extra frisson of danger and excitement for middle-class women, for whom saloons and many other liquor-serving establishments were off limits. In her memoir *Earth Horizon*, the novelist Mary Austin described going to San Francisco in the late 1880s and being excited and shocked by "the casual way in which wine appeared with meals":

> Mary's newspaper friend took her to one or two of these places, Zincand's, I think, and an Italian place where they were served with red wine and something else . . . could it have been Pisco Punch? . . . According to her bringing-up, Mary should have made the fine, shocked gesture of "turning her glass down"—that was out of a popular Temperance recitation— which she shamelessly didn't. She sipped a little courageously.[77]

This serving of alcohol provided a thrill often more exciting than the entertainment and the atmosphere. For example, after Annie Haskell visited the Louvre, a downtown café, with her estranged husband, "to hear the music, he said," she described not the music or the atmosphere but instead the alcohol that she drank: "I . . . had the nicest and prettiest *pousse café* that I have ever drunk or saw. I suppose I ought not to have drunk it."[78] A *pousse café* was a San Francisco specialty, made of "at least six cordials in perfect layers," topped with brandy, flambéed, then put out with a flip of an apron, and, as a finishing touch, a square of ice was "passed gently a dozen times or more across the fragile rim" of the iridescent glass. It was "a drink of varying temperatures, the top layer warm, the final mouthful as cold as a snowdrop. The last taste was of currant wine."[79] According to Charles Dobie, in *San Francisco: A Pageant, pousse cafés* were usually served in pairs, for "it was the fashion to have a lady along for such an occasion."[80] This and other elaborate cocktails, including the famous Pisco punch, made with a Peruvian liquor, could be obtained at downtown cafés. The theatricality of these drinks marked them as separate from everyday life, drawing attention to the rarity of drinking in the lives of the women drinking them. The less flamboyant red wine in Italian restaurants and beer in German ones were both part of the foreign atmosphere and part of the thrill of breaking a taboo. While in an ethnic restaurant, imagined as part of a foreign country, women could temporarily follow the rules that governed that country.

Upper-class women found amusement not only in the formal entertainments of downtown cafés but also in the thrill of eating in ethnic and bohemian restaurants, where they watched their ethnic and bohemian fellow diners rather than ballet girls or ice skaters. Slumming upper-class women usually visited these restaurants in the evening, always with an escort, and often as part of a group. The city had a wide range of these restaurants to choose from, as the cosmopolitan population of San Francisco was reflected in the range of ethnic restaurants it boasted. Charles Keeler's 1903 *San Francisco and Thereabouts* described a wide variety of ethnic restaurants besides the standard French and German:

> The Mexican restaurants of the Latin quarter at the base of Telegraph Hill, serve all sorts of hot concoctions—peppery stews, chicken tamales, frijoles, and the flat corn cakes so dear to the Mexican stomach, tortillas, with Chili con Carne and red peppers to warm up the meal. Italian restaurants stand side by side with the Mexican on Broadway, with their "Buon gusto" on the window pane to attract unwary flies within their webs. I have alluded elsewhere to the Chinese restaurants, but a Japanese tea house is more of a curiosity, even in cosmopolitan San Francisco. Up on Ellis Street is such a place, complete in all its appointments, set in a charming little Japanese garden. Here the Japanese are served precisely as in the land of chrysanthemum and the cherry blossom. There is even a Turkish restaurant in San Francisco where, surrounded by hangings and rugs of oriental richness, one may whiff the incense and sip the coffee of the Ottoman Empire.[81]

The excitement of an ethnic restaurant lay not only in the exotic foods available but also in the illusion of being in another country. The description of the Japanese teahouse above suggests that it was a perfect simulacrum of Japan, where Japanese patrons were served "precisely" as at home, and tourists could observe the natives as well as participate in Japanese practices.

Bohemian restaurants served less as a chance to travel the world in imagination as to play at traveling between social worlds, temporarily joining a disreputable but artistic, and often impoverished, underworld. The most prominent bohemian restaurant, Coppa's, was located downtown, in the Montgomery Block. The fame of Coppa's was widespread and drew women visitors as well as men. The suffragist Inez Haynes Irwin wrote in her unpublished autobiography of arriving in San Francisco in 1910: "Many, many were the stories I had heard about Coppa's and, so, the first night after I had arrived at the hotel I dressed myself in my best, summoned a taxi and went to Coppa's to dine. For the first time in my life, all alone, I ordered wine."[82] Other bohemian haunts, notably Luna's, a Mexican restaurant, and Sanguinetti's, an Italian restaurant, were also popular, especially for a slumming crowd. Both of these restaurants were less expensive and less elaborate than Coppa's and thus served an ordinary lower-middle-class clientele as well as bohemians and society folks out for a thrill. Burgess described a mixed crowd at Sanguinetti's (which he called Carminetti's in his novel): "For the most part the diners were all young—mechanics, clerks, factory girls and the like—though here and there, watching the sport, were up-town parties, reveling in an unconventional air" (Figure 3.4).[83] Just as in his description of Coppa's, Burgess describes the uptown patrons as separate from ordinary patrons, watching the sport, not participating in it. Just as these same upper-class diners would watch a floor show in a downtown

Figure 3.4. Illustration of Sanguinetti's restaurant, 1904. Sanguinetti's, noted for its revelry, was one of several Italian restaurants that upper-class San Franciscans visited for a safe thrill. Along with providing an exaggerated image of raucous entertainment, this drawing highlights the masculine pleasures of wine (on the table at right) and tobacco (the cigar, an upper-class mode of taking tobacco, smoked by the man in top hat seated just beyond the wine) and the presence of slummers. From Whittle, "The Humbler Restaurants of San Francisco," 364.

café, they would watch bohemians and working-class diners in bohemian restaurants. Of course, for the factory girls and other working-class diners, an ethnic restaurant served a different purpose. Rather than being an exotic haunt visited for thrills, it was an ordinary restaurant serving familiar food, which was impossible to make in their lodgings.

The Built Landscape of Dining for Entertainment

The geography of downtown cafés and bohemian restaurants reflects both their most common clientele and the activities with which they were associated. The most prominent large downtown cafés, the Techau Tavern, the Tait-Zinkand, and the Portola-Louvre, as well as their prequake predecessors, Tait's, Zinkand's, and the Louvre, were all located on or near Powell Street between Market and O'Farrell. This put them in a location almost precisely between the elite downtown shopping district, to their northeast, and the downtown theater district to their west, centered on Ellis Street. This fits well with their dual role of serving women eating alone in the daytime, who might combine a trip to a café with either shopping or a matinee, and mixed groups in the evening, whether before, after, or in lieu of a night at the theater. The notorious bohemian restaurant Coppa's was in the Montgomery Block downtown, at the other side of the shopping district from the downtown cafés, and quite solidly within the masculine downtown of offices. The geography of Coppa's and the other bohemian haunts underlines the class difference between them. In contrast to Coppa's relatively staid location, Luna's was at the corner of Vallejo Street and Dupont Street (now Grant Avenue), a location that Frank Norris describes getting to on a disreputable path: "It *can* be reached by following the alleys of Chinatown. You will come out of the last alley—the one where the slave girls are—upon the edge of the Mexican quarter, and by going ahead for a block or two, and by keeping a sharp lookout to the right and left you will hit upon it."[84] Sanguinetti's was "down near the harbor front, a region of warehouses, factories, freight tracks and desecrated, melancholy buildings, disheveled and squalid."[85] While Coppa's provided a comfortable look at literary bohemia, slumming in Luna's or Sanguinetti's carried more of a frisson of danger for their elite patrons.

Interior decoration and entertainment set the stage for the type of exotic experience to be found in each restaurant, an experience heightened by exotic food. Sanguinetti's maximized the experience of slumming and of disorder through a combination of sawdust on the floor and live music, often performed by African Americans. According to Clarence Edwords, in *Bohemian San Francisco,* shared tables further broke down a central rule of polite female conduct, not speaking to strangers, and forced slummers to participate in the behavior they came to experience: "One found oneself talking and laughing with the people about as if they were old friends. . . . If you wished to stay there in comfort you had to be one of them, and dignity had to be left outside."[86] A night at Sanguinetti's provided a temporary release from the rules of polite society and was a popular location for slumming, to the extent that tourists desiring a bohemian experience gradually came to be the only patrons, squeezing out the older clientele from "factories, canneries, shops, and drays."[87]

In contrast, Coppa's played up its artistic heritage rather than providing a class-crossing experience, and this was reflected in its decor. It was famous for its wall paintings and the center table, where the writers, artists, and journalists that made up San Francisco's artistic population held court. Gelett Burgess, who was a regular at this table, described Coppa's under the fictional name of Fulda's in *The Heart Line:*

> The walls were covered with cartoons and sketches. . . . It was a sort of mental and artistic hash spread upon the walls. The humor grew fiercer as one's eyes rose to the ceiling. There, a trail of monstrous footprints, preposterous, impossible, led, with divigations, to a point above the central table which was always reserved for the Pintos [the core group of bohemians]. To crown this elaborate nonsense, they had drawn a frieze below the cornice with panels containing the names of the frequenters of the place, alternated with such minor celebrities as Plato, Browning and Nietzsche.[88]

Coppa's murals were described in every guidebook to the city after they were painted in about 1903, and their destruction in the fire led to a great nostalgia for their former glory, poorly reflected in their replacements, which "lacked spontaneity" and were "painted in absurd imitation of the original outbursts of the artist frequenters of the place," according to one critic.[89]

Both the murals and the presence of the artists themselves made Coppa's a popular place for upper-class diners looking for the experience of bohemia. In *Bay Window Bohemia,* Oscar Lewis wrote that the inscriptions on the walls were created in part "to baffle the slummers, who by then made up the most numerous, and profitable, of Coppa's customers."[90] Burgess's descriptions of Coppa's always include the slummers, who are described trying to get themselves invited to join the bohemian table but otherwise sticking together and observing. The physical location of the table of bohemians, in the center of the restaurant, a centrality highlighted both by the footsteps on the ceiling and the presence of the bohemians as caricatures on the murals, made them into a sort of entertainment, performers on a central stage, visible from the surrounding tables full of slummers.

In exotic ethnic restaurants, interior decoration and food worked together to create the illusion of being in another country. Physical setting created a space apart from America. In the restaurants described by Keeler above, the Japanese garden and the Turkish hangings, rugs, and incense created exotic experiences only palely imitated by the orientalist decor of commercial tearooms run by white Americans. The inexpensive Italian restaurants of North Beach also provided an illusion of travel as well as delicious food. Helen Throop Purdy wrote, "In the Fior d'Italia, or the Buon Gusto, you may easily delude yourself for an hour with the thought that you are on Italian soil, and the waiters (so solicitous to please you, so anxious that you shall enjoy their food) add to the illusion."[91] While the settings of these restaurants were enchanting, the exotic food allowed an opportunity to play at being in a foreign country, complete with drinking alcohol. Even ethnic establishments that did not have the exotic decor of the Japanese tearoom or the Turkish restaurant provided an illusion of travel through taste. For example, at Luna's, a prominent Mexican restaurant, Purdy describes the pleasure of eating exotic foods in an exotic manner: "You could burn your throat with tamales, enchiladas, or chile con carne, eat frijoles from little individual pots, drink delicious chocolate, or water which had cooled in an olla."[92] The little individual pots and the olla emphasized the unfamiliarity of the food, thus heightening the pleasure of such simple experiences as drinking water.

The more expensive downtown cafés provided musical performances and spectacular architecture as well as food and drink. As Mary Pierce wrote concisely in her diary, "frog's legs and ballet girls" were the appeal of downtown cafés, which combined fine food, usually French or German, with entertainment.[93] Both the Tait-Zinkand (Figure 3.5) and the Portola-Louvre (Figure 3.6) provided entertainment throughout the day, serving both women in the afternoon and mixed-gender groups after the theater. The Portola-Louvre, which took over the basement space in the Flood Building from Tait's after the earthquake, provided "a fine orchestra, and vaudeville during the late afternoon and evening," encouraging "ladies [to] go there in the afternoon for tea, and to enjoy the entertainment."[94] Although their standard fare was orchestras and singers, downtown cafés also provided more spectacular entertainment, as when the Portola-Louvre introduced an ice-skating show in 1916, which Mary Pierce twice visited.[95] Similarly, the dining rooms of palace hotels and many midpriced hotels provided musical accompaniment.[96] Music and drinking combined to create a festive atmosphere.

Not only music, vaudeville, and ballet girls but also the architecture itself was used to provide entertainment. For example, the pre-earthquake Tait's, in the basement of the Flood Building, was distinguished by "its cascades and fountains and play of electric lights."[97] After the earthquake the Tait-Zinkand was still spectacular, according to Helen Purdy, who wrote, "The Tait-Zinkand restaurant is thoroughly San Franciscan, high-class but semi-Bohemian. The food is unsurpassed, the room is gaudily decorated, an orchestra in a gallery gives good music, while singers go about on the floor below and sing near one table and then another."[98]

Figure 3.5. Interior of Tait-Zinkand, one of the most popular downtown cafés. Courtesy of San Francisco History Center, San Francisco Public Library.

Figure 3.6. Portola-Louvre Restaurant. Like Tait's, the Portola-Louvre occupied a large hall-like space in which diners could watch performances as they ate.

In 1903, Charles Keeler grouped Techau's with Zinkand's (which later merged with Tait's as the Tait-Zinkand) as "among the best known of the German places, where orchestras liven the clink of steins and schooners."[99] He wrote that the Techau Tavern was "in an old church with pillars and recessed nooks decorated in green, where one may have rye bread and Frankfurters together with sundry other good things."[100] These nooks created a private space within a public room, still visible, and thus not too risqué, but intimate. Restaurants such as the Poodle Dog, which served French food, commonly provided more intimate spaces, more dangerous to the reputation, including private dining rooms upstairs.[101] In contrast, in the Tait-Zinkand and the Portola-Louvre, diners ate at one of a sea of tables, so they were part of the crowd and almost part of the entertainment, when singers performed at their tables.

Experiencing the Thrill of Dining Out

Downtown cafés were very much a space of the upper classes. The Techau Tavern, in particular, was regularly visited by both Ella Lees Leigh in 1903–5 and Mary Pierce in 1915–16. The importance of the Techau as an appropriate space for upper-class women is marked by its use as a lunchtime meeting place for the exclusive Daughters of California Pioneers, of which Leigh was an officer. Techau's (as Leigh and Pierce referred to it), like the Palace Hotel and the St. Francis Hotel, was privatized by upper-class women by serving as a meeting place for their clubs.[102] Aside from these lunch meetings, Techau's was visited by Leigh and Pierce in the evening, usually after going to the theater and always escorted by men.[103] Although the downtown cafés were visited regularly and with a sense of appropriation by upper-class men and women, they were also accessible to less well-off people for an occasional night out, when these patrons would be more likely to have a single drink, such as Annie Haskell's *pousse café* at the Louvre, rather than a full meal.

Exotic and bohemian restaurants were also more accessible to elite women. Through clothing and other status markers, elite women could show themselves to be clearly slumming when visiting Luna's or Sanguinetti's. Their class markers made it clear to everyone that they were simply trying on a role for a night and that drinking and otherwise breaking the rules of polite behavior were merely part of that role. The situation was more complex for less elite women. They could more easily be mistaken as regular denizens of these restaurants, and thus the distinction between who they really were and the role they were temporarily playing was less clear-cut. For some poorer women, of course, the restaurant that served as a thrilling glimpse of another life to elite women was a familiar space serving their home-style cuisine. If eating out for pleasure was primarily the province of the elite, eating out for a thrill was even more their territory, because their money ensured that the thrill would not harm their reputation.

The Class Geography of Dining Out

Just as women in different class positions experienced different geographies of errands, so these women also experienced radically different geographies of eating out. The intensity of their experience was also quite different, because upper- and upper-middle-class women ate out often, but meals out were much rarer for poorer women who had the means to cook in their homes. The class geography of eating out reproduced, in large part, the class geography of downtown shopping. The restaurants that Annie Haskell mentioned by name in her diaries were nearly all downtown, on Market Street and near it (Figure 3.7). She visited restaurants in the Emporium (a cafeteria, not the tearoom) and Hale's, as well as the Boos Brothers' Cafeteria and Campi's, all on the south side of Market Street. Her favorite place to eat, the Tivoli Café, was just the other side of Market Street, at 50 Eddy Street. All of these visits were for lunch, usually in combination with shopping. Mary Pierce, in contrast, only twice ventured across Market Street to its south side and then only to visit the unquestionably appropriate venues of the Emporium and the Palace Hotel. Her numerous restaurant visits ranged across the downtown area, from hotels on Geary Street near Taylor Street and on Union Square to tearooms and cafés along Post, Grant, Sutter, Powell, and O'Farrell Streets (see Figure 3.7).[104] She went out for all meals, including breakfast and tea, though lunches and dinners were her most frequent meals eaten out.

The landscape of places for women of all classes to dine in public expanded significantly from 1890 to 1915. In the late nineteenth century, upper-class women were firmly ensconced in the policed, enclosed, feminine spaces that had been introduced to hotels and the new department stores, while poorer women ate in mixed-gender restaurants and hash houses, which served families as well as single men and a few single women. By 1915, upper-class women were venturing farther afield, eating out alone or with other women in freestanding tearooms and even mixed-gender cafeterias. Most strikingly, the invention of the cafeteria provided female-appropriate meals for women of all classes, who often mingled in the same establishments. However, women's experiences of dining out remained deeply marked by class. For working women, meals out were both rarer and more pedestrian than for elite women. When not dining with a male escort in family restaurants on local main streets near their homes, working women who were concerned about their reputation primarily patronized inexpensive cafeterias and lunchrooms. For elite women, meals out spanned a greater spectrum. They ate quick lunches in cafeterias, hotels, and tearooms, particularly downtown. But they also regularly ate out for pleasure, at restaurants that provided not only food but also the chance to take in a spectacle or even to be part of one temporarily. For elite women, meals out could provide both comfortable and exotic experiences,

Figure 3.7. Restaurant visits of Annie Haskell and Mary Pierce, 1907–18. During these eleven years Haskell did not mention eating out often; the restaurants she did visit were along and near Market Street, in the same area as the majority of her downtown shopping. In contrast, during the three years from 1915 through 1917, Pierce ate out frequently, usually in the same general area as her shopping trips, though extending farther west of Powell Street as well.

including a wide variety of foods from all ethnic traditions, while less elite women were more likely to stick to their own ethnic traditions and the Anglo-American foods of the cafeteria or lunchroom. Elite women could more freely drink in public without compromising their morals, as they either drank elaborate concoctions in the downtown cafés, which catered particularly to them, or drank as part of a night of slumming, a temporary trying on of the roles of bohemian, poor, or immoral women. Their money opened up more of the city to them and made it possible for them to break the rules of propriety with impunity, as long as they broke those rules within the boundaries of exotic restaurants and in a group that included elite men.

FOUR
SPECTACLES AND AMUSEMENTS

Well, I have just got back from down town where I went to the Orpheum with Kate and Henry. I enjoyed it, though there is a great deal of silly business, but some other things are interesting and amusing. After, I went down to the clothing store where I met Roth and got him a blue serge suit. . . . Then I went back to the Golden West Hotel where we had dinner. After, we walked around the streets and looked in the windows for a while.

—Annie Haskell, August 15, 1903

AMUSEMENT WAS A COMMON REASON for women to go out in public at the turn of the twentieth century. During this period, working hours shortened and leisure time became more common, in large part because of the efforts of unions, which were particularly strong in San Francisco.[1] Just as the production of goods had largely moved from the home to commercial establishments, so leisure also increasingly moved from the home and the neighborhood into commercial establishments, often serving the city as a whole.[2] As the range of spectacles available expanded, theater owners concentrated their marketing on women, and as an increasing number of working women had some disposable income, more and more women went out to theaters and shows.[3] In addition, women were spectators of the many parades and public celebrations of the turn-of-the-century city.

In San Francisco as in other cities, amusement and spectacle brought women downtown and made them part of the observing and celebrating public, not only during the daytime hours, but increasingly in the evening as well. In this chapter

I discuss women's expanding participation in public spectacle as both spectators and participants and the consequences of their participation for their relationship to the city. Spectacle and amusement could take many forms: the theatrical spectacle of shows, the commercial spectacle of shops and store windows, and the civic spectacle of parades. Going to a show, window shopping, and watching a parade were all sources of amusement that took women to the downtown and other prominent public spaces of San Francisco. Although shows, windows, and parades were produced for different purposes, they were all consumed primarily as sources of amusement, and they all used the modern technologies of spectacle to draw spectators. Women's experience of these public spectacles increased their claim to the city, especially to the nighttime city, but also reinforced the class and ethnic differences and the unequal statuses among women.

Imagining Theatrical Entertainments

Going out to see a show was a regular form of amusement for women who could afford it. During the period from 1890 to 1917, the nature of shows changed as vaudeville expanded and movies were introduced into the landscape of San Francisco theater. With changes in the nature of theatrical entertainment came a broadening of the female audience for shows and changes in how all women experienced going to shows. One significant aspect of these changes in theatrical entertainment, particularly movies, was the creation of new types of spaces that did not carry the gendered history of theaters and, thus, could be gendered in new ways.

In the nineteenth century, women did not frequent theaters at night unescorted. Until the mid-nineteenth century, theaters were imagined as an overwhelmingly male space, with men sitting on the benches in the "pit" in front of the stage; poor men, blacks, and prostitutes in the gallery seats; high-class prostitutes in the "third tier," the top row of boxes; and wealthier patrons, including "women who wished to be regarded as ladies," seated only in the lower rows of boxes, the most expensive seats.[4] Around 1850, theaters began to be sanitized; a combination of higher prices, design changes, subdued performances, and rules barring unescorted women chased out both prostitutes and lower-class men.[5] By the 1890s women of a range of class positions sat in all the sections of theaters, which were newly defined only by class and not by respectability.

During the day, theaters were imagined as a largely female space, which women could patronize with other women and with children without fear of compromising their reputations; matinee performances were patronized almost exclusively by women. By night, in contrast, theaters were mixed-gender spaces in which women needed to be protected from strange men by the familiar men who escorted them. By the 1910s new ideas about the nature of the theater, shaped in part by the new theatrical forms of vaudeville and movies, expanded women's ease with the space of the theater. This was reflected in their growing willingness to go to the theater in the evening without a male escort.

In the 1890s, theaters in San Francisco fell into four main categories: establishments showing plays, operas, and other forms of "legitimate theater"; less expensive theaters that specialized in vaudeville; foreign-language theaters serving immigrant populations; and disreputable variety houses and concert saloons that provided a male audience with titillating fare and, often, liquor and access to prostitutes. This sorting into different types of theaters was a result of the process of cleaning up theater, making it more specialized and polite, which had begun in the mid-nineteenth century.[6] Each of these categories was differently imagined. The "legitimate theater" was seen as safe for women (although women were still to be escorted at night), largely because of its upper- and middle-class clientele and its high-class, artistic, uplifting plays. This refined form of theater, a quite new invention in the early twentieth century, helped to create a space for respectable women. Vaudeville was very much imagined as a popular theater, serving the working class as well as children. In vaudeville theaters, audiences could shout, stamp, and walk in and out, as they had in the mid-nineteenth century, but were no longer allowed to do in newly sacralized high-end theaters. For escorted working-class women, going to a vaudeville theater would not sully their reputations, but this category of theater was not seen as appropriate fare for a more elite female audience. Variety houses and concert saloons were imagined as the place to which all the disreputable males and disreputable acts of earlier theater were banished. They functioned as the "other" of vaudeville, marking the boundary between clean and salacious popular entertainment. Foreign-language theaters, for their part, were associated exclusively with the working-class immigrant groups they served, in San Francisco most notably Italians. These theaters combined high-class fare, such as grand operas and Shakespearean plays, with popular songs and low farce, melding the legitimate theater with vaudeville in a setting and at a price reminiscent of vaudeville. The appropriateness of foreign-language theaters for women and families varied somewhat with the attractions of the particular night, but they were generally patronized by mixed crowds.

The most significant change in theater types for women was the growth of vaudeville, which was in part a response to the squeezing out of poorer customers by the rising prices of high-class theater. Vaudeville theater offered short performances of all sorts for an inexpensive price, typically 10¢ to 50¢ ($2.64 to $13.20 in 2010 dollars), while prices for legitimate theaters more often started at 25¢ or 50¢ and went up to $2 ($52.70 in 2009 dollars).[7] Vaudeville promoters worked hard to keep the image of their theaters as clean, safe places for women and children in spite of being more raucous than high-class theaters. However, because many vaudeville theaters served beer and their theatrical fare consisted of variety shows rather than plays, they remained clearly working-class and were seen as an amusement rather than as a venue for art, as high-end theaters were. In San Francisco, vaudeville came into its own with the opening of the enormous Orpheum Theater, built specifically for vaudeville, in 1887 (Figure 4.1).[8] This theater seated over 1,680 people, and the highest price, for a box seat, was 50¢.[9] In the 1899 novel *McTeague*, Frank Norris describes an outing in which McTeague takes his girl, Trina, and her mother and brother to the Orpheum for a variety show. He describes the varied program, including acrobats, blackface minstrels, various comic acts, a caricaturist, yodelers, a kinetoscope, and "'the Society Contralto,' in evening dress, who sang the sentimental songs," captivating Trina, who "split her new gloves in her enthusiasm when it was finished."[10] Norris describes the space of the auditorium

Figure 4.1. Prequake Orpheum Theater, built 1887. The Orpheum was the first San Francisco theater built specifically for vaudeville. Courtesy of the Museum of Performance and Design, San Francisco.

as hot and smoky from cigars and "full of varied smells—the smell of stale cigars, of flat beer, of orange peel, of gas, of sachet powders, and of cheap perfumery."[11] Before the performance and during the intermission, "waiters hurried up and down the aisles, their trays laden with beer glasses," and a little boy walked the aisles, chanting, "Candies, French mixed candies, popcorn, peanuts and candy."[12] Norris describes the Orpheum, and vaudeville by implication, as a space of cheap and unending spectacle, from the painted curtain to the varied acts, filled with smoking, drinking, uncouth lower-class people trying hard to be proper.

Vaudeville producers marketed their shows to women in particular, in order to mark vaudeville theaters as respectable, even though inexpensive. Vaudeville theater managers actively courted women by providing free gifts, admitting them free of admission on ladies' nights, banning prostitutes, often banning smoking, controlling drinking, keeping the performances clean, and presenting acts such as sentimental singers calculated to appeal to women.[13] Women, especially working-class women, did attend vaudeville. Kathy Peiss notes that women made up one-third of the audience for vaudeville in 1910, but the price of tickets kept them from going often, unless they were being treated by a man, as Trina and her mother were treated by McTeague. Thus, vaudeville theaters expanded the theater attendance of many women, especially American-born women of limited means.[14] By creating a new form of theatrical amusement and working hard to gender it as female-appropriate, vaudeville impresarios were able to shift the gender and class mix of the audience for theater, expand their profits, and extend the runs of their shows.

With the addition of movie theaters to the landscape of theatrical amusements, the number and variety of women patrons increased significantly, in part because, unlike vaudeville, movies were eventually shown in a completely new kind of space. Motion pictures were introduced to many cities as part of vaudeville shows. Their role was as a novelty act, a specialty among the other shows. The first commercial projection of films was in 1896, with the invention of the Vitascope, which quickly made its way to San Francisco.[15] In June 1896, the Orpheum proudly advertised:

A Grand New Bill of Novelties!

THE VITASCOPE

The Sensation of the Nineteenth Century!

Which We Are the First to Introduce in San Francisco[16]

The Vitascope shared the spotlight with "twenty-four high-grade artists," including the four Marimba Virtuosi and a Wagnerian soprano. The novelty quickly wore off, however, and the Orpheum did not include films as a regular part of the bill until the Spanish–American War provided interesting footage. A "Biograph" of September 1898, for instance, was advertised as "New War Scenes, Including the Parade of the Victorious Battleships of the American Navy Passing in Review of New York Harbor," and was listed at the bottom of the bill, after acrobats, one-act comedies, opera singers, soubrettes, Great Danes, musical character comedy sketches, and juggling comedians.[17] Early films were typically short and unplotted, showing views of exotic parts of the world or topical material, such as the war scenes shown at the Orpheum. The novelty of projected film was itself the main attraction. The interest in this kind of footage waned relatively quickly, and after 1901 the Orpheum no longer included the Biograph among its features.[18]

The first real venue for moving pictures as a separate form of amusement, rather than as a part of vaudeville, was in nickelodeons in working-class neighborhoods of American cities. The nickelodeons and their affordable nickel shows, which began appearing throughout the United States in 1905–6, opened up a new space of amusement for working-class women.[19] A knowledge of English was not necessary to understand silent pictures, which mimed most action broadly, and the pictures were available to a working-class audience within their neighborhoods. Nickelodeons were frequented by an audience of mostly women and children. Even Italian immigrant girls, whose social activities were often curtailed by the strict rules of their families, went to the movies often.[20] Women's and children's attendance at nickelodeons was encouraged by theater managers, who typically advertised their theaters as catering "especially to the ladies and children" and showed slides between reels to make such welcoming announcements as "We are aiming to please the ladies," "Bring the children," "Ladies without escorts cordially invited," and "Ladies and children are cordially invited to this theater. No offensive pictures are ever shown here."[21]

The Built Landscape of Theatrical Amusements

The architecture and location of each type of theater that women patronized helped to reinforce their distinctions. For example, nickelodeons were small theaters, often simply storefronts filled with chairs, with a screen at one end and a projector at the other. The shows were brief, often as short as fifteen minutes, and were shown continuously, so that patrons could enter and exit whenever they wished. In addition to being located often in working-class neighborhoods, nickelodeons were integrated into local shopping streets as architecturally indistinguishable from other shops. All it took to transform a storefront into a nickelodeon was a projector, folding chairs, and paper over the windows. For example, the storefront on Fillmore shown in Figure 4.2, one of three identical buildings with a storefront below and flats above, was the location of a nickelodeon in 1911, the only year nickelodeons were used as a category for listings in the *Crocker–Langley San Francisco Directory*. Their ordinariness helped to signal their inexpensive and welcoming

Figure 4.2. In 1911, a nickelodeon was located in the current site of Extreme Pizza on Fillmore Street. Along this block, small storefronts are tucked below prominent flats.

nature. No one needed to feel discouraged from entering a nickelodeon because their clothes or schooling was not good enough. Additionally, nickelodeons' integration into the landscape of everyday shopping made them easily accessible to a wide range of women. Nickelodeons were located on a number of local and district main streets, as well as downtown, as can be seen in Figure 4.3, which shows the locations of nickelodeons listed in the 1911 directory. Clusters of nickelodeons were located along Mission, particularly between Twenty-first and Twenty-fourth Streets and Valencia and Thirtieth Streets, along Fillmore between O'Farrell and Bush, near the intersections of Castro, Noe, and Church with Market, and near Columbus in North Beach. The largest concentration of nickelodeons was on the south side of Market Street, the side opposite the majority of high-class theaters and department stores. Seven nickelodeons were located along Market west of Fifth, the area populated by the less expensive department stores that Annie Haskell most often patronized.

Movie theaters and many vaudeville theaters clustered on local and district main streets and on the south side of Market, particularly west of the central upper-class shopping district, in the area populated by discount stores (compare Figure 4.3

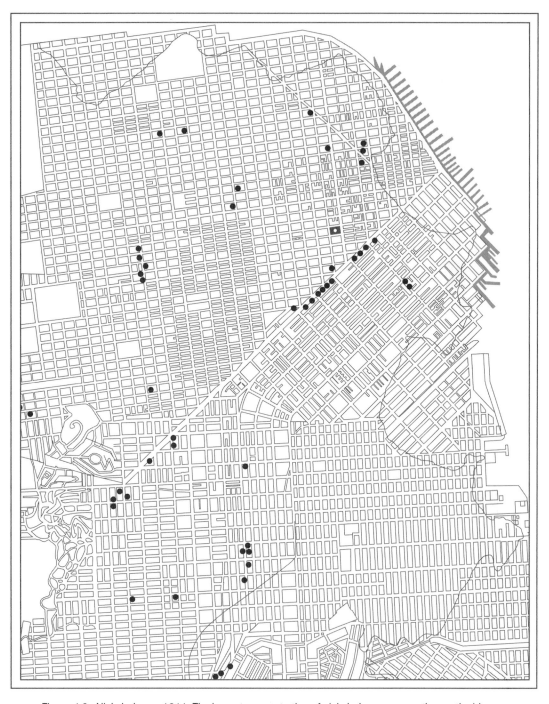

Figure 4.3. Nickelodeons, 1911. The largest concentration of nickelodeons was on the south side of Market Street between Second and Seventh Streets. Other clusters were on Mission Street near Twenty-second Street; on Fillmore Street between Bush and O'Farrell Streets; on Kearny near Columbus Avenue; and on Castro Street near Market Street. Locations from *Crocker-Langley San Francisco Directory,* 1911.

with Figures 2.3 and 2.8). In contrast to nickelodeons, however, vaudeville theaters and movie theaters were typically purpose-built buildings, architecturally distinct from the shops around them. Large, prominent vaudeville houses and movie theaters such as the Orpheum were imposing buildings that used essentially the same architectural language on their facades as high-class theaters. Stylistically they stood out from the storefronts that typically surrounded them. Similarly, smaller vaudeville and movie theaters often made use of a large entryway, often arched, to break the rhythm of shop fronts (Figure 4.4). However, these more popular theaters often made concessions to their location within a shopping district. For example, the facade of the Wigwam Theater (Figure 4.5), on Mission Street, revealed a store and a saloon within the same building, mixing its identity with that of the street it inhabited. The common placement of these theaters midblock (see Figure 2.13) further united theater and shops into one entity. Although more impressive than a storefront nickelodeon, the Wigwam and many other theaters shared the nickelodeon's intimate relationship to the shopping district.

Figure 4.4. Like other smaller theaters, the Grand View Motion Picture Theatre is the same scale as the residential and commercial buildings surrounding it, but its large arched doorway distinguishes it from other businesses. Courtesy of San Francisco History Center, San Francisco Public Library.

Figure 4.5. Wigwam Theatre, c. 1910, a major vaudeville house on Mission Street. Courtesy of San Francisco History Center, San Francisco Public Library.

Downtown "legitimate" theaters, in contrast to more popular theaters, were located near, but not strictly within, the downtown shopping district. In post-1906 San Francisco a distinct theater district was located directly to the west of Union Square and the downtown shopping district (Figure 4.6). Here theaters were sometimes built right next to one another and were surrounded primarily by hotels. These theaters were architecturally distinct, clearly separate buildings, and gave their entire street frontage to their lobbies, making the distinction between shopping and theatergoing clear-cut (Figure 4.7). As I will describe in more detail later in this chapter, the interiors of high-end theaters were also more specialized than the interiors of most vaudeville theaters. While most vaudeville theaters were open, flat halls with a stage, relatively indistinguishable from dance or meeting halls in their layout, high-end theaters were designed to create a clear sight line between each individual theatergoer and the stage, while also sorting those theatergoers into classes through their placement within the theater.

Experiencing the Landscape of Theatrical Amusements

The geography and typology of theatergoing were broader for women like Annie Haskell than for upper-class women like Mary Pierce and Ella Lees Leigh. The upper-class women went to plays, operas, and concerts in high-class downtown theaters, including the California, Alcazar, Majestic, Cort, and Columbia theaters, as well as feature films in downtown palace movie theaters. On occasion, Pierce also visited the Orpheum vaudeville theater downtown, on O'Farrell Street. Haskell, while she also visited several downtown theaters, mainly went to nickelodeons and theaters on Fillmore and especially in the Mission District, where she lived. Haskell went to vaudeville shows at the Orpheum, the Wigwam, and other theaters; visited nickelodeons; attended concerts in theaters, shops, and public parks; went to both grand and light operas at the Tivoli and other venues; and went to varied theaters to see plays ranging from what she called "wild melodrama" to Shakespeare. As an educated woman with an interest in culture and politics, Haskell was interested in many of the same plays, concerts, and films that attracted Pierce and Leigh. However, because she had little money, her outings often depended on friends and family members, and therefore she mostly frequented the less expensive vaudeville and melodrama shows that her family members went to regularly.[22]

Annie Haskell was very concerned with following the rules of propriety, which required that, while a woman might attend the theater alone or with other women when seeing a matinee, she needed a male escort at night. For example, in her 1890 diary, all eight of Haskell's references to attending a play, opera, or vaudeville show referred to evening shows to which she went escorted by her husband

Figure 4.6. Theaters, 1915. By 1915, theaters were once again concentrated downtown, adjacent to the downtown shopping district. In addition, the Republic and the Princess both showed films and were located on Fillmore; the Wigwam served the Mission District; and the Valencia was a single outpost between downtown and the Mission. (1) Republic; (2) Princess; (3) Columbia; (4) Alcazar; (5) Hippodrome; (6) Orpheum; (7) Cort; (8) Tivoli; (9) Savoy; (10) Empress; (11) Pantages; (12) Valencia; (13) Wigwam. Locations from *Crocker-Langley San Francisco Directory,* 1915.

Figure 4.7. Columbia Theater, c. 1910. Like other downtown "legitimate" theaters, the postquake Columbia Theater was an imposing, distinctive building, using classical details that emphasized its high-culture status. Courtesy of San Francisco History Center, San Francisco Public Library.

or another male relative.[23] The importance of being escorted by a male is clear in her entries. For example, she wrote on February 20, 1890, that because her husband was sick, her brother-in-law "undertook to escort" her, her mother-in-law, and a female friend to the opera. In 1890 Haskell also put up with the "horrid" and "impossible" behavior of her husband, Burnette, who typically took along a book to read during the play, so that she could be properly escorted.[24] The first reference that any of the diarists made to going to a play in the evening unescorted is not until 1910, and the circumstance, which made Haskell quite uncomfortable, occurred only because her male escort was ill.[25] By the 1910s, the necessity of a male escort for the evening was fading, at least for upper-class women such as Pierce, who felt perfectly comfortable going to see a play in the evening with female friends and relatives in 1915.

Annie Haskell's experience of theaters was quite different from Ella Lees Leigh's and Mary Pierce's experience of the same theaters. On June 5, 1915, Pierce and Haskell described going to see the same show, Pavlova at the Cort, but while Pierce sat in orchestra seats for the "truly inspired performance," Haskell described hurrying "up the long stairs that head to the Cort gallery."[26] Pierce and Leigh were able to take in the spectacle of a play, concert, or opera without interference, but after attending *Twelfth Night* on May 26, 1911, Haskell found it necessary to comment, "Though our seats were high, we could both see and hear." She was not as lucky at the Wigwam on February 3, 1910, about which she wrote, "I finally got a miserable seat in the back where I could hardly see or hear and amongst a lot of babes."[27] Although Haskell frequented some of the same theaters that richer women attended, she sat at the margins, just as many of the nickelodeons she visited were at the margins of the high-class area of the downtown.[28]

Mary Pierce and Ella Lees Leigh went to only those theaters that were designed to maximize a clear view from the audience to the stage, with a raked floor and seats angled to face the stage squarely (Figures 4.8 and 4.9). Although Haskell went to these theaters, where she perched high in the balcony, she also went to popular-price theaters, particularly the Tivoli, Orpheum, and Wigwam. These theaters were designed to maximize the number of people they could seat, with the prequake Tivoli and Orpheum seating sixteen hundred each, nearly a thousand more than most downtown legitimate theaters. To fit in the large crowd, seats in these theaters were arranged in gridlike rows, often on a level floor (Figure 4.10). The interior was more like a generic hall than a specialized theater. At the Tivoli, service for food and drinks, originally provided at tables but after 1880 offered at seats with racks to hold glasses, further interrupted patrons' ability to watch the drama onstage without impediment and distraction.

Beginning in 1907, Annie Haskell mentioned visiting nickelodeons and going to "motion picture shows." Her visits to nickelodeons were often quite casual, as when she and two other women "walked over to Fillmore St. had some lunch and visited a nickelodeon to relieve nervous tension" that had been created by taking the teacher's exam in 1911.[29] On another occasion, she and her sister Kate visited a nickelodeon as a break between viewing Sirius and Saturn through her brother-in-law's telescope, which he had set up on the sidewalk.[30] Haskell's nickelodeon visits, as well as her visits to other moving picture shows, were rarely planned in advance and were often combined with other activities, such as a shopping trip, a library visit, a meal out, or a trip downtown to see a concert at the music store. At times moving picture shows served purely as a place to rest or, on one occasion, a way to amuse herself while waiting for a streetcar.[31] This integration of nickelodeon visits into everyday activity was made easy by the relatively low price of admission, the short length of programs, and the continuous projection of the show.

Figure 4.8. Interior of Columbia Theater, 1895. The Columbia Theater was a major legitimate theater that served a high-class clientele. Courtesy of The Bancroft Library, University of California, Berkeley.

In contrast, when Mary Pierce went to see movies in 1915–16, they functioned more like plays. She never visited nickelodeons, and she nearly always referred to the subject of the film in her diary. While Annie Haskell simply mentioned going to a moving picture show, Pierce described her movie outings much as she did the plays she went to, writing on September 19, 1916, for example, "In evening Lucy and I see Theda Bara in 'Under Two Flags,'" without mentioning that this was a film and not a play. She was also more likely to visit films at night, for two-thirds of her film visits were in the evening, while fewer than half of Haskell's were in the evening.[32] Moviegoing also made up a much smaller proportion of outings for amusement for Pierce, who mentioned going to forty-five plays and operas in 1915–16 and to nine movies. In contrast, in 1915–16 Haskell mentioned going to eight plays and operas and six movies, while earlier, in 1910, she went to the movies eight times and only twice to plays or operas.

Mary Pierce did not see movies in nickelodeons but rather in theaters that had either been converted from live shows, such as the Savoy and the Tivoli, or built as movie theaters, such as the Portola and Grauman's Imperial. In the mid-1910s,

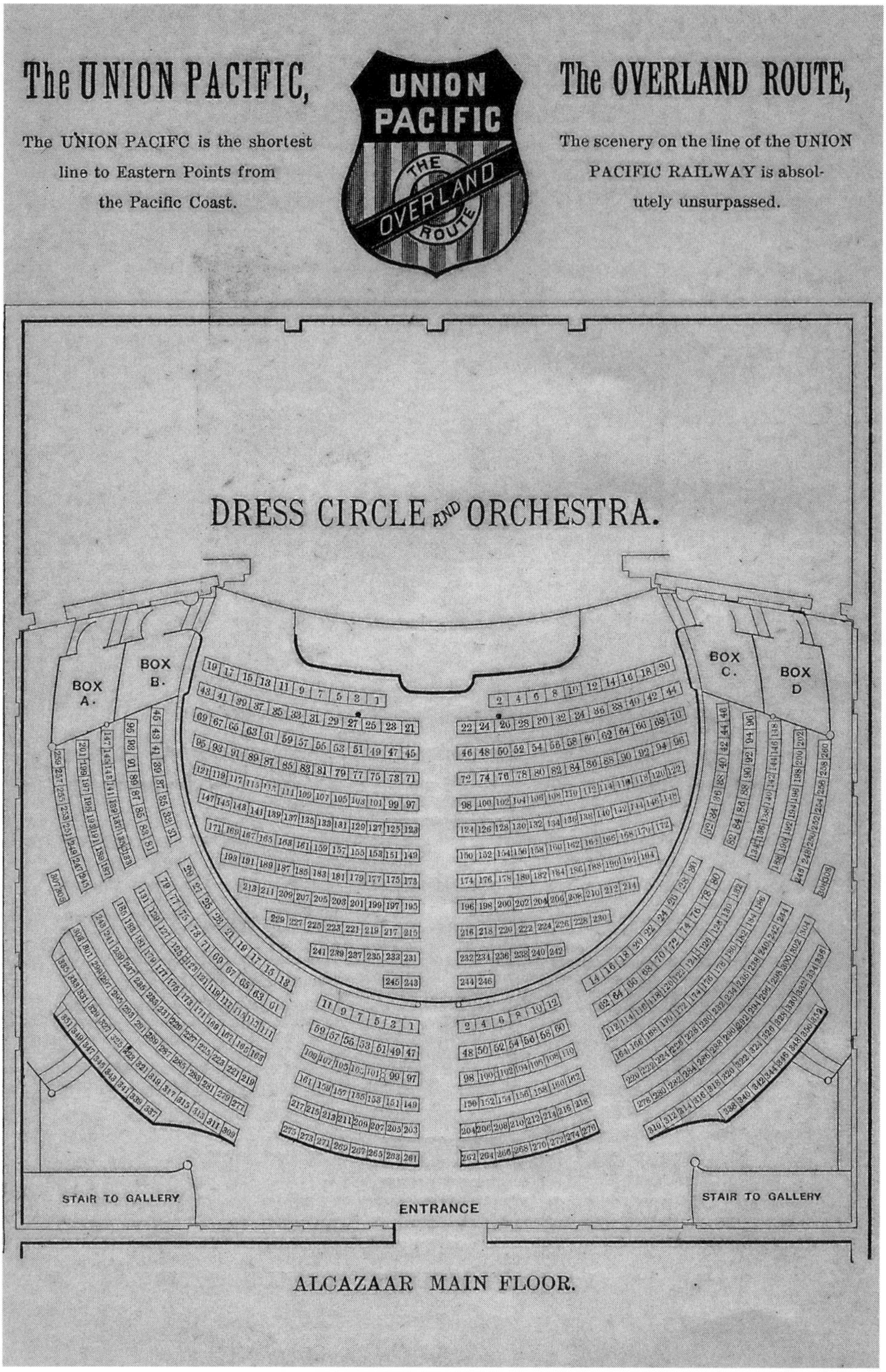

Figure 4.9. Plan of Alcazar, 1888. A high-class theater, the Alcazar had seats organized in a semicircle focused on the stage. Courtesy of The Bancroft Library, University of California, Berkeley.

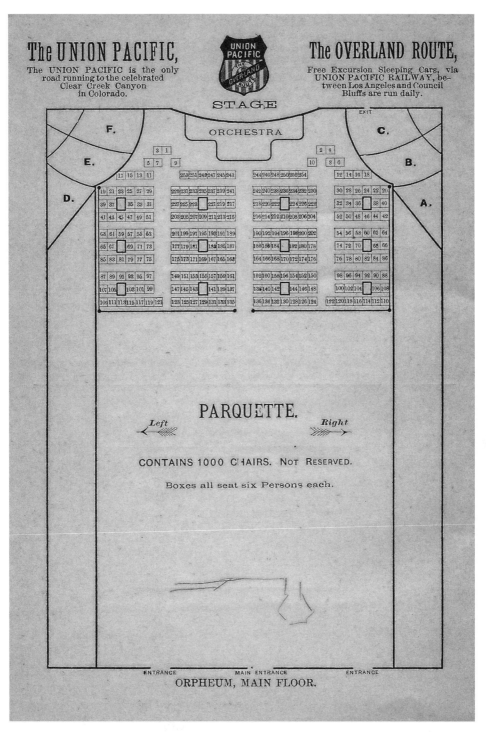

Figure 4.10. Plan of Orpheum Theater, 1888. The Orpheum Theater was organized in a strictly orthogonal fashion, maximizing the number of viewers with little consideration for sightlines. Courtesy of The Bancroft Library, University of California, Berkeley.

with the introduction of feature films with named stars, such as Theda Bara and Mary Pickford, films were marketed to middle- and upper-class women as well as to the working-class women to whom nickelodeons catered.[33] Instead of being advertised simply as "motion pictures," without detailing the subject, title, or actor, which was typical for most films included in vaudeville lineups, these new feature films were marketed like plays, with advertisements that emphasized the names of the star and the film and identified it as a film only in small print, if mentioned at all (Figure 4.11). By 1917, the *San Francisco Call and Post*'s regular feature on the week's theater offerings not only covered both films and plays (which it had been doing since 1913) but also announced the equality of the two in its headlines: "Before the Footlights and on the Picture Screen" and "News and Notes of the Players, Real and Reel."[34]

These newer films were usually shown in new, purpose-built movie theaters, often referred to as "palaces." These movie palaces featured more elaborate architecture and decoration, pipe organs and even orchestras to play accompaniment

Figure 4.11. Theater advertisements, 1916. *Temptation,* at the Tivoli, and *Destruction,* at the Empress, are both films, but the advertisements did not explicitly mention that fact. From *San Francisco Call and Post,* January 1, 1916, 16.

to the silent films, ushers to control behavior, and prices up to $1.50, a common high-end price for theater tickets.[35] In San Francisco, prices at palace theaters began at ten cents, twice the cost of nickelodeons. In addition, unlike nickelodeons but like theaters featuring vaudeville acts, plays, and operas, the movie palaces charged a range of prices depending on the seat and whether one was attending a matinee or an evening show.[36] The higher prices helped to ensure that the audience at these theaters was not primarily working-class and that those poorer patrons who did attend were likely to remain segregated in the cheaper balcony seats.

Thus, upper- and middle-class women saw movies in a very different sort of space from the nickelodeons frequented by poorer women. Richer women saw films much as they did plays, in the more expensive seats of proper theaters, or else they saw them as part of illustrated lectures in theaters or halls. Poorer women usually saw films in storefront nickelodeons, which had no reserved seats and no price differentiation among different seats. When they did see films in the larger theaters, they would typically sit in the inexpensive balcony seats, much as they did when they went to the live theater. For film, as for live theater, upper-class women experienced their amusements as a place and time apart from the everyday, in which ordinary annoyances did not intrude. Poorer women were less pampered. When they went to a nickelodeon or a vaudeville hall, their experience was more integrated with the everyday, including noise and the hustle and bustle of patrons entering and leaving or ordering refreshments. When they went to a more high-class theater, their experience was diminished by poor sightlines, and they were reminded with every step of the stairs to the balcony that this space did not exist to serve them.

Theaters and the Geography of Spectacle

In San Francisco the geography of theaters, whether high-class legitimate stages or nickelodeons, closely followed the geography of shopping. Just as the fancier department stores clustered around Union Square north of Market Street, so did the majority of theaters, although the downtown theaters were in an area adjacent to, rather than within, the downtown shopping district. The district main streets of Fillmore and Mission also boasted a few theaters showing live entertainment, generally vaudeville acts (see Figure 4.6).

Just as midday was prime time for women shoppers, it was also prime time for women theatergoers, who could comfortably go to low-price feminized matinees. Later in the evening, the downtown became a space more purely devoted to spectacle, inhabited by window-shoppers and mixed-gender theatergoing groups, availing themselves of the spectacle of the lit downtown as well as the spectacle within the theaters. Some performances were even held in shops rather than in theaters, further blurring the line between shopping district and theater district. In 1909 and 1910, Annie Haskell and her relations regularly attended free Saturday afternoon concerts at Sherman, Clay & Co. and Kohler and Chase, downtown music stores. These concert outings were always combined with shopping and other errands and sometimes also with visits to art galleries. Department stores also regularly provided free concerts; the Emporium, which Haskell mentioned visiting just to hear the music, offered concerts every Tuesday, Thursday, and Saturday night in 1902.[37] These downtown stores were the most popular-priced entertainment venues of all, and women of restricted means, such as Haskell and her sisters, took full advantage of their free shows, in some years attending free concerts more often than any form of paid entertainment. Performances were also a draw in many downtown San Francisco restaurants, especially the area's cafés, such as the Portola-Louvre and the Tait-Zinkand, which catered especially to after-theater patrons. Less expensive restaurants also provided entertainment. For example, Haskell and her sister Kate visited the Pompeian Court at Hale's department store for lunch "and heard the Hawaiians sing and play their guitars as if they were born with them in their hands."[38]

The location of theaters, in combination with concerts in large stores, reinscribed the centrality of the downtown and, to a lesser extent, local main streets in imagined maps of San Francisco. Market Street and the area to its north were by day the center of town, because they housed the shopping district and the business district, located to the east of the shopping district and most theaters. By day, theaters brought more women downtown to attend matinees and expanded the number of hours in a day a woman might spend downtown, as a play and shopping could easily be combined. By night, theaters brought both men and women to the brightly lit streets of the downtown, keeping Market Street and the shopping district peopled and active well after the shops and offices closed. For women, they provided an opportunity to claim the night, which, to this day, is seen as much more the province of men.

This combination of shopping and theater also reinforced the spectacular aspects of the downtown shopping landscape. Display windows and theaters shared the spotlight for evening strollers, who, going to and from the theater, would look in the elaborately arranged windows much as they would look on the stage within the theater. At night, with the shops closed, these windows served purely as theater and spectacle, to be looked at but not accessible for sale. Shop windows, lit in the same way the stage was lit, provided a spectacle mirroring the shows people were going to, prompting Wolfgang Schivelbusch to write, "The illuminated window as stage, the street as theatre and the passers-by as audience—this is the scene of big-city night life."[39] Concerts within stores blurred the line between stage and shop most fully, inviting patrons to think of the store as a theater and using the spectacular attractions of theatrical entertainment to draw in potential shoppers. In a weekday evening concert at the Emporium, the store embodied the downtown experience of theatergoing entirely within its walls, providing spectacles both theatrical and consumptive. The merchandise within the store, like the merchandise visible in the windows of the downtown, was not available for sale in the evening; thus, visitors combined their theatergoing with an enjoyment of the spectacular aspects of consumption, without the attendant pressures of purchasing.

Parades and Public Celebrations

Just as theater and the experience of downtown theatergoing engaged the downtown shopping district, the majority of public celebrations in San Francisco also focused on Market Street and the downtown, inspiring the writer of *Trips around San Francisco* to write, "Because of its festal characteristics by day and night, Market Street is excellently adapted to all those parades and pageants so popular with San Franciscans."[40] Parades and celebrations reinscribed Market Street as the center of the city, reinventing it from a space for movement and transportation to purely a space of spectacle (Figure 4.12). The street itself took on the central role usually taken by the storefronts and theaters that lined it. In preparation for parades, Market Street was decorated, often with electrical lights, which themselves became a separate spectacle to be visited the night before a parade (Figure 4.13).

Parades and public celebrations were another source of spectacle and amusement accessible to men and women of all classes. However, public celebrations were unlike theatrical entertainments in several ways. While plays, films, and most concerts were presented in specialized interior spaces, impinging on the streets only through signs, marquees, and barkers, parades and other public celebrations temporarily remade the ordinary space of the street into a space of spectacle.[41] The size of the audience in the darkened seats of a theater made little difference to a performance there, but the audience at a parade was an integral part of the spectacle. For informal public celebrations such as the annual celebration of New Year's Eve, the audience was the spectacle, and the crowd itself was what the revelers came to see. Women were often part of such spectacle, whether as participants in parades, spectators lining the street, or revelers in informal celebrations. While women were commonly spectators throughout the period I cover here, their participation both in parades and as revelers increased from the late nineteenth century into the twentieth.

The distinction between the formality of parades and the informality of public celebrations is significant. Parades made the civic order of the city visible in quite

Figure 4.12. Parade of soldiers home from the Philippines, 1898. Both men and women were spectators and, thus, part of the spectacle. Courtesy of The Bancroft Library, University of California, Berkeley.

explicit and self-conscious ways, and women's participation in them served as a highly conscious insertion of women into that civic order. As women claimed a role for themselves as civic representatives in parades, they reinforced the existing civic structure, even as they demanded a place for women within it. In public celebrations, in contrast, the lack of formality meant that women's participation held less explicit meaning. By participating in New Year's Eve and Christmas Eve celebrations downtown, women presented themselves as citizens of the city, but in a carnivalesque context in which breaking rules did not challenge, but rather reinforced, existing class and gender structures.

Public Celebrations

In San Francisco, two regular public celebrations, the New Year's Eve celebration on Market Street and the Christmas Eve concert at Lotta's Fountain (Market at

Figure 4.13. Market Street lit for celebration. The decoration of Market Street for parades and celebrations was often as much of a spectacle as the parade itself. Courtesy of San Francisco History Center, San Francisco Public Library.

Geary, Kearny, and Third), provided opportunities for women to be full participants in mass spectacles. In these informal public celebrations, to be a spectator was to be a participant. The annual New Year's Eve celebration on Market Street and other main streets was a mass celebration, typically made up purely of spectators, although occasionally including a parade early in the evening. This public celebration began in earnest in the late nineteenth century and grew in size and importance in the early twentieth. Beginning in the late 1890s, women were important and remarked-upon participants in this annual celebration.[42] The Christmas Eve concert, which began in 1910, similarly filled Market Street with a mixed throng (estimated between 90,000 and 250,000 in 1910).[43] While the Fourth of July parade celebrated the nation and the Labor Day parade celebrated the workers, both New Year's Eve and Christmas Eve celebrated the city of San Francisco in its entirety, crossing boundaries of gender, ethnicity, and class. The public New

Year's Eve celebration was a true carnival, fitting the description of the carnivalesque in Bakhtin's seminal discussion in *Rabelais and His World*. New Year's Eve celebrated death and rebirth in the end of one year and the start of the next; encompassed costumes, noise, bells, brooms, and mock battles with confetti; and was celebrated by "the people as a whole, . . . organized in their own way, the way of the people . . . outside and contrary to all existing forms of the coercive socioeconomic and political organization."[44] The Christmas Eve celebration, less carnivalesque than New Year's Eve, celebrated the rebirth of the city after the earthquake and fire and was focused on a single woman performer, initially the opera diva Mme Luisa Tetrazzini.

When in San Francisco, Annie Haskell went downtown for New Year's Eve and joined the crowds. In 1906 she wrote, "I was on Market Street last night. The blowing of the horns, the jangling of the bells, the pushing of the crowds, with the confetti, and the feather dusters made a pandemonium indescribable."[45] The one exception was in 1907, when she did not go to the celebration, because the downtown was still destroyed from the earthquake and fire. She wrote, "I did not want to go down to Fillmore Street and hail the new year in. I will wait till it goes back to Market Street."[46] The noise of New Year's is notable in Annie Haskell's diary entries, as in 1913, when she wrote, "I hadn't made a single good resolution anyway. Too much noise to think."[47] Noise was even more central to newspaper descriptions, which used headlines such as "Vast Throngs Noisily Usher in the New Year" and "Tumult Greets the New Year."[48] The New Year's coverage typically described the wide range of horns, from "the deepest of bassos to the shrillest of tenors," and other noisemakers, including cowbells, pots and pans, crickets (an "infernal machine that needs but to be twirled about its axis to furnish din unspeakable"), and resined cords connected to tin cans, and it emphasized the centrality of noise, as in the following: "Noise! More noise! Still more noise! All kinds of noise. Tinhorn noise. Noise of bells. Noise of rattles. Any old kind of noise, just so it was noise. San Francisco noise. Noise!"[49] The noise of people downtown was added to by whistles from all the factories, which joined the racket at midnight.

This "utter pandemonium" served to help remake Market Street from an everyday space of transportation, work, and shopping into a spectacular space of carnival, full of confetti, adults acting like children, and costumed people breaking the rules of public behavior.[50] "Gray-haired women played the pranks of their grandchildren," and "men and women were boys and girls."[51] In 1899, the *San Francisco Call* (hereafter the *Call*) wrote:

> On ordinary occasions boisterousness is supposed to be the especial prerogative of the
> male sex, but by long accepted custom the hilarity of New Year's eve in San Francisco
> has been about evenly divided between the entire human family and last night was no

exception to the rule. Thousands of women and girls made up for the other 364 days when they have to keep silent and gave full vent to their lungs through tin.[52]

The New Year's Eve celebration temporarily broke the gender rules, with women making up "for many days of domestic quiet" by blowing on tin horns and making a spectacle of themselves.[53] Women "entered into the frolic with the wildest enthusiasm" and "threw off conventionality for the time being and let their folly have its full fling."[54] Women's presence was regularly remarked upon in the papers, as was that of all ages of celebrants, from small children to grandparents.

The images used to illustrate newspaper accounts at the turn of the century emphasized both of these circumstances: women's presence and the centrality of noise to the celebration. All three major newspapers, the *Chronicle*, the *Examiner*, and the *Call*, illustrated their coverage each year with images showing a crowd of revelers, with a woman holding or blowing a horn front and center (Figures 4.14 and 4.15). The centrality of imagery of women in public, on the streets, at night,

Figure 4.14. New Year's illustration, *Examiner*, 1908. Like other San Francisco papers, the *Examiner* used women and horns in its coverage of New Year's during the first two decades of the twentieth century. From *San Francisco Examiner*, January 1, 1908, 1.

Figure 4.15. New Year's illustration, *Call,* 1910. Women, horns, and costumes are the central themes of this image. From *San Francisco Call,* January 1, 1910.

making noise, emphasized the temporary breakdown of rules of propriety in the carnival of New Year's. On this one occasion, the *Call* wrote, "San Francisco had forgotten classes and castes, and in one homogeneous whole was taking the night off."[55] "Street sweepers rubbed shoulders with men of millions. All social barriers were leveled along Market Street."[56] Even African Americans were included in the revelry. The *Chronicle* in 1912 told of a black woman whose mouth became filled with confetti when she opened it to sneeze, and who commented, "These here folks is treating me with as much disrespect as if I was white folks. . . . Most towns they wouldn't throw nothin' at me."[57] This temporary breakdown of class and gender roles was encapsulated by the friendly exchange between "Miss Pacific Heights" and a newsboy who attacked her with confetti or a feather duster, described in both 1905 and 1906.[58] In this encounter a male, working-class child mock-attacks an upper-class woman and is answered purely by laughter. Annie Haskell also remarked about the temporary breakdown of ordinary rules of conduct, especially of men toward women, writing in her diary in 1904: "Boys and men brushed the confetti from our shoulders with whisk brooms, or their hands as we passed, often chucking us under the chin, while myriad others behind blew mighty blasts in our ears, but as it was all part of the growing Mardi gras spirit, no offense was intended or taken."[59]

Unlike the noisy crowds of New Year's Eve, the Christmas Eve crowds were noted for their quiet politeness. As the *Call* announced, Market Street was turned into a "vast opera house," in which the population behaved like a proper opera crowd, cheering the diva but never interrupting her song. In fact, on this religious occasion, the crowd was even more polite than typical operagoers and was described in the papers as the equivalent of worshippers: "They stood with bared heads as people might stand in some vast Cathedral. This homage to the great artist who is loved by the town, and who loves the town, was to them something sacred."[60] This celebration remade Market Street into a temple in which was held a religious festival that celebrated the city of San Francisco and the opera singer the city claimed as its own. The participants in this festival came from both sexes and all classes, but the object of worship was a woman, the city's spirit embodied in the opera star.

As women's presence downtown (often making noise, as when women spoke on street corners on behalf of suffrage) became more common, the meanings of women's participation in public celebrations changed. Women remained part of the crowd, but rather than being remarked upon as breaking ordinary rules, they were described by newspapers simply as an attractive part of the crowd. By the 1910s, women were regular participants in the New Year's Eve and Christmas Eve celebrations and an ordinary presence downtown, no longer remarkable as they had been at the close of the nineteenth century.

Parades

In contrast to these public celebrations, in which San Francisco made itself visible through its crowds, parades have served as symbolic representations of a civic community, defined through different categories depending on the occasion.[61] The categories in each parade define the groups making up the public. Military parades, such as those associated with the Spanish–American War and World War I, and, to a lesser extent, Fourth of July parades, embodied the nation through its fighting forces. Fourth of July parades, while typically focused on the military in this period, also included the local police (a sort of local military), representatives of local government, ethnic fraternal organizations, and often schoolchildren. Admission Day parades, which were rotated among California cities and therefore only occasionally held in San Francisco, embodied the state through the members of the Native Sons and Daughters of the Golden West and other voluntary organizations. Labor Day parades embodied the city through its working people, organized according to the type of work they did.

In the 1890s, women participated in these parades primarily as spectators, cheering their working men or soldiers from the sidelines. A few women participated as allegories, such as the Goddess of Liberty in the 1890, 1894, 1895, and 1896 Fourth of July parades and Fraternity, Charity, and Loyalty in the Grand Army of the Republic float in the 1896 Fourth of July parade.[62] This continued a trend that had begun in the late 1860s in which, according to Mary Ryan, "woman had become spectacle" in parades when "the female body itself, with a minimum of iconographic trappings . . . became a focus of public ceremonial attention."[63] Women did sometimes read a poem or sing at the addresses after the Fourth of July parade, although they did not speak formally after the Labor Day parade, except in 1912, and they were participants in the picnics and dances that typically followed in local parks and halls. Although these activities were also usually public, they did not occupy Market Street, and they did not have the symbolic weight of the parade. Furthermore, these picnics and dances were conceptualized as family activities, so women participated largely as wives and daughters rather than as workers.

In the San Francisco Labor Day parade, women first marched as participants in their own right in 1902. Women of the Steam Laundry Workers' Union, the French Laundry Workers' Union, the Garment Workers' Union, and the Salesladies' Union dressed in white, rode in the parade, and were "loudly cheered during the counter-march by the various unions."[64] Their participation was highlighted in the *San Francisco Examiner* (hereafter the *Examiner*), which published a prominent photo of "the pretty girls on the Laundry Workers' Float" to accompany the detailed description of the parade.[65] The next year they were joined by a "goodly number" of saleswomen, and in 1906 women from the Bookbinders' Union also participated. By 1910, the *Call* wrote, "Unions there were of every conceivable kind, workers of every description—young and old, men and women, hale and weak."[66] Laundry workers, seamstresses, saleswomen, and waitresses all joined the march, not as embodiments of abstract virtues, but as workers themselves. According to the official order of the march, they participated under the category "miscellaneous," which marked their marginal position in the imaginary organization of the community through labor, but they were popular participants in the parade.

The Fourth of July parade was more exclusively male, in part because of its military nature and in part because it was largely discontinued after 1905, when women began to take part more regularly in such public spectacles.[67] With a few exceptions, women participated only as allegorical figures, such as Liberty and California, as they had in the preceding decade, or as the wife or daughter of a politician. Adult women were greatly outnumbered by schoolchildren, and Liberty was usually accompanied by schoolgirls representing the states. Unlike the Labor Day parade, which was organized by type of work, the Fourth of July parade was organized into military and civilian sections, with organizations representing different national groups, such as Italians, Germans, and Austrians, making up the bulk of the civilian section. While labor as an organizing feature made space for women to participate, especially because certain categories of labor, such as sewing and laundry, were largely female, the military and ethnic makeup of the Fourth of July parade did not create the same openings for women. As members of ethnic groups or as native-born women, they were considered to be represented by their men.

The exception to women's allegorical participation in the Fourth of July parade was their participation in debates around suffrage, although women also participated as members of sororal organizations in 1896 and 1898.[68] In 1895, Susan B.

Anthony and Anna Shaw, in town for the Women's Congress, joined the parade in a carriage following the mayor's. They "were recognized and cheered as they passed and were kept busy nodding all the way."[69] The following year, when suffragists were campaigning to pass a woman suffrage amendment in California, the Anti–Woman's Suffrage Association rode in private carriages at the end of the fifth division.[70] Women were not mentioned again as participants in their own right until 1912, the year after women had won the vote in California. In 1912 the *Call* announced, "For the first time in the history of San Francisco, a woman authoritatively addressed an Independence Day audience." Frances Potter's speech was described in the same paper with the headline "Eagle Dons Skirts, Woman Orator Thrills."[71] Except for these few exceptions surrounding the moments when suffragists were arguing for women's rightful position as full members of the body public, women participated in Fourth of July celebrations as spectators, cheering on the men.

While the Fourth of July celebration embodied the nation, Admission Day, September 9, celebrated the state. This celebration was tied to the fraternal organization the Native Sons of the Golden West (NSGW) and was celebrated in different California cities each year in conjunction with the organization's annual meeting. San Francisco hosted Admission Day celebrations in 1890, 1900, 1910, and 1915. The majority of participants in the parade were members of the NSGW or the Native Daughters of the Golden West (NDGW), but other fraternal organizations, including the Ancient Order of Foresters, the Improved Order of Red Men, and German, Austrian, French, and Italian clubs, participated as well, as did members of military, police, and firefighting units. The gendering of this celebration changed drastically over the years as the NDGW took on an increasingly large role.

In the 1890 parade, the grand officers of the NDGW rode in carriages with the grand officers of the NSGW, according to the announcement of the procession, but interestingly their participation was not noted in the lengthy newspaper coverage of the parade in the *Call*. A few other Native Daughters also joined the parade on floats, including one representing the San Francisco parlor of this organization, which featured "a Native Daughter, looking gorgeously beautiful," a Native Son, and a cinnamon bear, who acted as if "the young lady was a toothsome morsel for a lunch." Two female survivors of the Donner party rode in a carriage with one of their rescuers, a member of the Bear Flag party, and a man who accompanied Fremont on his expeditions. The remaining female participants embodied allegorical figures, inluding Agriculture, Columbia and her daughters, and the Goddess of Liberty. Women also participated from behind the scenes, making banners for the parade.[72]

By 1900, when the Admission Day parade was next held in San Francisco, the role of women within the parade was quite different. Many parlors of Native

Daughters from around the state rode in the parade on floats and carriages. Their presence was felt throughout the parade, because the organization was geographical, so that the NDGW marched with the NSGW from the same area of California, rather than in a separate section of the parade. In the tail end of the parade, peopled by other fraternal organizations, women served primarily as allegorical figures, such as the provinces of Sweden; Agriculture (in the Italian division); and the Goddess of Liberty and California (in the German division).[73] In the 1910 and 1915 parades, women no longer embodied allegories but were full participants, treated equally with their male counterparts in the coverage in the *Call*.[74] In 1915, all of the photos accompanying the coverage in the *Call* were of women, marching just as men did, rather than riding, as they had exclusively in the 1890 and 1900 parades. Annie Haskell and her sisters were among the Native Daughters "on foot and on horse and on carriages and on float" in the 1910 parade, while in 1890 they had been part of the admiring throng.[75] It was a great thrill for Annie Haskell, who wrote that it was "gorgeous and beautiful" and that she, her sister Rose, and the other riders in her tally-ho received many comments, even though they "were mostly old women. 'Oh, you Buena Vistas,' 'Oh, you fluffy ruffles,' 'California queens,' 'candy kids' and cheers, and all that sort of thing."[76]

By the 1910s women commonly participated in parades in large numbers, in contrast to the limited number of women in the nineteenth-century parades. Rather than embodying an abstract ideal or a civic symbol such as Liberty, Erin, or California, most of these twentieth-century parading women marched much as their male counterparts did, as female workers in Labor Day parades and as female club members in Admission Day parades and other parades of sororal and fraternal organizations. Within parades, women took their place as part of the body politic, representing themselves, rather than being represented by men.

The Geography of Spectacle in San Francisco

The Christmas Eve celebration, the New Year's Eve celebration, and the vast majority of parades all took place downtown on Market Street and surrounding business streets. Parades typically marched most of the length of Market Street, from Van Ness to the Ferry Building or vice versa, sometimes going one direction and doubling back. Parades also often left Market briefly to march up other major streets, such as Van Ness, Kearny, and Montgomery. The crowd on New Year's Eve typically converged on Market and Kearny Streets before the earthquake and fire and on Market, Fillmore, and Mission after.

Annual celebrations and parades celebrated Market Street and the downtown as the heart of the city and as the space of spectacle. On these occasions the everyday spectacle of window displays and downtown throngs was augmented by the dressed-up crowds watching parades, listening to the Christmas Eve concert, and participating in the New Year's Eve celebration; the floats and costumes of the paraders and New Year's Eve participants; the sounds of bands, opera singers, and tin horns; confetti; and banners and other decorations, including myriad lights.

Theaters, parades, and celebrations reinscribed the centrality of Market Street and the downtown, and to a lesser extent district main streets like Fillmore and Mission, to the life and identity of San Francisco. In their separate ways, theaters, parades, and other commemorations celebrated the downtown and both made use of and heightened its spectacle. Theaters created a routine nighttime population for the downtown shopping district by drawing people to the area after the shops had closed. The elaborate decorations in the show windows of downtown shops provided a free spectacle to theatergoers on their way to and from theaters, as well as for those who could not afford to go to the theater regularly. On Christmas Eve, the downtown was literally turned into a theater with the erection of a stage by Lotta's Fountain, where opera singers sang to vast crowds filling Market Street. Parades, organized in an orderly fashion and made up of people divided into logical categories, marched through the downtown, filling the sidewalks and windows with spectators. During these parades, the street was no longer a space of vehicular movement or even a space of commerce, but simply a space of spectacle. Bands and cheers filled the air, and banners, lights, floats, and other decorative elements remade both the marchers and the buildings along the parade route into objects to behold. The New Year's Eve celebration filled the streets of the downtown with people, noise, and confetti. In this carnivalesque celebration, all class and gender lines were transgressed, and the rules of proper behavior were broken, with adults behaving like children and women behaving like naughty boys. Similarly, the rules regarding the space of the street were broken too. Crowds made it necessary for streetcar lines to stop, because the growing number of people made it impossible for them to penetrate the space of the street. Rather than being a space of business and shopping and the center of transportation, the downtown became for this night purely a space of celebration.

As they reinforced the importance of the downtown, theaters, parades, and celebrations also increasingly inscribed women into the downtown and into the body politic. Female theatergoers and especially female filmgoers, drawn to the downtown by the new theater types that expanded women's participation in spectatorship, were an essential part of the evening theatergoing promenade. Female participants in the twentieth-century Labor Day and Admission Day parades marked the city as their own when they paraded as workers and as Native Daughters, members in their own right of the body politic of the city and the state. In their participation on New Year's Eve, women proclaimed themselves to be equal partners in merrymaking as well. Through their participation in all of these activities, women made a claim both on the territory of Market Street and the downtown and on full membership in the public.

Individual women's decisions to participate in the landscapes of spectacle and amusement and to make themselves visible downtown, as well as the decisions of theater owners to market their establishments to women, laid the groundwork for women's claims to full citizenship. This is not to say that by participating in informal public celebrations and downtown theaters women were explicitly making claims to space and citizenship. Parades, however, made the civic order of the city visible in a self-conscious way, so women's decisions to participate in parades on their own behalf were a conscious challenge to a status quo that did not recognize women as full participants in the civic life of the city. The fact that women first participated in San Francisco parades in the context of the suffrage movement underlines the political meaning of women's participation in these rituals of the public sphere. In contrast, while theaters were equally expressive of a social structure that separated San Franciscans by class, ethnicity, race, and gender, this social structure was implicit and therefore both harder to see and harder to challenge, because it seemed so natural.

FIVE

SPACES OF SUFFRAGE

IN 1896 AND 1911, California woman suffragists fought to win the vote in California, using a wide range of private and public spaces. In 1896, suffragists were very concerned with maintaining their propriety and femininity, often acting almost as visitors in public. In contrast, in 1911 suffragists acted as full participants in public space, secure in their rights to these spaces and willing to speak and sell publicly without fear of censure. In this chapter I examine the spatial tactics of suffragists in the California woman suffrage campaigns of 1896 and 1911 and argue that women's use of public spaces, and especially their sense of ownership of these spaces, had consequences beyond their felt relationship to the city. The increased range of nonpolitical public spaces in which women could and did move and act was an important aspect of their claim to political rights as members of the public and their ability to make that claim.

As the previous chapters have shown, from 1890 to the 1910s, women made increasing use of a range of public spaces, both as workers and as consumers. Downtown, upper- and middle-class women walked the streets as shoppers, and working women created their own relationships to the public spaces of the downtown as workers in its stores and also as shoppers there. Working-class and middle-class women also made local main streets their own as consumers. In their everyday movements through the city, whether visiting, shopping, or going to work, women of all classes made use of public transportation and peopled the streets. Eating out, going to the theater, and participating in public spectacles, women made the public spaces of the city their own. Their experience of the public spaces of the city as consumers of goods and services helped to construct women's relationships to the city and its neighborhoods, creating a sense of ownership over those places they frequented most often and in which they were served and accepted.

The California woman suffrage campaigns show that many different kinds of public spaces, including commercial spaces, were important both as spaces of discourse and as spaces that constructed participants' legitimacy to act as members of the public. The spaces of buying and selling, as well as other ordinary public spaces, are the ground on which the public sphere, a space of discourse in which people debate the public good, is built.[1] The importance of ordinary public spaces in constructing an argument for participation in the formalized political public sphere is demonstrated by the differences between the woman suffrage campaign in San Francisco in 1896 and the one in 1911. As the Berkeley suffragist and school-teacher Fannie McLean argued in her speech to women's clubs,

> The woman of today takes a larger and more gracious place in the world. We are now co-thinkers and co-workers with man, in the same world, living in the same houses, using the same public conveyances, attending the same colleges, buying our food and clothing at the same shops; and why not be co-voters as to the management of this common environment and as to the basic principles of the democracy which produces this environment?[2]

McLean argued that women's everyday use of public space should carry with it full rights in the public sphere, in the form of the right to vote. Women's ordinary use of public space also denoted a physical space within which they could make their arguments, and California suffragists made full use of all the public spaces at their disposal in order to convince men to give them the right to vote. In making use of these spaces for political speech, they reimagined them not only as spaces of work and consumption but also as spaces of politics. This shift in how these landscapes were imagined sometimes led to suffragists' making physical changes in them and altered how they and others experienced them and women's roles within them.

Using Space in the California Woman Suffrage Campaigns

The contrasts between the spaces used in the California woman suffrage campaign of 1896 and the campaign of 1911, only fifteen years apart, demonstrate the significant transformations in women's relationships to public space during the 1890s and into the early twentieth century, which the previous chapters of this book have documented. The unsuccessful 1896 campaign used a much smaller range of spaces than the successful 1911 campaign, and private spaces constituted a larger portion of them. The sites used in 1896 were also more controlled and enclosed than those used in 1911. Women's expanding use of public space in their everyday lives gave them a wider base from which to argue for their rights. As discussed in earlier chapters, women's expanding use of public spaces was uneven by class and ethnicity, and the actions of the woman suffragists in both 1896 and 1911 reflect the variations among women in terms of which spaces they engaged and in what manner.

At the turn of the century, suffragists were working to pass amendments to state constitutions to get the vote on a state-by-state basis, rather than focusing on a federal amendment. Although a federal amendment had been proposed in 1878, by Senator A. A. Sargent, of California, whose wife was a prominent San Francisco suffragist, it was rejected numerous times and was not even considered by U.S. Senate or House committees between the years of 1896 and 1913.[3] In this hostile federal atmosphere, suffragists turned to the states, hoping to build up women's rights and influence piecemeal in order to win suffrage eventually in all the states. Only five states gave women the vote prior to the California victory in 1911. Wyoming granted the vote to women from its beginnings as a territory in 1869 and was admitted to the union as a woman suffrage state in 1890. Colorado amended its constitution to allow women the vote in 1893. These were the only states in which women had the vote at the time of the 1896 California campaign. In 1896, two additional western states, Utah and Idaho, joined Wyoming and Colorado. Fourteen years later, in 1910, the people of Washington amended its state constitution to give women the vote. The California campaign helped to turn the tide, and California's 1911 victory was followed by Oregon, Kansas, and Arizona in 1912, Illinois in 1913, Montana and Nevada in 1914, and several other states soon afterward. These state victories helped lead to the passage of the federal amendment in 1920.

In both the 1896 and the 1911 California campaigns, suffragists fought first to get a referendum on suffrage on the ballot, and once they had achieved this, they worked to convince the men of the state to vote for it. Although suffragists used a variety of spaces and tactics in an attempt to reach a large number of men in both campaigns, the unsuccessful campaign of 1896 was waged primarily in the traditional public political spaces of commercial halls and in the private spaces of suffragists' parlors and voters' homes. The campaign was organized by one central suffrage organization, which was closely tied to the East Coast woman suffrage movement and had a membership that consisted mainly of upper-middle-class, white, nonimmigrant women, although it did include less elite women such as Annie Haskell.

Fifteen years later, in 1911, suffragists made use of these same spaces but also moved into retail and commercial spaces, commercial places of entertainment, and the streets, using techniques of persuasion borrowed from these realms. The 1911 California woman suffrage campaign was the largest and broadest waged in the United States to that date and borrowed some strategies from the radical suffragettes in England. This campaign was actually several interlocking campaigns, waged by organizations as diverse as the College Equal Suffrage League, largely made up of middle- and upper-class educated women, many of whom were active in other sorts of reform activities; the Club Women's Franchise League, a largely elite group; the Wage Earners' Suffrage League, closely tied to the Waitresses' Union; and a coalition organization, the State Central Committee, that coordinated efforts.[4] Each of these groups made use of different sets of spaces, with the least overlap in the polite space of hotels, used mostly by the club women, and the streets, which were never used by the Club Women's Franchise League and were used most actively by the middle-class reformers.

The 1911 campaign also targeted voters beyond the middle and upper classes. Focusing on working-class voters, the Wage Earners' Suffrage League addressed all 185 unions in the city.[5] Newspaper coverage in the *Call* emphasized the support of the union members for suffrage, reporting, for example, "The postal clerks gave their indorsement by a rising vote in which every man in the hall rose to his feet Saturday night. The pattern makers pledged themselves to a man."[6] Members of the Wage Earners' Suffrage League did not confine their speeches to union meetings but also spoke to workers "at political meetings in the districts where the workingmen live" and "in the factories and foundries where they toil."[7] For example, on October 2, 1911, they held noonday meetings in the city's lumberyards and the Union Iron Works, and on October 6, 1911, suffragists spoke at various places along the waterfront and again at the Union Iron Works.[8] Interestingly, the Union Iron Works was also the only workplace where a suffrage address was reported in 1896.[9] Other suffrage organizations also spoke to workers at their workplaces, targeting different classes of workers. Members of the Club Women's Franchise League visited commission and wholesale houses and railway offices to speak to employees there about suffrage, and the College Equal Suffrage League spoke to schoolteachers in the public schools and addressed merchants' employees during their noon hour.[10]

Middle-class reformist suffragists self-consciously addressed voters of racial and ethnic backgrounds different from their own. Churches were used as a space to speak to African American voters in both the 1896 and the 1911 campaigns. At least three addresses were made in 1896 in African American churches, by Naomi Anderson at the African American Baptist church on Powell Street on July 31 and at the African Methodist Episcopal Zion Church, on Stockton Street, on July 30, where Susan B. Anthony also spoke on May 3.[11] In 1911, a large meeting was held at the Third Baptist Church, at Hyde and Clay Streets, presided over by Julia Sanborn, "well known in almost every state of the union as a missionary among the colored people."[12] This use of a missionary as a speaker is expressive of the relationship between less powerful groups and suffragists, who were often middle-class reformers doing settlement and other reform work with immigrants and the poor. In the 1911 campaign, suffragists, particularly those active in the College Equal Suffrage League, also courted immigrants. Suffrage flyers were printed in Italian, French, German, Portuguese, and Chinese (Figure 5.1), and advertisements were run in all the foreign papers in San Francisco and Oakland during the last week of the campaign.[13] Because suffragists "found that it was impossible to get foreigners . . . to come out to . . . public meetings," they also used other means to target immigrant populations. For example, a committee of the College Equal Suffrage League arranged to give a talk on woman suffrage to every gathering of every German association in San Francisco.[14] Suffragists similarly spoke to meetings of French and Italian groups. In addition, mass meetings were held in Swedish, French, and Italian to target those populations. These meetings were held in prominent locations within the immigrant neighborhoods; for example, a mass meeting addressing the Italian population was held at the Italian theater in North Beach. At these meetings most speeches were given in the native language of the immigrant population, by prominent members of their community as well as by native-born suffragists. In addition, at the Italian meetings "a vocalist gave several operatic selections" in order to please the audience's presumed love of music. These meetings were actively announced by street speakers and through advertisements in foreign-language and neighborhood papers, on window cards in shop windows, and on flyers distributed throughout the neighborhoods.[15]

In both the 1896 and the 1911 campaigns, suffragists made use of both domestic spaces and public spaces, engaging each of these realms with different sets of tactics. Any targeted group, whether workers, immigrants, or the elite, was addressed both within the private spaces of their homes and the homes of their acquaintances and within the public spaces of churches, public halls, workplaces, streets, shops, and commercial amusements, although, as we've seen, the public realm was much more heavily engaged in 1911.

Politics in Private Space: Engaging the Domestic

Women employed domestic space as political space for practical and ideological reasons. In addition to being inexpensive, domestic space evoked the home as the

LISEZ — RÉFLÉCHISSEZ

Les Femmes ont le droit de
Voter
à toutes les élections
—en—

Australie	Norvège	Ile de Man
Nouvelle Zélande	Finlande	Tasmanie

Elles votent aux élections municipales
—en—

Angleterre	Islande	Danemark
Ecosse	Canada	Suède
Pays de Galles	Natal (Afrique)	

AUX ETATS UNIS

Les femmes votent aux élections municipales et
scolaires dans

28 ETATS

Elles ont le même droit de voter que les hommes
dans les états suivants:

Wyoming	depuis	1870
Colorado	depuis	1893
Idaho	depuis	1896
Utah	depuis	1896
Washington	depuis	1910

ET EN CALIFORNIE ??

En France, un project de loi a été déposé, il y
a deux ans environ, à la Chambre tendant à donner
à la femme le droit de voter, comme à l'homme.
Nous laisserons nous dépasser ici?

Le Donne Hanno Completo Suffragio

—IN—

Australia	Norvegia	Isle of Man
Nuova Zelanda	Filanda	Tasmania

Le Donne Hanno Suffragio Municipale

—IN—

Inghilterra	Iceland	Danimarca
Scozia	Canada	Sweden
Wales	Natal (Sud Africa)	

NEGLI STATI UNITI
LE DONNE VOTANO
IN VENTOTTO STATI
In Affari Municipali E Scolastici

Le Donne Hanno Ugual Suffragio Degli
Uomini Negli Stati

Wyoming
Utah
Colorado
Idaho
Washington

Perché Non In California?

Frauen Haben Eine Allgemeine Wahlstimme

—IN—

Australien	Norwegen	Insel Man
New Seeland	Finnland	Tasmania

Frauen Haben Die Municipale Wahl

—IN—

England	Island	Dännemark
Schottland	Canada	Schweden
Wales	Natal (Süd Africa)	

IN DEN VEREINIGTEN STAATEN
WÄHLEN FRAUEN
IN ACHT UND ZWANZIG STAATEN
In Municipalen und Schul Angelegenheiten

Frauen Wählen Unter Gleichen Bedingungen
Wie Die Manner In

Wyoming
Utah
Colorado
Idaho
Washington

Varum Nicht In California ?

As Mulheres Teem Suffragio Completo

———EM———

Australia	Noruega	Isle de Man
Nova Zelandia	Finlandia	Tasmania

As Mulheres Teem Suffragio Municipal

———EM———

Inglaterra	Islandia	Dinamarca
Escocia	Canada'	Suecia
Paiz de Galles	Natal	(Africa do Sul)

NOS ESTADOS UNIDOS
AS MULHERES VOTAM
EM VINTE E OITO ESTADOS
Nos Negocios Municipaes e Escolares

As Mulheres Votam em Termos
Eguaes aos Homens em

Wyoming
Utah
Colorado
Idaho
Washington

POR QUE NÃO NA CALIFORNIA?

Figure 5.1. Multilingual suffrage flyers, 1911. California suffragists targeted a number of
immigrant groups, including French, Germans, Italians, and Portuguese. Courtesy of the
Huntington Library, San Marino, California.

woman's sphere. This gave suffragists a certain latitude in how they employed domestic space, as well as making it a proper space for women to use. By engaging the home as a political space and by using the social conventions of tea parties and visits as the bases for their political activism, suffragists underlined their femininity and made their political activity seem nonthreatening.

Domestic Space: Using Private Space for Public Purposes

Because women were associated with and had the most access to domestic space, suffragists often used this space for meetings. *Parlor meetings* is a term encountered early in the California suffrage fight. In April 1896, before the official push to organize precinct clubs, the *Call* wrote that suffrage leaders had "decided to adopt the plan of parlor suffrage meetings conducted with such success in the east. Already clubs are organized in each district."[16] These parlor meetings were similar, if not identical, to precinct club meetings, and the article implied that they were organized, or at least conceived of, in relation to the political space of the district. However, the term *parlor meeting* emphasizes their hominess rather than their organization based on political maps. This term expressed a desire to conceive of these meetings as part of a private landscape of domesticity. In a parlor meeting, politics was domesticated, and suffrage meetings were imagined primarily not as part of a political network but rather as part of a social network of like-minded women.

Neighborhood suffrage-club meetings in 1896 were probably held at the houses of leading local suffragists who had enough space to accommodate a meeting. Annie Haskell referred to several of the meetings she went to in 1896 as "parlor meetings," although she only once mentioned in whose parlor a meeting was held. That meeting was at the house of Mrs. Sargent, the prominent suffragist and wife of Senator A. A. Sargent, who had proposed a federal suffrage amendment in 1878.[17] Across the bay in Berkeley and Oakland, meetings were held in the private homes of precinct presidents and other activists, such as Mary (Mrs. William) Keith, the secretary of the Alameda County suffrage organization.[18] These parlor meetings had an important practical advantage: they did not require significant financial outlay. In contrast, men's organizations more often had access to rooms in clubs, union halls, and the offices in which members worked. This world of nondomestic, semiprivate spaces was less accessible to women, although not entirely so.[19] Public halls could also be rented for meetings and often were for other organizations. Because 1896 was a presidential election year, many political organizations had precinct- and district-level clubs with regular meetings. The precinct club meetings announced or reported in the three major San Francisco daily papers, the *Chronicle*, the *Call*, and the *Examiner*, were those of Republican and Democratic clubs. When a meeting place was mentioned, it was most often "at their headquarters," which implies that these organizations had offices of some sort at the district level, unlike the Woman Suffrage Association, which had an office only at the state or city level, and then only well after the campaign had begun. Local meetings of political parties were also held in other public halls and spaces but were never listed as meeting in private homes. Renting space in a hall for a small-scale meeting was an expense, but the decision to hold meetings in suffragists' home parlors rather than public halls was likely a cultural and strategic choice more than a financial one.

Because a major purpose of precinct meetings was outreach to the neighborhood, holding meetings in the parlors of private homes was symbolically useful, because it marked them as occasions of friendship and sociability, as much as of political action. A meeting in a home could almost masquerade as a tea party or sociable visiting; the space of the parlor put these gatherings into the imagined realm of the domestic, even as the substance of and access to the meeting were public. Suffrage leaders recognized the importance of sociability as a way of pulling in potential converts to the suffrage cause; one of the important points of their action plan after the defeat of the amendment in 1896 was to "interest the young people in a series of entertainments, dances, contests, socials, teas, campaign songs."[20] Holding smaller meetings in parlors rather than public halls also associated the suffrage movement with the home, the "proper" place for women. Anti-suffragists often based their arguments against suffrage on the idea that giving women the vote would threaten the centrality of the home for women and destroy its sanctity. Suffragists countered by describing the vote as an extension of women's duties in the home, a way for women to protect the health and morality of their children.[21] The argument that motherhood provided a logical basis for public power was not limited to the suffrage movement; arguments for reform politics of all sorts, from city beautification to welfare, often displayed the image of woman as a maternal figure, housekeeper of the city, protecting her children and all children by exerting her moral power to keep the city clean, safe, and good.[22]

However, the term *parlor meeting* was also not without its problems in 1896, because the emphasis on domesticity embodied in the term could undermine the political seriousness of the suffragists' endeavor. Therefore, the suffrage organization eventually downplayed that term in favor of a more gender-neutral term. After the *Call* first mentioned the formation of small clubs and referred to their meetings as "parlor meetings,"[23] emphasizing the feminine nature of the space where the meetings took place, later articles replaced *parlor meeting* with *precinct meeting,* emphasizing the tie between suffrage-club organization and the formal landscape of male electoral politics. This shift made 1896 suffrage-club meetings potentially part of two imagined landscapes: the landscape of domesticity and the

landscape of politics. This ambiguous imagining was highly expressive of the difficult tightrope suffragists were trying to walk. They were simultaneously demanding a formal role in the public sphere and reassuring voters that they did not desire
to change women's social roles, arguing, for example, that it was precisely because
they were mothers that women needed the vote.

Just as domestic spaces were used in 1896 to emphasize the femininity and propriety of suffragists, the imagery of domestic spaces was also transposed onto
public spaces in order to feminize them. For example, the 1896 suffrage headquarters, in a rented downtown office directly behind the facade of the Emporium
department store building, functioned similarly to a parlor. An August 18, 1896,
article in the *Call*, "Suffragist 'At Homes,' New Social Feature to Be Inaugurated
during the Present Week," described fortnightly evening receptions to be held in
the Woman Suffrage Bureau offices for women "whose occupations at home or at
work prevent[ed] their visiting the bureau during office hours." These receptions
were referred to as evenings "at home," with Mary E. Hay as the "hostess par ex-
cellence." The evening receptions, and perhaps the reception of visitors during
regular office hours, functioned much as visiting hours and days did for a refined
lady in her parlor, and the language of polite visiting was used to refer to the
Suffrage Association in much the same way as it was for a lady in the society pages.
Similarly, in 1911 the Oakland Suffrage Amendment League announced weekly
at-homes in their headquarters in the Albany Block, on Broadway in Oakland. The
Examiner announced that this office would be opened with a "suffrage housewarming," elaborating, "All their friends have been cordially invited . . . and true
hospitality in the shape of equality tea, will be dispensed by the receiving party."[24]

The 1896 suffrage headquarters was also feminized and domesticated through
its decoration, which made use of the style and accoutrements of a domestic parlor, including draperies, parlor tables, throw rugs, flowers, and plants (Figure 5.2).
A short note at the end of an article about the Woman Suffrage Bureau headquarters stated, "The lady managers of the bureau desire to return special thanks to the
kind friends who keep the rooms fragrant and lovely by means of their generous
donations of flowers."[25] This emphasized the "lovely" feminine quality of the office
and downplayed any relation it may have borne to typical "rational" masculine
office decor and function.[26] Flowers were similarly used to feminize meeting halls
and other public spaces and were even used to decorate polling places the first time
San Francisco women voted.[27] Not only did flowers add color and otherwise visually feminize a space; their scent similarly marked the space as feminine, masking
and counterbalancing the scent of cigar smoke of traditional male politics.

In the 1911 campaign also, individual suffragists' houses were used as sites for
sociable meetings, but suffragists worked to associate these meeting with the imagined spaces of politics rather than those of domesticity. They dropped the term

Figure 5.2. Woman Suffrage Bureau headquarters, 1896. The headquarters were located in an office space in the facade of the Emporium. They were feminized through the use of plants, draperies, rugs, and parlor tables, all items that furnished domestic parlors. Courtesy of the Huntington Library, San Marino, California.

parlor meeting, which emphasized the private space of the parlor, in favor of terms such as *suffrage tea* and *suffrage reception,* which described activities that sometimes took place in hotels and other nondomestic spaces. Teas and receptions remained part of a feminine realm of sociability, but a realm familiar from semi-public club and charity work and thus not necessarily tied to the domestic realm. This renaming also emphasized the political purpose of the meeting by using *suffrage* in the term, while the 1896 term *parlor meeting* was more coy about the reason for the meeting. Regular "pink teas" were also held every Wednesday and Thursday from mid-August through the October 1911 election by the Club Women's Franchise League to win over anti-suffragists. These teas masqueraded as purely sociable occasions, to which anti-suffrage women were invited. After the guests had been "made perfectly comfortable with tea, wafers, and conversation about their babies and their cooks . . . a little suffrage [was] adroitly applied." According to the *Chronicle,* "That the achievement [support for the suffrage cause] is finally reached . . . is inevitable, because no woman is permitted to go until her name is enrolled as a member of the league. . . . Mrs. Johnson [a member of the Club Women's Franchise League] not only enrolls her new members, but provides against any backsliding by immediately putting them to work on their anti-neighbors by suggesting that they themselves set other dates for more pink teas."[28]

Some suffrage teas were described in the newspaper in purely social terms, much like the items of social news that shared the In Woman's World page with suffrage events in the *Call* or the "What Society Is Doing" column that ran next to the "Doings of the Women's Clubs" column, which detailed suffrage activities in the *Chronicle*.[29] For example, an item in the *Call* on August 22, 1911, read, "Mrs. George Wale of the Votes for Women Club, assisted by Mrs. Oscar Eckman and Miss Ruth McDonald, kept open house at her residence in the Sunset district yesterday from 1 to 4 P.M. in the interest of the suffrage movement, and received many guests."[30] Other teas were described in more detail, the listings of speakers and entertainments making it clear that the teas followed the format of meetings and were not merely social affairs.[31] However, the domestic social language of the "tea," which was more feminine and less political than a "meeting," was sufficiently dominant that it was even carried over to describe suffrage meetings outside the home, such as the weekly equality tea held in the assembly room of the Richmond branch of the Carnegie Library.[32] Thus, most suffrage meetings remained part of an imagined landscape of female sociability, while masculine party precinct meetings were imagined as part of a political landscape, however, one that was based in part in spaces of masculine sociability, such as the coffeehouse and the saloon.

Suffrage teas and parlor meetings were also gendered through their timing. All of the teas and meetings held in suffragists' homes in 1911 were held in the daytime, usually in the afternoon. This made them primarily accessible to women of leisure and marked them as following the class and gender norms of middle- and upper-class women's sociability. Similarly, the more public teas of the Club Women's Franchise League were held in the afternoon at the St. Francis Hotel, and those of the Women's Suffrage Party were held at ten in the morning in the party's offices.[33] The regular meetings of both of these groups were also held during the daytime,[34] making use of the domestic space and circuits of female domesticity, in contrast to the party precinct meetings and other public meetings that aimed at a mass audience, thus were usually held in the evening.

Private spaces were also mobilized in force on October 10, 1911, election day, with more than a hundred women holding open houses for the over four thousand suffrage picketers and poll watchers, serving light luncheon and tea, and providing resting rooms with "couches and easy chairs where the weary workers [could] snatch a few moments rest during their long vigil."[35] These accommodations in private homes were supplemented by equivalent services provided by the California

Club in its clubhouse and by the Club Women's Franchise League in rooms at the St. Francis Hotel, spaces typically open only to elite women. Here private spaces were used less as truly public spaces, equivalent to rented halls or headquarters where one might hold a meeting, and more as highly controlled semipublic spaces, equivalent to private clubs that, in both their men's and women's incarnations, used a design language of domesticity.

Domestic spaces mattered to both the 1896 and 1911 campaigns, but they were imagined in distinctly different ways in the two campaigns and were much more central in 1896. In 1896, domestic spaces were used as primary meeting places, and they were imagined as simultaneously part of a private landscape of female domesticity and part of a more public landscape of politics, with the domesticity often dominant. Although suffrage teas remained an important recruitment tool in 1911, in this later campaign domestic spaces more often functioned as auxiliary spaces; they were used as sites for meetings much less often than clubs, hotels, halls, and headquarters in downtown office buildings. When the 1911 suffragists made use of domestic spaces, they reimagined them as the equivalent of hotels and clubs, sites of elite women's sociability but tied to the organized world of women's clubs rather than the domestic world of family. In 1911, suffragists no longer felt it necessary to meet in homes in order to emphasize their propriety, in part because middle- and upper-middle-class women could inhabit many more types of public space without compromising themselves.

Visiting for Suffrage: Door-to-Door Canvassing

Door-to-door canvassing similarly used domestic space for political speech, although with this tactic potential voters were engaged in their own homes rather than invited into the homes of suffragists. In early July 1896, the leaders of the California State Suffrage Association began a campaign to establish suffrage clubs at the precinct level throughout San Francisco and the state. By August 7, over fifty clubs had officially been established in the city.[36] These clubs were the first and most important step of a strategy of spatial expansion and saturation, through which suffragists hoped to reach every voter, often by means of the voters' female relations. The clubs were to function as a home base for canvassing, outreach to neighborhood women and sympathetic men, and "a system of calls, loaning and distributing literature, [and] extending invitations and meetings."[37]

One precinct chairwoman was Annie Haskell, who had recently moved to the Mission District from South Park. She wrote in her diary on July 23, 1896, "This p.m. I went down to the Head Quarters of the Suffragists as I agreed. They want me to represent the precinct. I didn't want to but I could hardly refuse as I am the only one they know in this precinct." As precinct chairwoman, she took on the responsibility of single-handedly canvassing door to door throughout her district, going out for several exhausting hours every day for over three months.[38] When Haskell described her "suffraging," the canvassing she did in the Mission District, she sometimes used the language of visiting. She usually referred to her suffrage work briefly, saying simply that she "went out" and "got a number of names." However, she also wrote about suffrage canvassing as a social activity, a form of visiting, as in this diary entry from August 4, 1896: "Well, I went out again this afternoon. I only got four names, but I did not visit many hours, and I met some nice women and we talked too long I guess." She was also frustrated by the pressure to solicit money as she canvassed, writing, "It makes me sick to think of asking for money."[39] Asking for money did not harmonize with the idea of canvassing as visiting; besides that, she wrote of the Mission District, "There is no money—everyone pleads poverty."[40]

Door-to-door canvassing, organized through local suffrage clubs, was also an important tool in the suffrage campaign of 1911 and was announced in an August 19 article in the *Call* titled "Campaign Carried to Voters' Homes." It declared, "Every man who votes in this city may expect to receive a call. If on their first call the suffragists find the man is not at home, they will ascertain the best time to catch him in and will return as often as necessary to make a personal plea for his vote."[41] In this article the terminology of polite visiting, "receive a call," was used to describe this political activity, marking it as continuous with women's ordinary sociable visiting. Also important was the "personal" relationship between a suffragist and a voter in canvassing, which occurred in the voter's home, making it quite different from the public address used in speeches in halls, publications, and other forms of education. Persuading voters, primarily through canvassing them in their homes, was the first and primary task of local suffrage organizations in 1911 as well as in 1896. Thus, the private space of the home, or its threshold, was used as a part of the public realm when suffragists engaged individual voters in rational discourse on the political subject of women's rights. Women made use of their conventional association with the home and the feminine social activities of teas and visiting to activate the home as a political space, but the language they used to describe these political encounters marks them as part of an imagined landscape of domestic sociability, not a public, political realm.

Suffrage Politics in Public Space

As women became associated with a wider range of spaces through their everyday activities, they engaged them more broadly as political spaces. While in 1896 suffragists used public space relatively cautiously, the 1911 suffragists engaged the wider range of public spaces that they had begun to encounter more commonly in their everyday lives. In 1896, the public spaces employed by suffragists were those associated with department stores and downtown shopping, because the downtown shopping district was the first nondomestic part of the city to be feminized and was a district in which the upper-middle-class women who made up the bulk of suffragists were most at home. In 1911, suffragists employed hotels, lunchrooms and tearooms, theaters, streetcars, the streets themselves, and the parades that filled them—the spaces and activities they had made their own through everyday use. Because the 1911 suffragists were more diverse than those engaged in the 1896 campaign, not all of them engaged all of these spaces equally. Educated middle-class suffragists most aggressively used commercial public space, in keeping with their status as the primary group of consumers served by that space.

Selling Suffrage in the Downtown Shopping District

The landscapes and districts defined by the everyday activity of errands were central to the campaigns of both 1896 and 1911. In keeping with the largely upper-middle-class leadership of the 1896 campaign, the only errand landscape actively engaged in 1896 was the downtown shopping landscape. Again in 1911, the downtown shopping landscape was a central space of political activity, engaged largely by middle- and upper-middle-class suffragists, both to speak to men and women of their own class and to address women who worked downtown, through a suffragist-run lunchroom as well as advertisements on streetcars. The suffragists of 1911, however, also used local main streets and grocery stores, which were often targeted by reformist middle-class women hoping to reach immigrant and working-class women and their voting kin.

   At the beginning of the 1896 campaign, the headquarters of the California State Suffrage Association was the home of its president, Ellen Clark Sargent, at 1630 Folsom Street.[42] In late June it moved to the brand-new Emporium building, on Market Street (on the same block as the Society of California Pioneers, the Academy of Science, and the Metropolitan Temple), where the association held most of its large public meetings. There the association took three rooms, two to be used as offices and the third as a reception room, where members received visitors and held committee meetings.[43] Thus, just as the language shifted from the private "parlor meeting" to the more public "suffrage tea" in references to the meetings, the headquarters also moved from a private space to a more public space, albeit a thoroughly feminized commercial space. The choice of the Emporium building was important. The site was on a prominent block on the main street of San Francisco, in keeping with the respectability of the association, and within a building named after its major tenant, a brand-new department store, which was the epitome of female-dominated commercial public space. With the offices located in a space dominated by a department store, these suffragists walked the line between the masculine-coded space of the office and the feminine-coded space of the store. Although these offices shared the ambience of the Emporium's feminized retail space, the only direct engagement of that retail space in 1896 consisted of "a number of artistic hand-painted placards" placed by the Emporium management "in every prominent portion of the interior of the building," inviting shoppers to visit the Woman Suffrage Bureau offices.[44] The suffragists stayed within the more private zone of their offices, decorated, as we have seen, to be reminiscent of a parlor, and did not venture into the store itself to win over recruits. While they made use of their proximity to feminized retail space, their headquarters was not thought of as part of the landscape of shopping. Instead, it was imagined as simultaneously part of the landscape of public politics, as a headquarters office, and of the landscape of female sociability, as a parlorlike space that held at-homes.

In 1911, in contrast, middle-class suffragists regularly engaged retail spaces, including the rebuilt Emporium, to sell suffrage tea and postcards, hand out literature, and advertise the suffrage cause. In 1911 suffragists used retail space in general in two main ways: selling, combined always with campaigning, and advertising. Throughout the 1911 campaign, suffragists served and sold "Equality Tea" in their offices, booths at fairs, and, as we've seen, even inside department stores. This tea was "prepared at their [the suffragists'] expense, packed in boxes of their design and sold at their prices at the interest of the case," and it was "talked of, sold, and drunk wherever suffragists [were] gathered together."[45] The Women's Suffrage Party set up a booth in the Emporium to sell and serve tea and to proselytize for the suffrage cause.[46] From this booth they also distributed two hundred *Votes for Women* buttons to Emporium employees.[47] The booth was kept running for a month, and then the sales were expanded to other San Francisco stores and throughout the state. This represents a very different relationship to the space of the department store from that of the 1896 suffragists, who perched next to it. In 1896, suffragists behaved like polite shoppers, while in 1911 suffragists acted more like salesgirls.

Tea selling and serving by the Women's Suffrage Party were expanded beyond stores and suffrage headquarters to booths at fairs throughout the state, including the Pure Food Exhibition in San Jose, the California State Fair in Sacramento, the Cherry Festival in San Leandro, and the annual Industrial Fair of the Retailers Protective Association in San Francisco.[48] The suffragists' sales, however, were not limited to Equality Tea. They also made money from the sale of a novel titled *An American Suffragette,* which they apparently did not sell themselves but was sold by bookstores and newsstands on behalf of the Club Women's Franchise League.[49] Some retailers also sold Equality Tea on behalf of the suffragists.

A more public spectacle of selling was "postal day," held October 5, 1911, five days before the vote. On this well-advertised day suffragists, described by Selina Solomons in *How We Won the Vote in California* as "prettily costumed young saleswomen, with golden bannerettes, offering their wares," sold postcards downtown.[50] A *Call* article, illustrated with a charmingly flirtatious picture, *Miss Florence Dunnuck, A Militant Suffragist* (Figure 5.3), described the activity this way: "At every street corner where traffic is busiest, at the entrance to all the big office buildings and the most patronized stores, stands will be maintained by members of the various clubs, and cards and literature will be sold to further the campaign for equal franchise in California."[51] The suffragists enlisted the help of "many

Figure 5.3. *Miss Florence Dunnuck, a Militant Suffragist*. This illustration announced the selling of postcards on downtown streets. The incongruity between the label "militant suffragist" and the picture of a sweet, pretty young woman with flowers plays on the contrast between old stereotypes of suffragists and the new image of young, stylish suffragists. From *San Francisco Call,* October 5, 1911, 7.

prominent business houses," which supported them in many ways, including providing rest stations in their stores for the "pretty girls" selling postcards. These supportive stores included Paul Elder, the White House, the Emporium, Roos Bros., and Sherman, Clay & Co.[52]

Suffragists also set up shop in a storefront just a few doors down from the Emporium, decorating their window with yellow placards and posters, yellow chrysanthemums, and *Votes for Women* banners. They pulled sympathizers in with the "constant distribution of leaflets on the sidewalk in front of the store, day and evening, until 9 P.M."[53] With this storefront headquarters, suffragists made themselves visible and easily accessible to a wide range of the populace, including workingmen and workingwomen who came in during their lunch hour and on their way home from work. The storefront headquarters functioned as a suffrage store as well as a political office, as is clear in this description of a typical headquarters visitor: "... the pretty High School student who gushingly asks for a button. 'I saw a girl with one,' she says, 'and I thought it was a fraternity pin. It is so cute. Only five cents? Ain't they sweet? She told me I could get them in this building. . . . I think they're awful cute. Oh no, I don't want to join. I just want a pin.'"[54]

Most dramatically, suffragists also used the windows of stores as a space for advertising, not just in San Francisco's downtown, but also on local and district main streets throughout the San Francisco Bay area. In San Francisco, they focused particularly on the downtown, Fillmore Street, and the Mission District.[55] In this campaign the College Equal Suffrage League asked merchants to give a suffrage window exhibit from August 21 to 28. For that week more than fifty stores, including the City of Paris, Shreve & Co., and I. Magnin and Company, displayed yellow goods in their windows, as yellow was the color used for the suffrage campaign in the United States.[56] A member of the College Equal Suffrage League described the scene this way:

> Shopwindows, from one end of the city to the other, blossomed in every known shade of yellow, and to point the reason for the color, copies of the prize poster, in dull olives and tan, lightened with yellow and flame, gave the campaign cry "Votes for Women." . . . One large furniture store gave two great front windows to a beautiful autumn color scheme in browns and yellows, and one book shop put up several dozen copies of the prize poster and filled his window-shelf with copies of such books as Olive Schreiner's "Woman and Labor," and Miss Addams' "Newer Ideals of Peace." . . . The city wore the color that was soon to be the color of success.[57]

The decoration of windows in suffrage colors was continued periodically throughout the campaign, and on the eve of the vote, many shops hung suffrage flags in their windows.[58]

Contemporary advertising practices were explicitly used by California suffragists to promote their political position. In a speech on tactics for the 1911 campaign, the Berkeley schoolteacher and suffragist Fannie McLean wrote, "The chief feature of all our campaign will have to be dignified advertising. The visible sign—Votes for Women—must appeal to the eye everywhere."[59] According to the suffrage historian Ellen DuBois, California pioneered the "modern methods" of advertising within the suffrage movement.[60] One important advertising technique used in this campaign was the repetition of the official *Votes for Women* poster. This poster (Figure 5.4) was the result of a well-publicized competition, and the winning design was an image of an elegant woman "clad in Indian draperies, standing against the Golden Gate as a background with the setting sun forming a halo around her head."[61] The youth and elegance of the female figure on this poster, described by one speaker as "the official 'Votes for Women' posters with the pretty girl upon them," were important aspects of the image suffragists tried to project in the 1911 campaign.[62] As was reported in an article saved by McLean,

> The "shrieking sisterhood" of suffragists is a thing of the past. No more shall man be compelled to defend himself against the short haired, vituperative enthusiasts of the last century. In contrast with the "old order that passeth" is the suffragette of the present day, who must be a dainty feminine creature with the prettiest of manners and clothes and a vast store of logical argument on the tip of her tongue.[63]

Articles and authors often remarked on the beauty and modernity of the young suffragists, who "put to ridicule that statement by some 'anti' that 'the difference between a suffragette and a debutante is 20 years.'"[64] For example, in a *Chronicle* article, the ushers at the mass suffrage meeting at Dreamland Rink on October 5 were described as "fifty members of local suffrage organizations who . . . will refute the popular impression that the cause is only espoused by the advanced and the unbeautiful."[65] Similarly, the *Examiner* wrote that the ushers at a meeting in the Scottish Rite Temple on September 29 were "a brilliant throng of beautiful women gowned in a style benefiting a gala occasion, and made a very pretty picture in itself an argument for equal suffrage it would take a mile of logic to overcome."[66] This image of modernity was strengthened by the use of automobiles, movies, billboards, electric signs, and other modern inventions by the suffragists.

The repetition of the official *Votes for Women* poster, which was not only posted throughout the state but also reproduced on stickers and postcards (fifteen thousand of each) (Figure 5.5), was explicitly patterned on contemporary retail practices, as was the use of a single color. The official report of the committee on design wrote, "The psychology of advertising teaches us to repeat, with slight variations, a familiar design until the public eye is caught by the manifold repetitions of the same arresting idea."[67] The prize poster, the slogan "Votes for Women," and the color yellow were all repeated to such an extent that some suffragists eventually

Figure 5.4. *Votes for Women,* poster by B. M. Boye. This was the winner of a poster competition sponsored by a coalition of San Francisco woman suffrage organizations and was the main image used in the campaign. It was designed in a range of shades of yellow, the suffrage color. Courtesy of The Schlesinger Library, Radcliffe Institute, Harvard University.

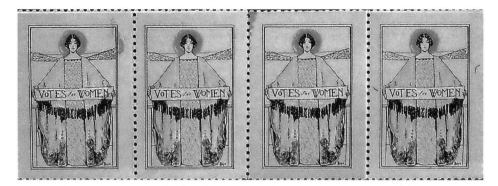

Figure 5.5. *Votes for Women* stickers. The poster was reproduced on postcards and stickers. Courtesy of the Huntington Library, San Marino, California.

found the color "violent and pestilential" and wished that they might have chosen "a new and prettier color."[68]

Window displays as well as other forms of advertising used repetition heavily. Indeed, the major display strategy for windows of this era was patterned repetition. Model window after model window was organized entirely out of handkerchiefs, shoes, canned goods, or other commodities, arranged to create a striking visual effect (Figure 5.6). Repetition was also created through the use of a single color. Windows, interior displays, and sometimes even entire stores were often decorated in shades of a single color, creating an image that simultaneously expressed unity and harmony through color and abundance through the variety of objects and shades. The repeated use of a single color was a marketing technique particularly associated with department stores. The historian William Leach described this 1907 use of the color green at the New York store Greenhut's: "Carpets, side walls, stool seats, and desk blotters wore different shades of green; window backgrounds were green velvet, and the store attendants dressed in green; there were green stationery, green stock boxes and wrapping paper, green string, even green ink and green ribbon for the green store typewriters."[69] California suffragists adopted this single-color marketing ploy when they decided on the color yellow as a unifying motif for all material related to the state's suffrage campaign. Other political organizations had also employed the repetition of color; the Woman's Christian Temperance Union, for instance, used a white ribbon, and British suffragists had used purple, white, and green. However, California suffragists were the first to combine a politically coded color with window displays, suggesting that they were specifically adopting the tactics of modern department store marketing.[70]

The use of the color yellow was questioned, however, both by people who simply did not like it and by those opposed to woman's suffrage: "Miss Martin of the

Figure 5.6. Model window displays in the early twentieth century showed effects created through the repetition of a single object. From *The Art of Decorating: Show Windows and Interiors,* 341.

anti-suffragist cause of California declared that the yellow emblems of the suffragettes indicated that they came from 'pest houses,' and the color indicated cowardice on the part of men who wear the yellow buttons."[71] In answer, suffragists gave many arguments in its favor. Alice Park, the Palo Alto booster of yellow as a suffrage color (all her correspondence was on yellow paper, stamped "Votes for Women"), wrote about why they had chosen that color:

> We knew the suffragettes in England tried to catch the eye with colors, and our yellow was easier to use than their purple, white, and green. . . . We said it was the most beautiful color in the world, and especially in the golden state; that California owed its life to the gold in the hills; that the golden poppy is the state flower; that the golden orange grows here, and golden grain.[72]

Yellow had also been used as a suffrage color elsewhere in the United States, first in the Kansas campaign of 1887 and, since then, in Washington State, where suffrage was won in 1910.[73] In California, yellow was repeated in suffrage posters, pins, sashes, banners, stickers, displays, postcards, flower packets (of yellow flowers), and other paraphernalia. The color yellow and the official suffrage poster were the unifying symbols of suffrage in the show window campaign and throughout the entire suffrage battle. In the window campaign individual merchants chose which yellow goods to display, but the color and the poster marked the display of goods as part of a political display as well as a commercial one.

For the most part, suffragists were not themselves shop owners or managers, so they gained access to the store windows through their social connections and purchasing power. According to the official committee report on the window display campaign, the committee chairman "was a member of a family long known in the city. She started a list with the signatures of some of the most important firms in San Francisco, and each consent, of course, made the next easier to win."[74] Suffragists not only encouraged the participation of store owners through personal contacts but also used the mass media. They published the names of prominent stores that participated in the campaign in the daily newspapers in advance of the display week to pressure nonparticipants to sign on. In the window display campaign and throughout the entire 1911 suffrage campaign, women used their influence as shoppers to pressure stores to support them, whether by decorating their windows in yellow, supporting the postal day by providing rest areas for suffragists, or not displaying anti-suffrage signs, for fear of a threatened boycott.[75] California suffragists also made use of their power as consumers to gain access to store employees. Visiting large stores and if possible speaking to young managers, whom they considered "a better risk than old ones," suffragists convinced owners and managers to include suffrage arguments in their pay envelopes, place suffrage pamphlets on the time clock, and allow suffragists to address workers personally and distribute literature.[76]

In the window display campaign, suffragists took advantage of the conventional department store practice of providing space to women's clubs and church groups for charity activities. For example, the July 4, 1903, the *Dry Goods Reporter* described a church apron sale held in a Minnesota department store. The store built and decorated a booth for the sale in a corner of the store, served coffee and lunch to the women working at the sale, and advertised the sale heavily.[77] This sale and similar in-store charity activities were reported in the *Dry Goods Reporter* and the *Modern Grocer* and touted for creating goodwill, extra trade, and advertising for stores. Women's clubs' public, though nonpolitical, use of store space set a precedent for suffrage clubs' political use of store space. For store owners, promoting suffrage in their window displays simply continued a policy of accommodating female consumers, treating the store as the women's club it was often described as being. It also was a way of attracting the middle-class women who were major suffrage boosters and competing with stores that did not sign on to the campaign.

The show window campaign engaged not only the downtown shopping district but also local and district main streets, such as Mission and Fillmore Streets. Main-street shop windows were also essential in advertising meetings targeted at a local population, such as the mass meetings conducted in Italian in North Beach, advertised in part by "window cards in the local shops."[78] Shop windows throughout the city were essential spaces for suffrage propaganda aimed at the specific audiences who frequented each neighborhood. Working-class women grocery shoppers were also targeted by suffragists, who stamped a suffrage message on thousands of paper bags in grocery stores.[79] In 1910, Brooklyn suffragists similarly printed thirty thousand paper bags with suffrage information and gave them away to grocers as a way of getting the message to "the faithful mothers, sisters and aunts who are to be found working in the kitchens."[80] The Brooklyn suffragists argued that these bags were inexpensive to print, elaborating, "The class the bags will reach is exactly the class of women who have always been the despair of our workers, because they are so hard to get at; and yet they are of the bone and sinew of our land, and constitute a splendid future electorate."[81] California suffragists, following the New York suffragists' example, expanded beyond their main focus on the downtown shopping landscape and reached the women least likely to shop there by placing suffrage messages in grocery stores. Suffragists reached further consumers by "tucking pamphlets in the pockets of clothes about to be delivered by tailors."[82]

Serving Up Suffrage: Tea, Lunch, and Women's Rights

The suffragists in 1896 may well have served tea in their offices for their evenings "at home," but if they did, they used the model of the tea party, a private ritual of sociability, mapped onto the more public space of an office. In 1911, two suffrage organizations, the Club Women's Franchise League and the Women's Suffrage Party, regularly served tea in their offices. When suffragists in 1911 served tea in non-domestic spaces, rather than arranging them to mimic domestic parlors, they used the model of the commercial tearoom, a female-friendly space of consumption most often found in the polite middle-class spaces of the hotel and the department store.

The Club Women's Franchise League had their headquarters in the St. Francis Hotel, an expensive and nationally prominent hotel located on Union Square. They served Equality Tea in their rooms on Saturday afternoons. The newspapers never described the space in which tea was served but did regularly announce the league's "tea time." The language used in newspapers to describe the league's tea time walked a fine line between the domestic and the commercial. Although the rooms were never referred to as tearooms, the newspapers also never used the terms *tea party* or *a tea* (as in a social affair) to describe the serving of tea.[83] Thus, the club women's serving of tea rhetorically engaged both the civilized, commercial tea taken in the polite space of a hotel tearoom and the more exclusive club social, which similarly used the spaces of the hotel for more private purposes. Not far away, the less elite Women's Suffrage Party served tea at ten every day in "a model tearoom in the club headquarters, room 125 of the Lick building."[84] This room was organized on the model of a commercial tearoom, and much was made of its design. One article described the interior as a typical suffrage space, elaborating, "The room will be tastefully decorated with yellow bunting, suffrage posters and bowls of flowers, which seem to have bloomed in yellow and purple for the express purpose of furthering the cause."[85] A later article declared that the tearoom would be decorated "in true Chinese style, with oriental decorations on the wall and far eastern tea sets on the tables."[86]

This design emphasized the tea over suffrage and more closely approximated commercial tearoom design. Whatever the final decorative scheme, the Women's Suffrage Party tearoom was not described as an ersatz parlor in which ladies gave teas; rather, as one newspaper attested, "The object is not so much to have a suffrage room as a tearoom that will attract visitors to taste some of the delights the suffrage party has in store for its adherents."[87] The commercial, as opposed to the domestic, model of the tearoom was further heightened by the presence of a table where suffragists sold different varieties of Equality Tea in half-pound, whole-pound, and five-pound boxes.[88] Selling tea was in keeping with a commercial tearoom space but would have been out of place in a parlor. The Club Women's Franchise League's teas most likely attracted primarily other elite club women, who would have felt comfortable partaking of the league's hospitality. In contrast, the commercial space of the Women's Suffrage Party tearoom could have attracted a larger range of respectable middle-class female patrons, including any woman who might have frequented downtown tearooms. As discussed in chapter 3, this audience could potentially extend into the lower middle class.

The more reform-minded middle-class suffragists of the Votes for Women Club used the model of another commercial space of refreshment, the cafeteria lunchroom. In order to reach out to the population of working women and make some money, they ran a lunchroom for "business women" (that is, shopgirls and office workers), serving five-cent dishes in an upstairs room at 315 Sutter Street, near the intersection with Grant Avenue and in the immediate vicinity of high-end department stores. Understood as a wholesome space, the lunchroom was furnished with unpainted yellow pine tables, naturally showing the suffrage color. According to a newspaper description of its decoration, "All sorts of enthusiastic votes for women banners make their appeal from the walls and yellow paper flowers grow on the chandeliers."[89] The restaurant was "not run for the girls alone, but on a sound business basis," so it served as a potential source of income for the suffrage cause and at least paid for itself. More important, however, it served as a way to expose young working women who might never go to a suffrage meeting to suffrage ideas. Although it was run as a business, a newspaper article emphasized its homeliness with its descriptions of the cook ("mothering from the gray-haired woman who prepares your lunch"), the food ("just plain home cooking),", and the cashier's language ("'Come again, dear,' just as if you were visiting and did not have to hurry back to an office or store").[90]

In running an eating place for working women, the suffragists of the Votes for Women Club followed a reformist example set by women in several other cities, women who opened lunchrooms to serve working girls good food in moral and healthy surroundings. Articles in the *Woman's Journal* in the early years of the twentieth century described several women-run lunchrooms for working women in New York, Boston, and Chicago.[91] In these lunchrooms, which served women exclusively, meals were provided hot from a steam table at an affordable price, as in New York's Woman's Home Club, where "no dish is over five cents and bread, butter, and some sauces and relishes are but a penny apiece."[92] The suffrage lunchroom thus followed a tradition of women's activism and business, serving a real need and making money while also spreading the word about suffrage to a working-class population.

In public eating establishments that suffragists did not run themselves, they used other methods to make their mark. In a letter to Alice Park describing her suffrage activities, M. J. Bearby wrote, "I stamp the paper napkins in all the Ice Cream Parlors and all the Restaurants I come in contact where they will permit with no refusals."[93] In this way suffrage messages were spread in restaurants and other eating places even when the suffragists were not there. Although suffragists confined their presence to tearooms and lunchrooms serving a primarily, if not exclusively, female clientele, napkins could travel more broadly, reaching men as well as women, particularly the less elite men eating in restaurants that used paper napkins. With the use of slogan-bearing paper napkins in lunchrooms that focused on working women, tearooms that served middle-class women, and restaurants that served working- and middle-class men, suffragists kept their cause visible, furthering their goal of making their slogan ubiquitous and simultaneously reinforcing their image as respectable, businesslike hostesses.

Converting the Commuters

In 1896, the streets were not explicitly activated as a space of suffrage activity, although canvassers walking house to house must inevitably have engaged some people in debate and conversation on the street as they went on their rounds. This use of the street was incidental to the task of going to private houses and occurred primarily within residential neighborhoods, ordinarily the neighborhood in which the canvasser resided. In 1911, in contrast, suffragists actively engaged the street as a forum for speeches. The window displays in shops and the posters in the windows of offices also marked the space of the street with the signs of suffrage. The campaign of advertising, like the selling of suffrage paraphernalia, moved beyond the space of shop windows and into the street itself. Speakers such as Mrs. Orlow Black encouraged suffragists to put up posters throughout the city (Figure 5.7): "There are a lot of fences in this city that are not working. Now, whenever you see a fence that is not working paste some of these on it . . . these official 'Votes for Women' posters with the pretty girl upon them."[94] Larger advertisements, including billboards and a "large, permanent, electric sign" at Market Street near Fourth, "the largest business center of the city," also addressed people on the streets.[95] Suffragists used four different billboards (Figure 5.8), each focusing on different sorts of women who needed the ballot. One posted at Sutter Street near Powell read, "Vote Yes on Amendment No. 8. Justice for California women. The women pay taxes. Give some say to those who pay."[96] Two hundred fifty seven-by-ten-foot "great, stern, black-and-white billboards—undecorative and uncompromising," were placed throughout the city in September and were joined by fifty twelve-by-twenty-foot billboards later in the campaign.[97] As Selina Solomons pointed out, the street was also full of suffrage symbols draped from cars and "carried 'accidentally' through the streets from one headquarters to another." On the day of a big mass meeting, she reported, "Mrs. Mary T. Gamage carried an enormous and very beautiful silk pennant through the entire length of Fillmore Street."[98]

Suffrage advertising also addressed commuters and others riding streetcars and ferries. Six hundred eleven-by-fourteen-inch placards with crisp copy, such as "Give your girl the same chance as your boy,"[99] were placed in streetcars for five weeks. Two to four placards were placed in each of the streetcars that ran into Market Street because of Market Street's centrality to the city and the streetcar system. Suffragists believed that "more people who might be influenced by street-car advertising rode on these lines than on any other."[100] The Market Street lines carried a high volume of riders, which made them an efficient location to place advertising. In addition, suffragists may have believed that the middle-class riders on these lines, commuting to white-collar jobs and going downtown to shop, were particularly open to being influenced by the suffrage message. Six three-by-ten-foot signs were used to catch the eye of ferry commuters, who were likely to include many middle- and upper-class residents of Berkeley and Oakland traveling to work at downtown offices. The method of placing these signs, however, was less professional than the paid advertising on streetcars. After ascertaining that it was not strictly illegal to plant signs in the bay, intrepid suffragists "made their way, in a heavy wind, to the crazy structures in the bay called 'duck-blinds,'" and "made

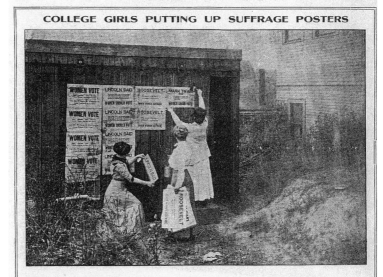

Figure 5.7. Women pasting up suffrage posters. Suffrage posters were put up wherever space was available, as well as on rented billboards. From *Western Woman Voter* 1, no. 9 (September 1911): 1.

four . . . quaking signs fast." Though they had a problem with boys who cut "the better half . . . from women" and changed one sign to read "Votes for __men," these suffragists succeeded in addressing ferry commuters traveling both to and from San Francisco.[101]

If ferry commuters could have ignored the signs, they would have found it harder to ignore the members of the Club Women's Franchise League, who "applied influence, literature, and discreet conversation to the commuter as he was in the act of commuting at the ferry" on October 6 and October 9, 1911. In addressing commuters, they were careful not to speak too long, because anything that interfered with the boat schedule "might mitigate against the cause."[102] With the signs, they had prepared ferry commuters for their message, although through impersonal appeals. In person, the club women could potentially be more persuasive, presenting commuting men with specific arguments for woman suffrage. More

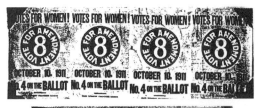

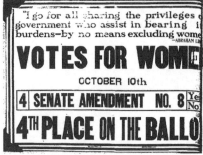

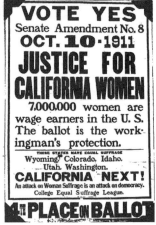

Figure 5.8. Posters on billboards, 1911. During the 1911 woman suffrage campaign, 250 large billboards were posted throughout San Francisco. Courtesy of the Huntington Library, San Marino, California.

significantly, they themselves acted as an argument for suffrage, showing the men commuting from suburban communities to jobs in the downtown that refined club women, much like their own wives, were supporters of woman suffrage.

Speaking in the Streets

While in 1896 suffragists may have used smaller neighborhood streets in the course of door-to-door canvassing, the streets used in 1911 were the most prominent in town, major thoroughfares, especially Market and Mission Streets. These were the streets of shops, the natural place to advertise. They were also sites with large numbers of passersby, thus ideal for making speeches. Suffrage speeches were usually made from automobiles, which provided a physical platform from which to speak. Automobiles also allowed speakers to move from site to site in the city, getting the word out to as many people as possible, particularly throughout the downtown and the Mission District. The most common sites for street speeches were on Mission at the corners with Twenty-third, Twentieth, and Seventeenth Streets; at Post and Fillmore; and along Market Street on the corners with Grant, Stockton, Seventh, and Fifth Streets (Figure 5.9).[103] These locations were also common sites of other political speech and civic displays. The activity on Grant and Market (Figure 5.10), a corner frequented by suffrage speakers, is described by Mary Austin in her 1917 novel, *The Ford:*

> Close to where he stood, a bearded anarchist brandished his red banner. . . . Farther up, somebody raucously advertised the Secret of Vitality, as disclosed in the tag ends of some obsolete philosophy; and highest of all, under the flare of the street lamp, half a hundred people surrounded a soap box from which a woman's tossed head and gesticulating arms gave her the appearance of swimming in their midst. Young Brent mistook them at first sight for suffragists, until his idle glance was corrected by the betraying lack of yellow pennants.[104]

On this corner, suffragists were just one type among many political and religious speakers, distinguishable only through their trademark, the color yellow.

Suffragists took over the downtown public space of Union Square in the week preceding the October 10 election. On the afternoon of October 5, 1911, campaigners went into Union Square Park, "absolutely virgin soil, so far as suffrage is concerned," and, after a disagreement with a gardener and an encounter with a policeman, who declined to be "decorated by suffragists," "hastily procured the soap box, so popular in the suffrage campaign, and the services of Professor Edward Dupuy, and with the assistance of the crowd a meeting was evolved."[105] A second takeover of Union Square, held on the eve of the October 10 election, was more impressive, involving five thousand people, at least four automobiles, multiple speakers, and the famous singer Mme Lillian Nordica. The meeting began on Stockton Street, at the east side of the park, where the audience heard Mme Nordica give a pro-suffrage speech and sing "America," changing some of the lyrics to reflect her pro-suffrage stance, and "The Star Spangled Banner," with the crowds singing along.[106] This was followed by a speech by Dr. Charles E. Aked, a prominent pro-suffrage debater, which Mme Nordica publicly approved of "by nodding her head and crying 'Hear, hear' when the speaker clinched the points of his argument."[107] Then Mme Nordica went back to her hotel, and automobiles filled with suffrage speakers took up posts at the four corners of the square and carried on four separate open-air meetings.

The *Chronicle* announced that suffrage organizations concentrated on the street meeting: "Every evening suffrage arguments and suffrage principles may be heard without other expenditure than that of strength sufficient to stand in a crowd."[108]

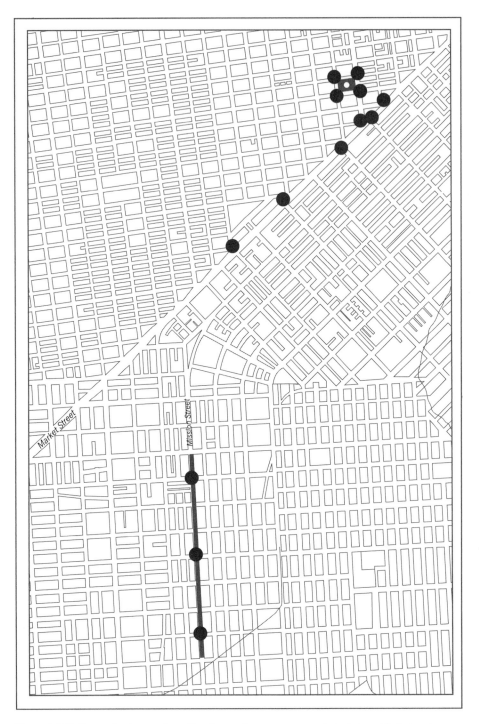

Figure 5.9. Suffrage street speeches. Street speeches were concentrated along Market and Mission Streets, and each dot represents a street speech mentioned in the San Francisco newspapers. The line along Mission Street denotes mention of speeches "on Mission Street" for which no intersection was named.

Figure 5.10. Intersection of Market, Grant, and O'Farrell Streets, c. 1915. This was a popular site for street speeches, including those made by suffragists in 1911. Market Street is to the right, and Grant is toward the center of this photograph. Courtesy of San Francisco History Center, San Francisco Public Library.

Because there was always a crowd where the street speakers located themselves, this method was successful for reaching a range of people, especially voting men, who might not have come to formal meetings. Street meetings were usually held at night, so they were accessible to working men and women. Members of the College Equal Suffrage League, who focused on reaching immigrant and working-class voters but were themselves middle- and upper-class native-born women, were the most active street speakers. In order to entertain the crowd as well as educate it, their speeches were usually interspersed with songs (many popular songs had new suffrage lyrics written to them for this purpose), and sometimes a bugle was used to draw a crowd.[109] Jokes were also used, as when Rose French commented when standing on a soapbox at Grant and Market that "although it was her first appearance on a soap box, it was not her maiden appearance, as she was then a grandmother."[110]

Suffrage speakers usually used automobiles instead of soapboxes for outdoor suffrage speeches. They were so common that the *Call* referred to street speeches as part of the "automobile campaign," and the photograph accompanying one article was mostly filled by a banner-draped car.[111] A car known as the Blue Liner, driven all over the state carrying the suffrage message, was often featured in photographs and articles, and the city automobiles may be seen as little sisters to that icon of the California suffrage campaign.[112] Ida Finney Mackrille, of the College Equal Suffrage League, wrote that initially conservative suffragists had opposed speaking from automobiles, saying, "It will never do. Such sensational methods will lose us votes." She argued that, in contrast, automobile speaking was "one of the best ways of reaching the voter. The man who was not interested in suffrage, who could not be inveigled into a hall or to an indoor meeting of any kind, would yet stop on the street corner to 'hear what the women have to say.'" She wrote, "We had to get the attention of men, and as they would not come to us, we went to them."[113] In the context of San Francisco, automobiles were used as easily portable and tall soapboxes. In contrast, in New York City, although street speaking was regularly used to attract listeners who would not attend a conventional meeting, suffragists did not use automobiles, because they were seen as "suggest[ing] class distinction" that would wound the pride of the sensitive New York street audience.[114] Apparently the class implications of automobiles were not seen as a problem by San Francisco suffragists, although downtown street speeches were often described as being made from soapboxes rather than cars.[115]

San Francisco suffragists took over the streets to the greatest extent on October 5, for postal day, discussed earlier, and on October 10, election day. On election day, between two thousand and four thousand women from across the spectrum of suffrage activists took to the streets for picket duty, handing out reminder cards to voters. Several other suffragists watched the polling itself and the counting of votes, as they had done in 1896.[116] This takeover of the streets was reported at length in the *Call*, which featured three pictures of very respectable looking suffragists in the street on the front page of the October 11 paper and wrote at length on women's experience on the pickets. Similarly, the *Examiner* featured a two-page spread on suffragists active in the campaign, centered around images of them campaigning on election day. Alice Park described election day as a pageant of yellow: "Women overseers rode in automobiles with golden banners and as they neared the polls, there was always a spot of gold in sight, where a large 'votes for women' sign was displayed, one or more women with yellow ribbon badges, and holding yellow cards in their hands."[117] On this day women were present throughout the streets, not marching or speaking from cars or soapboxes as spectacular performers, but instead handing out literature and talking logically as rational and political persons in an attempt to persuade voters (Figure 5.11). Women's presence was described as a civilizing influence, such that "that dreadful thing called politics, raised as a phantom bugbear by the opponents of equal suffrage, subsided under the feminine touch . . . and became just a quiet, orderly election."[118]

Performing for Suffrage

The 1896 campaign used theaters and similar spaces of amusement to present fundraising entertainments consisting of performances, usually combining a number of musical numbers and skits, which were put on purely for the purpose of making money to pay for the campaign. These entertainments were quite different from the mass meetings held in 1911, which were free and were dominated by

Stopping Voters at the Polls in San Francisco

Figure 5.11. Suffragists stopping voters at the polls, 1911. Suffragists took to the streets in force on Election Day to convince voters to support them. From Selina Solomons Papers. Courtesy of The Bancroft Library, University of California, Berkeley.

speeches, although musical interludes were common. These suffrage entertainments were part of a general type of fund-raising entertainment regularly organized by club women for charities such as hospitals and orphanages. One 1896 suffrage entertainment was a "society concert," held on October 6 at Metropolitan Hall, which, for the occasion, sported new decorations "which were probably the most diversified and artistic that the big hall ever saw. The stage itself had been transformed into a regular arbor of flowers, potted plants and evergreens."[119] This concert consisted primarily of classical musical numbers by a variety of performers. The other 1896 suffrage entertainment reported in the newspapers was a "professional theatrical matinee" at the Tivoli on October 22, which involved "professional talent from every theater in the city."[120] This performance was at a much larger scale and was aimed at a broader audience.

Suffrage entertainments were also used as fund-raisers in 1911. Two well-publicized fund-raising entertainments were held not in a theater but in the colonial ballroom of the St. Francis Hotel. These performances, a classical concert by Nellie Widman-Blow, mezzo-soprano, on September 5, and a dramatic reading by Marion Craig-Wentworth, on September 12, were notably different from many other entertainments and suffrage meetings incorporating entertainment, because they were not organized along the lines of vaudeville, as multiple short, unrelated performances, but were instead carefully considered wholes, with a unity of type, style, and performers, similar to the Metropolitan Hall concert in 1896, although with further refinements.[121] The numbers in the Widman-Blow concert, for example, were not only all classical but were also "so arranged as to deal consecutively with sorrow, sentiment, love and happiness."[122] This unification of style is one of the important aspects of what Lawrence Levine characterizes as "the sacralization of culture," the tendency in the late nineteenth century to "call into question the traditional practice of mixing musical genres and presenting audiences with an eclectic feast."[123] By their unity of genre and style, these suffrage performances were marked for the sophisticated, cultured elite, in keeping with their location in the St. Francis Hotel. The scheduling of the dramatic reading, on 2:30 P.M. on a Tuesday, further reinforced the message that this performance was intended for an audience of the leisure class, primarily upper- and upper-middle-class women.

A more popular event was the benefit concert by the "Australian boys" at the Valencia Theater, at Valencia and Thirteenth Streets, on the evening of Thursday, September 28, 1911. Australia had granted non-Aboriginal women the vote in 1902, so the Australian entertainers were in a position to speak of the positive effects of woman suffrage there. This concert was organized by the College Equal Suffrage League, whose efforts focused primarily on immigrant and working-class voters. The Valencia, like other theaters in the Mission District, primarily hosted vaudeville shows, attracting a lower-middle- and working-class audience. In keeping with its vaudeville setting, the night's entertainment included a band program, athletic stunts, and several suffrage numbers, including "a quaint dance in costume," "several novel features in which yellow balloons and flags (were) used," and "a new suffrage song to the tune of 'Yankee Doodle,'" with an accompaniment "hummed in chorus by the members of the Boys' band."[124] There was only one suffrage address, a ten-minute talk, with the rest of the night reserved for performances. As this was a nighttime concert and included acts to amuse everyone, the concert probably attracted a fair share of men, unlike the entertainments in the St. Francis. The space of the theater was decorated as befits a suffrage space, "decked with flags and bunting bearing significant suffrage phrases. Yellow and purple [were] used as indicative of the movement for woman's political rights."[125] In contrast, the St. Francis was not bedecked with banners for the highbrow suffrage entertainments, although the suffrage colors were present at the Widman-Blow concert in the attire of the young girls who distributed programs there and were dressed "in white lingerie frocks and wearing aprons and ribbon bows in pretty shades of yellow and lavender."[126] The Valencia Theater was one of the main venues for mass meetings as well as entertainments, although the decoration of the space was not discussed in the news coverage of meetings there. It was a large space used both as a hall for various group meetings and rallies (including those of anti-suffragists) and as a theater for theatrical performances.[127] Other mixed-use spaces used by the suffragists in 1911 included the Cort Theater and Dreamland Rink (also used for a big rally for the mayoral candidate James Rolph).

Suffragists in 1911 not only held rallies and sponsored entertainments in theaters but also expanded their purview, producing suffrage plays and presenting suffrage information in movie theaters. They moved beyond the conventional amateur sponsorship role of club women in relation to entertainment and became full-fledged producers of amusements. Just as suffragists expanded from merely being patrons of tearooms and lunchrooms when they decided to run eating places as businesses, woman suffragists took on a somewhat professional role in theater production. In 1911, suffragists produced several short suffrage plays in the San Francisco Bay area, including Mary Lambert's *The Winning of Senator Jones,* performed by members of the California Writers' Club at Golden Gate Hall in Oakland on September 22, at the First Unitarian Church in Oakland on October 3, and on at least one other occasion; Beatrice Harraden's *Lady Geraldine's Speech,* performed nearby in Piedmont under the direction of the College Equal Suffrage League; Selina Solomons's *The Girl from Colorado, or The Conversion of Aunty Suffridge,* which was read publicly in the St. Francis Hotel and performed in San Francisco on October 7; and a suffrage play by Henry Kirk, produced by the Club Women's Franchise League in San Rafael.[128] Although these performances are evidence of women taking on the format of popular entertainment as a way of communicating a political argument, these plays were not performed in the spaces typically used for theatrical productions. Instead, they were more similar to club theatricals.

Suffragists also made use of the ordinary genre of movies and landscape of movie theaters in their 1911 campaign. In her "campaign of education" speech, Fannie McLean emphasized movie theaters as a site for suffrage action:

> The most popular educator of today is the Moving Picture. I have never seen any suffrage pictures excepting ridiculous ones that did more harm than good, but there must be some good ones—representing the parade in London, or Child Welfare slides showing what could be done for children; or the polls in Colorado, or slides with arguments for suffrage upon it.[129]

Also, suffrage films and slides were shown in a number of theaters throughout the San Francisco Bay area on a regular basis. In Mill Valley, "regular suffrage films . . . with all the pictures of what women [were] doing in all lines of work" were shown by members of the Club Women's Franchise League as part of a show that also included singing and dancing.[130] In San Francisco, suffrage films focusing on the history and condition of women in the Americas since their discovery by Europeans were shown to a meeting of the Retailers Protective Association, and plans were made to show these same films in North Beach nickelodeons.[131] A film of California pictures by Marie Alice Perrin was also used as the basis for a suffrage program (including a "humorous monologue" and "five minute speeches") in the Princess Theater on Ellis Street. This program, like ordinary film showings and unlike suffrage entertainments and meetings, was repeated more than once in the day, without any increase in the price of admission.[132] All of these programs were aimed at the working- and lower-middle-class audiences who frequented vaudeville theaters such as the Princess, where programs typically combined films with live performances in a variety format.

Other suffrage programs made use of the space of movie theaters and nickelodeons but did not include the showing of suffrage films. The most common suffrage activity in movie theaters was the showing of suffrage slides, often stereopticon slides. The California Equal Suffrage Association created a collection of slides and made several sets, which were distributed throughout California. Ida Finney Mackrille, who presented slides with talks in a variety of locations, including nickelodeons, a big theater, and an industrial fair, described the process of getting the slides shown:

> We would go to the proprietor of a nickelodeon and make a business proposition, something like this: "If you will show our suffrage slides, in addition to your regular run, allowing an accompanying explanation by one of our speakers—in all to occupy fifteen minutes—we will advertise your show for that night through the newspapers, posters and handbills." We were not once refused the privilege. As a matter of fact it was a favorable arrangement for the showman, for we always secured a good audience.[133]

Just as suffragists gained access to shopwindows in part because suffrage displays would encourage suffragists to shop at those stores, they appealed to nickelodeon owners on a purely business basis. In gaining access to nickelodeons, they were not asking for charity but rather making a deal; their model was not club women but entrepreneurs.

In Oakland, woman suffrage slides were shown in the Orpheum, the Broadway, and the Bell theaters.[134] Similar slides, showing "the various pursuits, many of them manual labor, followed by women in this state," "views of women in other countries," "episodes in various suffrage campaigns," and "actual pictures of many of the lower type of men who are allowed to vote," were displayed to audiences in small towns throughout California.[135] Stereopticon slides were also used by the College Equal Suffrage League to entertain and inform audiences. In San Francisco, the *Call* reported that special suffrage slides designed for the California campaign, with accompanying explanation, were shown at the Sixteenth Street Theater at Mission and Howard.[136] At the nickelodeon at Nineteenth Avenue and H Street, weekly suffrage addresses were made by members of the California Equal Suffrage Association, and every night a suffrage number was included in the musical selections.[137]

Another popular theatrical form, vaudeville, was also used by woman suffragists. A vaudeville troupe traveled the state in a touring car that held themselves, their sets, and suffrage flyers, persuading voters "not only by the usual song and speech, but by song and dance as well." The *Chronicle* deprecatingly wrote of the process as "taking the message to those voters who prefer it sugar-coated with vaudeville."[138] In San Francisco, at the Princess Theater, a suffrage monologue by Marie Alice Perrin was made part of the vaudeville program on September 2, 1911. "It has been particularly emphasized that Miss Perrin's contribution to the entertainment will not be a lecture, but a monologue, and will have all of the characteristics of the vaudeville stage." Not only would the monologue be properly entertaining, but it was also expected to draw a large audience.[139] This extensive use of the space of movie and vaudeville theaters demonstrated a desire to reach a broad range of the populace. In particular, it showed an intent to engage working- and lower-middle-class voters, especially those who were not interested in politics and might not otherwise encounter suffrage arguments. Movie theaters also quickly became a feminized space, in which both young single women and married women could enjoy themselves and to which a large number of women could afford to go without being treated by a man.[140] Suffragists in 1911 made use of this female-appropriate space by producing and showing slides and films and presenting accompanying talks. They were not spectators but producers and performers.

Joining in the Parade

While there were no suffrage parades in San Francisco (although one was held in Oakland in 1908), the Wage Earners' Suffrage League and the College Equal Suffrage Association, with the assistance of other suffrage associations, entered a float in the Labor Day parade, on September 4, 1911, engaging Market Street in yet another way (Figure 5.12). The float, which was featured in a large photograph in the *Call*, included many examples of California womanhood.

In the front sat Miss Maud Younger, a prominent exponent of the equal suffrage cause, beneath a banner with the words "Justice for Women." The figure of Justice was shown in the act of handing the ballot to California. On one side stood a trained nurse, on the other a college woman in cap and gown, while the working women were represented by a stenographer at her typewriter, a saleswoman at the ribbon counter, a factory girl at a sewing machine and another in the act of pasting labels on fruit cans.[141]

Figure 5.12. Suffrage float in Labor Day parade, 1911. The float featured the figures of Justice and California, as well as women workers from representative professions and trades. From *San Francisco Call*, September 5, 1911, 2.

The float was cheered by the crowd and received an honorable mention from the judges. At the end of the parade, in response to a crowd "cheering and clamoring for flowers and bits of ribbon, calling 'Speech! Speech!'" several suffragists spoke in front of the Ferry Building on the importance of suffrage to working women.[142]

The decision to participate in the Labor Day parade in San Francisco was highly symbolic. Not only were laborers an important targeted segment of the voting populace, but in addition a major argument in this campaign was that women workers needed the vote in order to have better control over their work and the use of their taxes. Rather than participating as a few honored guests or members of a women's auxiliary, women workers were, in the Labor Day parade, claiming their status as full-fledged workers. In other towns and cities, suffragists also participated in parades, but these parades were purely celebratory and did not have the political significance of the Labor Day parade. In San Francisco, a highly unionized city, the Labor Day parade was an event of great importance, taking over the symbolic heart of the city with an extensive display of the presence of unionized workers.

Gendered Landscapes and the Public Sphere

In the California woman suffrage campaign of 1911, suffragists reshaped the public spaces of their everyday lives into spaces of political speech. They expanded their activities well beyond the private spaces that were so central to the 1896 campaign, following the changes in their daily use of space and in their association with the public realm as well as the private sphere. In this campaign, women took on new roles, often employing spaces that they had access to because of their everyday activities. Employing their power as consumers and adopting the advertising methods targeted at them, they advertised and sold suffrage through the stores and windows of the downtown shopping district, local and district main streets, and grocery stores. In selling suffrage, they engaged familiar spaces of consumption but radically shifted their roles within those spaces. They marked the streets and streetcars of the city with their message through posters and billboards, becoming advertisers rather than remaining the objects of advertising. They employed their authority as reformist middle-class women to give speeches on the main streets of the city, going where the voters were rather than waiting for the voters to come to them. To gain more sympathizers among women, including those of the working class, as well as to make money for the cause, they sold tea to middle-class shoppers and hot lunches to working girls. They produced suffrage plays and showed slides in nickelodeons, reaching a broad sweep of the populace by once again going where the voters were, including immigrant and working-class women and men in general. They paraded with other workers in the Labor Day parade, taking part in a shared spectacle while marking their inclusion in the public spheres of work and politics.

In many of these political activities, suffragists utilized spaces they had made their own through everyday use, as consumers and workers. Only because these spaces had first become part of women's everyday lives, and people were used to seeing them there, were suffragists successful in their efforts to refashion them as political spaces. In using these spaces for political purposes, however, women radically reshaped their relationship to them. Rather than being shoppers, middle-class suffragists sold suffrage; rather than watching movies, they acted as theatrical producers. Women's increased everyday use of public space from 1890 to 1911 paved the way for the dramatic expansion of tactics in the 1911 suffrage campaign. The landscape of downtown shopping, the first public zone to be feminized, was engaged by both the 1896 and the 1911 suffragists, although more cautiously in 1896. Cafeterias, theaters, public transportation, and the streets of the downtown were engaged in 1911, a point at which these spaces had become an unquestioned part of women's everyday lives.

Just as the public commercial realm opened to a wide range of women—those served by restaurants and high-end theaters as well as those who frequented cafeterias and nickelodeons—the suffrage campaign also embraced women from a range of classes and ethnicities, both as activists and as recruits. However, the roles of different women within the campaign were not equal. Ethnic and working women spoke to men and women like themselves and, thus, remained largely in the neighborhoods and workspaces of their everyday lives, although significantly changing the kinds of activities they engaged in there. While middle-class women used their status as consumers to expand their roles (as when they produced advertising and theatrical performances), working women used their status as workers to give them the right to speak to working men and women throughout the city. Middle-class women also used their class position and the norms of charitable and reform activity to enter spaces outside their daily circuits and speak to people unlike themselves. While both the daily lives and the political activities of working-class and ethnic women were constrained by neighborhood affiliation, middle-class suffragists claimed the whole city and everyone within it as their political domain.

Suffragists in 1911 learned the techniques of selling and other aspects of business both as consumers and as workers, and they employed these techniques in selling their political opinions to others, much as shop owners and manufacturers had sold hats and baking soda to them. Women's everyday use of public space enabled them to employ space for their own ends. Without having encountered public spaces in the multiple everyday ways that have been chronicled in this book, women would not have had the access to space and control over it that were central aspects of the suffrage campaign. Equally essential, women's everyday use of public space helped them imagine themselves as part of the public sphere, for they, like men, had a sense of ownership in the city and its symbolic center. Women's presence in public also made it easier for male voters to imagine them as a constituent part of the public. Thus, built space and women's actions within it were central to their full participation in the public sphere.

EPILOGUE
EVERYDAY LANDSCAPES

THIS BOOK ARGUES FOR A COMPLEX RELATIONSHIP between gender ideology and the built environment, a relationship that positions the modern downtown created in American cities like San Francisco at the turn of the century as central to changing attitudes about the lives of women. The built environment of San Francisco's downtown neither directly reflected changing gender ideologies nor created them. Instead, the built and imagined landscapes of the downtown interacted with each other, often harmonizing and at other times conflicting, creating gaps that women negotiated in their everyday use of the downtown. In the 1880s, at the beginning of the story told in this book, only a few discrete public spaces within the city were imagined as female-dominated or female-appropriate: dry goods stores; other shops catering to women; ladies' dining rooms in hotels; respectable theaters but during matinees only; and streetcars at very particular times of day. In only one generation, the gendered nature of the downtown landscape transformed radically. By the 1910s the larger downtown landscape surrounding the old islands of femininity, as well as many new businesses, were seen as female-appropriate. This was a dramatic change in how the gendered landscape of the city was imagined, a change created through the actions of many individuals, including women who made use of downtown spaces and business owners who tried out new architectural and business forms to accommodate women without compromising their virtue. Change happened incrementally, as a result of the constant feedback among imagined, experienced, and built landscapes, powered by women's everyday experiences.

Downtown shopping was arguably the vanguard of this change, as middle- and upper-class women ventured into the just-emerging downtown to shop at elaborate dry goods shops and department stores in mid- to late-nineteenth-century cities. These stores created a foothold for women in the new specialized American downtown, initiating the process through which women made large elements of the downtown theirs, whether as elite shoppers or as shop clerks. Most directly, the presence of women in downtown shops necessitated their presence on the streets and on public transportation, turning streetcars into a mixed-gender as well as a mixed-class realm. By the early twentieth century, the presence of women on the streetcars was so normalized as to obviate the need for men to pay them special courtesy. Their presence downtown in shops also led to their presence other places downtown, in tearooms and eventually cafeterias and restaurants for refreshment, and in stage theaters and movie theaters for amusement. As the streets of the downtown became increasingly feminine territory, women could also use them as participants in public celebrations and as suffragists arguing for women's right to vote. Women also increasingly became part of the downtown when they were not shopping, such as when working in the shops, restaurants, and other businesses that served women, as well as working in clerical jobs in male-dominated offices. Beyond the downtown, similar transformations were taking place in other public spaces as women, including poorer and non-Anglo women, shopped, ate, and went to amusements on local and district main streets.

While the activities of shopping, eating out, and entertainment took women of all sorts out of their homes and into public space, the spaces they made their own and the nature of their interactions there were quite different depending on their class and ethnicity. Elite women's money and status allowed them to negotiate the built landscape more easily, so their experiences more closely matched the imagined gendered ideal. For example, upper-class, American-born, white women's shopping, eating, and entertainment activities all converged on areas of the downtown off Market Street, areas they visited frequently and with a great sense of ownership. Many of the spaces they frequented were single-gender, and others, such as theaters and downtown cafés, were sorted by class. When they ventured into mixed-gender and mixed-class spaces, in visits to bohemian restaurants, for example, their class position allowed them to remain unsullied. The task of making experience match up with the ideal was more difficult for less elite women, such as Annie Haskell. The stores she could afford to shop in downtown were on heterogeneous Market Street, mixed in with stores serving men; the restaurants she patronized served a mixed clientele, so she had to be vigilant if she wished to be perceived as respectable; and her experience of public transportation required her to loiter on the streets.

In each of the landscapes described in this book, women of different class and ethnic positions constructed their imagined relationships to the city as a whole. Elite women's experiences continually reinforced their sense that the city, and particularly its downtown, was theirs. Their money bought them service and access; downtown shops, theaters, and restaurants existed to serve them. While other women also used the downtown, their experiences in the same spaces were radically different, often placing them at the margins of institutions that focused on the well-to-do, such as the basement sales in department stores and the upper balconies of downtown theaters. For Annie Haskell, who was often short on money in spite of her middle-class education and marriage, negotiating the city was a process of constant friction. When shopping sales and discount stores, she was frustrated with the quality of goods and with the nature of her interactions with shop clerks. Sitting in the balcony of theaters, she found it hard to see and hear properly. Although she disliked cafeterias, she ate in them because they were the only respectable downtown restaurants she could afford. Taking the streetcars to navigate the city, she was frustrated by long waits and the lack of seats. While she certainly knew her way around the downtown as well as she did her local neighborhood, any interaction with the city was one of negotiation; she was of the city but never comfortable with it. Working-class and ethnic women may have been more comfortable in their immediate neighborhoods than Annie Haskell ever seemed anywhere, because their daily grocery shopping and occasional visits to local restaurants could be transacted with people who were much like themselves and spoke their native languages. However, the downtown, as well as the sense of being a citizen of San Francisco as a whole, was largely closed to them; they might sometimes window-shop and go to an occasional basement sale, but ethnic women were unwelcome downtown, not only as shoppers, but also as workers because of their accented English.

All women's use of public space expanded from the late nineteenth to the early twentieth century. All the streets and public spaces of the city became increasingly feminized, and the downtown particularly so. This change in the gendered meaning of the downtown was especially important, as Market Street was the symbolic heart of the city. Parades and other public celebrations, in which women were increasingly visible participants, continually reinscribed Market Street as the center of San Francisco. Women's regular daily presence in the downtown and their visible presence in these rituals of communal identity helped to place them symbolically into the body politic. As chapter 5 shows, woman suffragists took advantage of the shifting gender meanings of the downtown and other public spaces of the city in their 1911 campaign. They capitalized on women's increased presence in and cultural ownership of the symbolic center of the city by making the downtown the locus of much of their campaigning. They also employed all the public spaces women had claimed through everyday use, from department stores to cafeterias and nickel-odeons and especially the street, as political space where they could legitimately argue for their rights. Because of the dramatic change in women's everyday use of this wide range of public spaces, these spaces were newly imagined as feminine or at least as places where women had a legitimate reason to be seen and heard.

This story of the change in women's public landscapes in one American city has significance well beyond its particular geographical and historical context. The social processes and urban patterns that characterize the story of San Francisco, as told here, are typical of cities throughout the United States in this time period. Other cities similarly experienced an expansion of businesses catering to women within their increasingly specialized downtowns and women's expanded use of public space both downtown and on local and district main streets. Tea-rooms, lunchrooms, cafeterias, nickelodeons and movie theaters, and the other institutions described here were built in cities throughout the United States at approximately the same time to serve their female populations. Thus, this study of San Francisco can help us understand American women's uses of cities in the late nineteenth and early twentieth centuries and particularly the consequences of these experiences for American cities as a whole.

This study also casts light on the important interrelationship between every-day use and the shape of our social landscape and built environment. It proposes a spatially focused mode of social inquiry that can help us better understand the cities we live in, not just historically, but in the present as well. By exploring the relationship between how spaces are produced and experienced and by positing that both of these processes are expressive of as well as constitutive of their cul-ture and society, we can gain new insight and ask new questions. For example, given what I have argued here about the relationship between downtown shop-ping and women's public lives, how can we make sense of the changes that have happened in the shopping landscape since? How might this mode of inquiry help us explore the larger cultural motives for and consequences of the move to car-oriented shopping malls in the 1950s and beyond? How might we understand the more recent expansion of shopping malls within the downtown? Beyond the realm of shopping, how might exploring the distinctions among the populations of different classes, races, ethnicities, and genders in their everyday experiences of urban space help us understand the form of our cities, both now and in the past? What are the potential consequences of these experiences for how people imagine themselves as urban citizens? Paying attention to the patterns of urban life as man-ifested in and shaped by the form of cities will enrich our understanding of how cities work and what meanings they hold for all of their inhabitants.

NOTES

Introduction

1. Dunn, *Care-Free San Francisco*, 19–20.

2. Southern Pacific Company, *Trips around San Francisco*, 11.

3. Sangster, *Good Manners for All Occasions*, 228–29, repeats the advice against walking quickly and speaking loudly twice in two pages.

4. The word *gender*, as I use it, refers to the culturally constructed social categories imposed on sexed bodies. Gender functions as a system, based on the poles of male and female, and its forms are always culturally and historically contingent.

5. Stansell, *City of Women*; Ryan, *Women in Public*; Deutsch, *Women and the City*.

6. These categories build in part on Henri Lefebvre's categories of representations of space, spaces of representation, and spatial practice, discussed in his book *The Production of Space*; however, my categories do not map cleanly onto his. In particular, it is hard to figure out exactly how real physical space fits into his model.

My use of the term *landscape* follows the tradition of cultural landscape studies, in which "*landscape* denotes the interaction of people and place: a social group and its spaces, particularly the spaces to which the group belongs and from which its members derive some part of their shared identity and meaning" (Groth, "Frameworks for Cultural Landscape Study," 1). On cultural landscape, see the collections Bender, ed., *Landscape*; Cosgrove and Daniels, eds., *The Iconography of Landscape;* Conzen, ed., *The Making of the American Landscape;* Groth and Bressi, eds., *Understanding Ordinary Landscapes;* Groth and Wilson, eds., *Everyday America;* Meinig and Jackson, eds., *The Interpretation of Ordinary Landscapes.* See also Foote, *Shadowed Ground;* Jackson, *Maps of Meaning;* Norton, *Explorations in the Meaning of Landscape;* Rowntree, "Cultural/Humanistic Geography"; Schein, "The Place of Landscape"; and Stilgoe, *Common Landscapes of America, 1580 to 1845.*

7. Southern Pacific Company, *Trips around San Francisco,* 11.

8. Ibid., 22.

9. Post Street Improvement Club, *A Brief Outline of Interesting Jaunts in and about San Francisco,* 1.

10. Bowden, "The Dynamics of City Growth."

11. Murphy, Vance, and Epstein, eds., *Central Business District Studies.*

12. Edward Filene, quoted in Benson, *Counter Cultures,* 76.

13. Vance, *The Continuing City,* 390–424. Vance argues in part that the extent of trolley lines in 1890, combined with the nearly universal nickel flat fare, made the downtown particularly convenient for shopping. In addition, increasingly specialized retail businesses, which were separated both from wholesale business and from manufacture (as artisanal manufacture was replaced by factories), required a higher volume of sales to break even.

14. Peiss, *Cheap Amusements;* Nasaw, *Going Out.*

15. Arendt, *The Human Condition,* 50.

16. See Kasson, *Rudeness and Civility,* 128–32, especially illustration 20; Pollock, *Vision and Difference,* 50–90; Gardner, *Passing By,* especially 134–36; and Ogborn, "The Pleasure Garden," in *Spaces of Modernity.*

17. See Walkowitz, *City of Dreadful Delight;* and Wilson, *The Sphinx in the City.* Current anxieties about women in public tend to be focused on women in public at night and on women who are perceived to be in the wrong place. Walkowitz and Wilson both argue that the ideology of endangered womanhood served to limit women's freedom in public space in the nineteenth century. Gill Valentine, in "Images of Danger," argues further that in the present day this ideology also tends to make women turn to those most likely to sexually abuse them, male relatives and acquaintances, in order to be protected from unknown men.

18. Lefebvre, *Everyday Life in the Modern World,* 35–36.

19. The use of existing buildings as a source is a major premise of vernacular architecture studies, which use fieldwork on ordinary buildings to learn about the architecture and beliefs of the culture that created them. See Carter and Cromley, *Invitation to Vernacular Architecture;* Upton and Vlach, *Common Places;* Glassie, *Vernacular Architecture;* and *Buildings and Landscapes* (formerly *Perspectives in Vernacular Architecture*), the journal of the Vernacular Architecture Forum.

20. Diaries, and especially those available in archives, more typically cover voyages and other unusual periods in people's lives rather than the banalities of everyday life. Thus, of the diaries available in the Bancroft Library, San Francisco History Room, and California Historical Society, many more cover journeys to San Francisco than cover everyday life in San Francisco. The diaries used here have also been used by others less extensively

than those covering travel. Of the three, to my knowledge only Annie Haskell's diary has been cited in a published work; it is very briefly used in Mary Ryan's *Women in Public.*

21. Leigh was born in 1859 in San Francisco.

22. Leigh moved into 1133 Hayes in 1905. Her apartment building, which had fourteen apartments, was next door at 1141–1153 Hayes. Details on Leigh from Lees Family Papers, BANC MSS C–B 654, Bancroft Library, University of California, Berkeley.

23. Pierce was born in 1872. Details on Pierce from various items, especially Mary Eugenia Pierce Diary, in Pierce Family Papers, BANC MSS 75/35 c, Bancroft Library, University of California, Berkeley.

24. Hal Johnson, "So We're Told," clipping in Pierce Family Papers.

25. Annie Fader Haskell Diary, in Haskell Family Papers, BANC MSS C–B 364, Bancroft Library, University of California, Berkeley.

26. Traditionally, class or stratification is determined at the level of the family, and the social class position of the family is defined as the position of the family head, usually an adult male. See, for example, Hodge and Siegel, "Stratification, Social," 15: 317. However, this is often a poor marker for women. For example, Annie Haskell's husband was a lawyer, but especially after she left him, her position was more economically precarious than that of her sister, who was married at least twice, once to a policeman. (For an overview of empirical and feminist critiques of the use of the family as the unit of class analysis, see Edgell, *Class,* 39–52.) However, my approach is in keeping with the sociological tradition of treating class and stratification as not purely a question of relation to the means of production (the Marxist definition) or as purely a function of income, but instead as fundamentally multidimensional. See Barber, "Stratification, Social," 292; Bendix and Lipset, *Class, Status, and Power;* and Breen and Rottman, *Class Stratification.*

27. The idea of cultural capital is primarily associated with the work of Pierre Bourdieu, especially *Distinction,* but can be traced back at least as far as Thorstein Veblen's 1899 *The Theory of the Leisure Class,* and is a central focus of Paul Fussell's *Class.* Much recent historical work has also focused on the creation and reproduction of class cultures, beginning with Thompson's *The Making of the English Working Class.* See, for example, Auslander, *Taste and Power;* Blumin, *The Emergence of the Middle Class;* Bushman, *The Refinement of America;* Davidoff and Hall, *Family Fortunes;* Grier, *Culture and Comfort;* Halttunen, *Confidence Men and Painted Women;* Kidd and Nicholls, eds., *Gender, Civic Culture and Consumerism;* Moskowitz, *Standard of Living;* and Ryan, *Cradle of the Middle Class.*

28. In 1890, women made up 47 percent of San Francisco's white population and 43 percent of San Francisco's population overall. Women were slightly fewer than 10 percent of the "colored" population in the 1890 census, because the Chinese population was almost entirely male. The category "white" in the 1890 census included Hispanics but not persons of Asian, African, or Native American descent. U.S. Department of the Interior, Census Office, "Table 1: Population of the Cities on June 1, 1890, by Ages, with Distinction of Sex, Color, Nativity, Parental Nativity, and Birthplaces of Mothers."

29. San Francisco ranked fourth in the nation in the value of its imports and fifth in the value of its exports. See Issel and Cherny, *San Francisco, 1865–1932,* 24.

30. Gibson, "Population of the 100 Largest Cities and Other Urban Places in the United States."

31. Ibid., Table 14. In addition, the square-foot value of its retail real estate was sixth in the country, and it was fifth for both wholesale business and residential properties, according to Speck, "Real Estate."

32. "In 1900, nearly one San Franciscan in five lived south of Market, in the area between Market and Townsend, from the waterfront to Eleventh Street" (Issel and Cherny, *San Francisco, 1865–1932,* 59).

1. Sidewalks and Streetcars

1. U.S. Bureau of the Census, *Historical Statistics of the United States, Colonial Times to 1970,* part 1, "Series D 26–28: Gainful Workers, by Sex, by State: 1870 to 1950," and "Series A 195–209: Population of States, by Sex, Race, Urban–Rural Residence, and Age: 1790 to 1970." The proportion of women in California who worked in each census year is as follows: 1870, 6.54 percent; 1880, 8.13 percent; 1890, 11.84 percent; 1900, 13.22 percent; 1910, 16.58 percent; and 1920, 17.77 percent.

2. Ibid., "Series D 183–232: Major Occupation Groups of the Experienced Civilian Labor Force, by Sex: 1900 to 1970."

3. Kasson, *Rudeness and Civility,* 4–5.

4. Montgomery, *Displaying Women.*

5. Young, *Our Deportment,* 145.

6. Louis, *Decorum,* 122; Young, *Our Deportment,* 145–46; Wells, *Manners, Culture and Dress of the Best American Society,* 414. Etiquette books often directly copy advice and wording from earlier books. This passage is used identically in these three. Dale, in *Our Manners and Social Customs,* 139, uses the same passage but changes the wording slightly.

7. Young, *Our Deportment,* 145; Bunce, *What to Do.*

8. Hartley, *The Ladies' Book of Etiquette and Manual of Politeness.*

9. Louis, *Decorum,* 122; Wells, *Manners, Culture and Dress of the Best American Society,* 132.

10. White, *Success in Society.*

11. For excellent discussions of turn-of-the-century working women and style, see Enstad, *Ladies of Labor, Girls of Adventure;* Peiss, "Putting on Style," in *Cheap Amusements,* 56–87; and Stansell, "The Bowery," in *City of Women,* 89–100.

12. Ryan, *Women in Public,* 68–92.

13. Kasson, *Rudeness and Civility;* Bushman, *The Refinement of America.*

14. Wharton, *The Age of Innocence* (2000), 213.

15. Young, *Our Deportment,* 14; Louis, *Decorum,* 122; Wells, *Manners, Culture and Dress of the Best American Society,* 414.

16. White, *Success in Society,* 188; White, *Polite Society At Home and Abroad.* See also Hartley, *The Ladies' Book of Etiquette and Manual of Politeness,* 114.

17. White, *Polite Society At Home and Abroad,* 36.

18. Hartley, *Ladies' Book of Etiquette and Manual of Politeness,* 112–13. Kasson, *Rudeness*

and Civility, 131 n. 36, also cites an 1866 manual, the *Hand-Book of Etiquette,* that advised against stopping to look at windows.

19. White, *Polite Society At Home and Abroad,* 36.

20. Enstad, *Ladies of Labor, Girls of Adventure,* 181–83.

21. Kingsland, *The Book of Good Manners,* 320.

22. Louis, *Decorum,* 119.

23. Cooke, *Social Etiquette, or Manners and Customs of Polite Society.*

24. Ibid., 337.

25. Hall, *Social Customs,* 355.

26. Ibid., 354.

27. Ibid., 355.

28. Koslofsky, "Embracing the Night."

29. Peiss, *Cheap Amusements;* Stansell, *City of Women.*

30. Cooke, *Social Etiquette, or Manners and Customs of Polite Society,* 31.

31. Sangster, *Good Manners for All Occasions,* 37–38; Green, *A Dictionary of Etiquette;* Everett, *The Etiquette of Today.*

32. Stewart, *Perfect Behavior,* 77.

33. Everett, *The Etiquette of Today,* 101.

34. Roberts, *Putnam's Handbook of Etiquette.*

35. Harland and Van de Water, *Everyday Etiquette.*

36. Hersey, *To Girls,* 104.

37. White, *Polite Society At Home and Abroad,* 45.

38. Sangster, *Good Manners for All Occasions,* 38.

39. Jansen, *San Francisco Cable Cars,* 51.

40. Green, *A Dictionary of Etiquette,* 236.

41. Sangster, *Good Manners for All Occasions,* 36.

42. Everett, *The Etiquette of Today,* 97–98.

43. Unnamed 1892 author cited in Middleton, *The Time of the Trolley,* 109.

44. Smallwood, *The White Front Cars of San Francisco,* 254–58.

45. Smallwood, ibid., 162, writes of complaints about the lack of smoking sections in these cars. In 1927, as part of a modernization of the new cars, they were provided with a smoking compartment. Later streetcar designs for San Francisco usually were not enclosed but rather included an open-air section; however, longitudinal benches remained common (ibid.).

46. Helen Dare, "One of the Advantages of the P.A.Y.E. Cars—For Passengers," *San Francisco Chronicle,* August 18, 1911, 7.

47. Ryan, *Women in Public,* 76–79; Wiley, *A Free Library in This City,* 102; Jansen, *San Francisco's Cable Cars,* 51.

48. "Great Success Achieved by the Local Improvement Clubs," *San Francisco Call,* August 20, 1910, 11; "King Tells of Good Work of Great Association of San Francisco Merchants," *San Francisco Call,* January 18, 1904, 7.

49. San Francisco Board of Supervisors, *San Francisco Municipal Reports,* Fiscal Year 1904–5, 343.

50. The fact that riding the ferry was essentially an ordinary occurrence is marked both by Mary Pierce's frequent trips to San Francisco and by Roth Haskell's using the ferry to commute daily from San Francisco to Berkeley in 1904 so that he could complete his final year of school at Berkeley High and not have to change schools.

51. Doxey, *Doxey's Guide to San Francisco and the Pleasure Resorts of California.*

52. O'Shaunessy, *Street Railway Transportation Requirements of San Francisco,* 4–5.

53. Smallwood, *The White Front Cars of San Francisco.*

54. Thirteen of the twenty-nine lines listed in the 1897 *Doxey's Guide to San Francisco* began or ended at the Ferry Building, while seven additional lines began on Market. Of the remaining nine lines, four crossed Market, two served the Mission District exclusively, one served the Potrero Hill district, one ran mail from the railroad terminus at Third and Brannan to the Pacific Mail Dock, and one ran from Third and Townsend, south of Market, to the Union Iron Works, Pacific Rolling Mills, a sugar refinery, and other industrial sites along the bay (Doxey, *Doxey's Guide to San Francisco and the Pleasure Resorts of California,* 30–37).

55. Haskell Diary, Sunday, March 16, 1902. Haskell mentions riding in a carriage for funerals on Saturday, March 23, 1895; Wednesday, April 9, 1902; and Monday, August 28, 1911, and complains of not having a carriage for a funeral on Monday, August 14, 1916.

56. Pierce Diary, Saturday, March 27, 1915. Although Pierce was sometimes given a lift to Oakland by friends with automobiles, she was more likely to ride in an automobile for an excursion, as Haskell also did. Pierce, auto rides for a purpose in 1915–16 (twelve): February 26, 1915; March 8, 1915; March 27, 1915; April 29, 1915; and June 1, 1915; March 1, 1916; May 16, 1916; July 3, 1916; July 6, 1916; September 7, 1916; September 16, 1916; and October 7, 1916. Pierce, auto rides for an excursion only in 1915–16 (twenty): February 20, 1915; March 1, 1915; May 28, 1915; June 3, 1915; June 6, 1915; June 17, 1915; June 23, 1915; June 26, 1915; August 4, 1915; August 5, 1915; September 3, 1915; September 23, 1915; and September 27, 1915; February 27, 1916; April 12, 1916; July 23, 1916; July 25, 1916; August 20, 1916; September 15, 1916; and December 17, 1916. Haskell, auto rides for a purpose in 1900–1917: none. Haskell, auto rides for an excursion in 1900–1917 (four): July 30, 1911; August 17, 1916; June 12, 1917; June 16, 1917.

57. Samuel H. Williamson, "What Is the Relative Value?" Economic History Services, April 2004, http://www.eh.net/hmit/compare/. Kathy Peiss cites working women in New York who took regular excursions on trolleys and subways because "everything was so cheap" (Peiss, *Cheap Amusements,* 121 n. 21). James Vance, in *The Continuing City,* 390–93, argues that the nickel fare was essential to the growth of the downtown as a specialized, nonresidential space, as it made both housing in the suburbs and commuting to the downtown for work and shopping inexpensive.

58. Enstad, *Ladies of Labor, Girls of Adventure;* Peiss, *Cheap Amusements,* 52.

59. New York Factory Investigating Commission, *Fourth Report,* 4: 1512–13, quoted in Peiss, *Cheap Amusements,* 53.

60. Haskell Diary, Saturday, October 30, 1909.

61. Ibid., July 4, 1895; March 17, 1897; December 29, 1913; June 26, 1914; June 9, 1916; July 25, 1917.

62. Ibid., Friday, August 17, 1897, emphasis in original.

63. Ibid., Monday, May 31, 1897; Monday, July 5, 1897.

64. Ibid., Sunday, May 30, 1915.

65. Ibid., Tuesday, August 29, 1916.

66. Ibid., Thursday, June 29, 1916.

67. "King Tells of Good Work of Great Association of San Francisco Merchants," *San Francisco Call,* January 18, 1904, 7.

68. Smallwood, *The White Front Cars of San Francisco,* 161, 167, 179, 229, 239.

69. Haskell Diary, September 27, 1907; see also August 19, 1906.

70. Harlan, *San Francisco Bay Ferryboats.* Passing references in Olmsted, *The Ferry Building,* to fares led me to believe that other ferries also typically cost a nickel.

71. While the Ferry Building did include waiting rooms on the second floor and off the main hall, the building was largely a pass-through space. With 180 trips every weekday in 1913, carrying 120,000 fares daily, the waiting time for a ferry was typically quite short (Olmsted, *The Ferry Building*). See also "Tiny Baby Found in Ferry Depot," *San Francisco Call,* March 13, 1910.

72. Haskell Diary, Wednesday, May 31, 1916; Thursday, August 24, 1915; see also March 12, 1899; February 19, 1905; and December 17, 1905.

2. Errands

1. Veblen, *The Theory of the Leisure Class.*

2. Benson, "Palaces of Consumption and Machine for Selling"; Benson, *Counter Cultures;* Bowlby, *Just Looking;* Friedberg, *Window Shopping;* Laermans, "Learning to Consume"; Leach, *Land of Desire;* Miller, *The Bon Marché;* Nava, "Modernity's Disavowal"; Williams, *Dream Worlds.*

3. Abelson, *When Ladies Go A-Thieving;* Benson, *Counter Cultures;* Bowlby, *Just Looking;* Friedberg, *Window Shopping;* Leach, *Land of Desire;* Nava, "Modernity's Disavowal"; Reekie, *Temptations.*

4. Baudelaire, *The Painter of Modern Life;* Benjamin, "Paris, Capital of the Nineteenth Century."

5. On the masculinity of the flaneur, see especially Wolff, "The Invisible Flâneuse." On shopping and the flaneuse, see Friedberg, *Window Shopping,* 36–38; and Nava, "Modernity's Disavowal," 57–59, 69–72.

6. C. E. Cake, "Arranging Goods to Make the Shoppers Buy," *System* 18 (December 1910): 593, quoted in Benson, *Counter Cultures,* 76.

7. Keeler, *San Francisco and Thereabouts,* 37.

8. *How to Advertise to Men* contrasts selling to women, which uses emotion and desire, with the only successful mode of selling to men, which is logical argument, aimed at convincing buyers that the product will save money and time. The book argues that, unlike a woman, "a man does not buy ALL that he wants. To DESIRE a thing is not to immediately buy it" (10).

9. Paco Underhill, in *Why We Buy*, argues that engagement with objects with all the senses, particularly touch, leads to increased sales.

10. Paul Dubuisson, "Les voleuses des grands magasins," 1903, quoted in Abelson, *When Ladies Go A-Thieving*, 46. Women's emotional abandon when faced with seductive displays of wares is also described in several long passages in Émile Zola's *Au bonheur des dames* (translated into English as *The Ladies' Paradise*).

11. Quoted ibid.

12. See Benson, "Made, Not Born: From the Shopgirl to the Skilled Saleswoman," chapter 4 in *Counter Cultures*, 124–76, for an overview of the history of the training and education of department store saleswomen.

13. Ibid., 140.

14. Even those scholars who have focused on the space of the window and its display have largely ignored the experience of women on the streets outside the store. Leach, in "Land of Desire" and in "Strategists of Display and the Production of Desire," in *Consuming Visions*, 99–132, and Reekie, in *Temptations*, discuss window display techniques at length but do not address the observer's position. Friedberg, in *Window Shopping*, and Nava, in "Modernity's Disavowal," both discuss the gaze of the female observer on the street but are more interested in the modernity of that gaze and its relationship to the cinematic gaze than the experience of the woman shopper. Nava also assumes that the street, like the store, is feminized, writing, "The streets and the pavements in the main shopping centers were monopolized by women" (70–71). Longstreth, in *City Center to Regional Mall*, does address the shopping district as a whole, but his focus is on the period following the one under discussion here.

15. Bowden, "The Dynamics of City Growth."

16. Dunn, *Care-Free San Francisco*, 22.

17. De Witt, *An Illustrated and Descriptive Souvenir and Guide to San Francisco*. When it opened the Emporium also impressed Annie Haskell, who wrote in her diary that it was "run on a new plan for San Francisco—a great department store—with everything in it imaginable." Haskell Diary, June 2, 1896.

18. Purdy, *San Francisco*.

19. Onken Younits advertisement, *Modern Grocer*, 1911; Butler Brothers advertisement, *Modern Grocer*, March 4, 1911, 32.

20. In her diary Mary Pierce mentioned visits to Dr. Levinger, at 177 Post Street, on September 25, 1915; October 4, 1915; October 6, 1915; October 8, 1915; February 21, 1916; March 7, 1916; and August 8, 1916.

21. Dr. Lundberg had an office at 219 Geary Street in 1890, and in 1899 Dr. Frances C. Treadwell moved from her office in room 94 of the Murphy Building, 1236 Market Street, to "real nice rooms in the Supreme Court Building," 305 Larkin Street (Haskell Diary, March 6, 1899).

22. de Certeau, Giard, and Mayol, *The Practice of Everyday Life*, vol. 2: *Living and Cooking*, 11.

23. Sangster, *Good Manners for All Occasions*, 69.

24. Dunn, *Care-Free San Francisco*, 22.

25. Annie Haskell's diary for June 5, 1916, described looking up Ruth in I. Magnin, where she was working. In the 1910 manuscript census, for which Annie Haskell was a census taker, Ruth Hutchinson is listed as a seamstress in a shirt factory.

26. Benson, *Counter Cultures,* 23–26, 128–31.

27. Sangster, *Good Manners for All Occasions,* 267.

28. Leslie, *The Behavior Book,* 77.

29. The Emporium advertisement in *San Francisco Daily News,* August 14, 1911, 3.

30. Pragers advertisement in *San Francisco Bulletin,* August 21, 1911, 16; Owl Drug advertisement in *San Francisco Bulletin,* August 10, 1911.

31. Haskell Diary, Monday, June 26, 1911; Friday, May 15, 1914.

32. Ibid., Monday, May 22, 1911.

33. Ibid., Friday, August 4, 1916.

34. Ibid., Friday, January 31, 1902.

35. Ibid., Monday, July 10, 1905.

36. Ibid., Thursday, February 16, 1905.

37. Ibid., Tuesday, December 8, 1896; Monday, July 3, 1905; Wednesday, June 2, 1909; Saturday, December 18, 1909; Saturday, August 3, 1912.

38. Ibid., Tuesday, June 8, 1915.

39. Ibid., Saturday, August 21, 1909.

40. Ibid., Friday, July 23, 1909; Monday, July 20, 1914; Monday, June 25, 1911; Thursday, June 4, 1914.

41. Ibid., Tuesday, December 8, 1896; Thursday, December 21, 1905; Monday, July 6, 1908; Saturday, August 21, 1909; Saturday, December 18, 1909.

42. Ibid., Wednesday, June 2, 1909.

43. De Witt, *An Illustrated and Descriptive Souvenir and Guide to San Francisco,* 42.

44. Haskell Diary, Tuesday, June 2, 1896. Also went to the Emporium for a concert with her sister Katie, September 19, 1903.

45. Ibid., Saturday, December 18, 1909; Saturday, January 8, 1910.

46. Dunn, *Care-Free San Francisco,* 19–20.

47. Haskell Diary, Friday, April 30, 1915. See also Saturday, February 22, 1896; Tuesday, July 21, 1903; and Friday, May 28, 1909.

48. Ibid., Friday, May 28, 1909, in which Haskell complains about changes to the downtown; Thursday, August 26, 1909; and Friday, November 3, 1909.

49. Dobie, *San Francisco,* 265.

50. Haskell Diary, Monday, August 24, 1916.

51. "Joyous Thousands Acclaim New Year," *San Francisco Call,* January 1, 1907, 1; "All San Francisco Joins in Joyous Din of Greeting to 1908," *San Francisco Call,* January 1, 1908, 16; "Hail New Year, Rejoicing That City is Reborn," *San Francisco Call,* January 1, 1909, 1.

52. Dobie, *San Francisco,* 269.

53. Another large theater, the Valencia, was relatively nearby at Thirteenth and Valencia. In 1911, seven nickelodeons were located on Mission Street itself.

54. In the 1911 *Crocker–Langley San Francisco Directory,* these are the Anglo-California

Trust Company, Mission Branch, at the northwest corner of Sixteenth and Mission; the Mission Bank, at Sixteenth and Julian; and the Mission Savings Bank, at Sixteenth and Valencia.

55. Annie Haskell's diary mentions the names of several dentists: in 1903, Dr. Christiansen at 2701 Mission; in 1906, Dr. Porterfield at 3403 Sixteenth; in 1911, Dr. Richards at 3350a Sixteenth; and in 1915–16, Dr. Craigie at 467 Castro.

56. At least one of the two Christian Science practitioners that Haskell consulted had offices on Mission Street: Dr. Willet at 2560 Mission. The other practitioner she visited, Mrs. Gilbert, was in the Mission District but was not listed in the directory.

57. Logan, *Bring Along Laughter,* 41.

58. Ibid., 201–2.

59. Forbes, *Mama's Bank Account.*

60. Haskell Diary, November 30, 1896; July 3, 1903; November 3, 1903; July 6, 1910; August 7, 1915.

61. Ibid., December 20, 1895; February 15, 1896; October 12, 1896; December 24, 1896; March 31, 1903; April 13, 1903; January 12, 1905; May 25, 1906; August 21, 1914.

62. Ibid., Sunday, October 31, 1909.

63. Self-service really began with the self-service Piggly-Wiggly stores of Tennessee, which opened in 1916, and it was spread by grocery stores in Los Angeles, which experimented with self-service during the 1910s. See Charvat, *Supermarketing,* 13–14; Mayo, *The American Grocery Store,* 89–92; and Mueller and Garoian, *Changes in the Market Structure of Grocery Retailing,* 11. On Los Angeles, see also Longstreth, *The Drive-in, the Supermarket, and the Transformation of Commercial Space in Los Angeles, 1914–1941.*

64. Fifty-nine of the female grocers in the 1911 *Crocker–Langley San Francisco Directory* were listed as widows in the alphabetical listing of residents. Six female grocers were listed as "Miss," and at least five had no man listed in the directory with their same last name and address. In 1890, fourteen female grocers were listed as widows, two as "Miss," and twenty-three had no man listed in the directory with the same last name and address.

65. George E. Place, "The Los Angeles Grocer," *Retail Grocers' Advocate,* February 9, 1908, 40. For grocer's wives, see "The Grocer's Wife," *Retail Grocers' Advocate* (San Francisco), January 3, 1908, 9. For women clerks, see "The Woman Grocer," *Retail Grocers' Advocate* (San Francisco), January 17, 1908, 14.

66. Place, "The Los Angeles Grocer."

67. "The Woman Grocer."

68. Ibid.

69. Place, "The Los Angeles Grocer."

70. In addition, 3.4 percent of female grocers lived immediately next door, in comparison to 2.5 percent of grocers overall.

71. Many of the listings of grocers in directories give addresses stating the corner where the grocery is located, such as "NW corner 15th and Noe," rather than the building number.

72. I checked the home addresses of a random sample of 121 grocers in the 1890 *Crocker–Langley San Francisco Directory;* of these 63 had a residence listing with the same address as the store listing, and a further 8 lived on the same block as the store. In the 1911

Crocker–Langley San Francisco Directory, I checked the home addresses of a random sample of 120 grocers; of these 69 had a residence listing with the same address as the store listing.

73. The editors of journals such as the *Modern Grocer* encouraged window displays, publishing model displays and suggesting display ideas. However, the number of items in these journals arguing that display was worthwhile suggests a certain resistance to display and stands in contrast to journals for department store owners, which take the importance of display windows for granted. The local San Francisco grocers' journal, the *Retail Grocers' Advocate,* concentrated largely on questions of supply, labor management, fixtures, and prices and only rarely mentioned display.

74. Levy, *920 O'Farrell Street,* 139.

75. *The World Our Field* (catalog–magazine of Goldberg, Bowen & Company), summer 1914.

76. *Master Grocer* (catalog–magazine of Goldberg, Bowen & Company), February 1906, 9.

77. Mayo, *The American Grocery Store,* 72–73; personal discussion with Richard Longstreth. In the 1920s, the Emporium also opened a downtown department grocery store, the Crystal Palace Market (Charvat, *Supermarketing,* 12–13).

78. Haskell Diary, cash accounts for 1916 and 1917. Annie Haskell was living with her sister Helen or her son, Roth, during these years and thus was not solely responsible for household shopping, a task that she shared with her sister and her daughter-in-law.

79. Haskell Diary, July 20, 1916. See also July 24, 1916; August 1, 1916; and August 23, 1916.

80. Ibid., Tuesday, July 14, 1903; Monday, August 21, 1911.

81. Ibid., Saturday, June 20, 1914; Tuesday, June 30, 1903. See also Friday, December 11, 1903; Monday, January 25, 1904; Saturday, January 14, 1905; Saturday, July 14, 1906; Thursday, July 26, 1906; Friday, June 25, 1909; Wednesday, July 6, 1910; and Tuesday, July 11, 1911.

82. Ibid., Saturday, July 14, 1906.

83. Milla Zenovich Logan, in *Bring Along Laughter,* 237–39, describes the regular visits of Matia, the Dalmatian grocer, to take orders and to gossip with Logan's mother; the weekly visits of Stevo, the wine man; and the visits of Velo, the laundryman; Danilo, the coffee man; and Milan, who came by to deliver chickens.

84. Ibid., 43, 116, 218, 220.

85. The importance of credit to the grocery business is underlined in Findlay, *Paul Findlay's Book for Grocers,* 86–87, which argues, "Credit is a definite worthy service . . . one of the most valuable services which can be rendered by the grocer and . . . is as good business, as profitable and as much a legitimate retail service as to carry a stock of goods."

3. Dining Out

1. Paul Groth, in *Living Downtown,* 114–19, discusses the growth of inexpensive and abundant commercial eating places in the new rooming-house districts of late-nineteenth-century American cities.

2. On the expansion of downtown lunchrooms in the United States and their ties to office and retail work, see McIntosh, *American Food Habits in Historical Perspective,* 113; and Levenstein, *Revolution at the Table,* 185–86.

3. Sangster, *Good Manners for All Occasions,* 41.

4. Tearooms, especially those in small towns and rural settings, were often part of houses and quite explicitly made use of the trappings of domesticity, as Cynthia Brandimarte argues in "'To Make the Whole World Homelike.'" Department store and hotel tearooms, in contrast, more often used exotic and garden motifs.

5. Sewell, "Tea and Suffrage."

6. Donovan, *The Woman Who Waits,* 109.

7. Ibid.

8. Ibid.

9. *The Tea Room and Coffee Shop,* 7.

10. Elliott, *Tea Room and Cafeteria Management,* vi–vii.

11. Southern Pacific Company, *Trips around San Francisco,* 12.

12. In the 1915 *Crocker–Langley San Francisco Directory,* only two of the establishments recommended to women by Helen Throop Purdy, in *San Francisco,* 152, the Golden Pheasant and Swain's, are listed under restaurants in the classified business directory. Of these, the Golden Pheasant was also listed under confectionery, as was the Pig 'n' Whistle, and Swain's described itself in the listings as a "bakery and restaurant." Foster & O'Rear's, which was visited by Mary Pierce, was also listed only under confectionery.

13. Doxey, *Doxey's Guide to San Francisco and the Pleasure Resorts of California,* 28.

14. Ibid., 29.

15. Kinchin, "Interiors."

16. Donovan, *The Woman Who Waits,* 109.

17. Jan Whitaker, "Doing Good in the Cafeteria," paper delivered at Boston University, January 31, 2009; 1915 *Crocker–Langley San Francisco Directory.*

18. Purdy, *San Francisco,* 152. Leigh mentions going to three of these: the Pig 'n' Whistle, the Emporium, and the Tea Cup.

19. Keeler, *San Francisco and Thereabouts,* 47.

20. The association of light colors with female space and dark with masculine was very common at the turn of the century. See Kinchin, "Interiors."

21. Doxey, *Doxey's Guide to San Francisco and the Pleasure Resorts of California,* 28.

22. Mentioned in both Mary Pierce's diary and Annie Haskell's.

23. Leigh Diary, Sunday, January 1, 1905; Sunday, January 15, 1905; Sunday, January 29, 1905.

24. Mary Pierce was born in 1872 and thus was in her early forties in 1915 and 1916. She ate at the St. Francis with Mr. Poole on December 1, 1915; March 17, 1916; and March 26, 1916; and with Stewart Anderson on March 14, 1916. In addition, she dined at the Palace Hotel with her brother Elliott on December 20, 1916, and with Mr. Holmes at the Hotel Oakland on December 1, 1915.

25. Pierce Diary, February 2, 1916, April 25, 1916.

26. Haskell Diary, Saturday, August 15, 1903. The Golden West Hotel is listed in the

1916 *Official Hotel Red Book and Directory* as a "first-class house," but its prices were half those of the Palace and the St. Francis (from a dollar a day at the Golden West, and from two dollars a day at the Palace and the St. Francis) (*Official Hotel Red Book and Directory,* 1916, 50, 52, 55, 62).

27. Haskell Diary, Friday, September 9, 1910.

28. Pierce Diary, April 8, 1916; Haskell Diary, August 27, 1914; June 5, 1916.

29. Donovan, *The Woman Who Waits,* 109.

30. Pierce Diary, Friday, April 9, 1915; Thursday, December 2, 1915; Saturday, January 15, 1916; Friday, September 8, 1916; Tuesday, December 19, 1916.

31. Haskell Diary, Friday, June 4, 1915.

32. "Mammoth Café Zinkand," *San Francisco Call,* January 1, 1891, 6. As with hotels, the ladies' dining room, gentlemen's grill room, and the barroom each had a separate entrance, with a flower stand at the entrance to the first and cigar stands at the entrance to the last two.

33. De Witt, in *An Illustrated and Descriptive Souvenir and Guide to San Francisco,* 87, claimed that one could "satisfy a craving appetite to its fullest desire for the remarkably small sum of fifteen cents," roughly three dollars in current terms.

34. Doxey, *Doxey's Guide to San Francisco and the Pleasure Resorts of California,* 28.

35. *San Francisco* (1901), 52.

36. Rosenzweig, *Eight Hours for What We Will,* 63. Stern and Stern argue that saloons were not patronized by shopgirls and female office workers, because they were "for men only," and the new white-collar workers were "too refined for free lunch in saloons" ("Cafeteria," 40).

37. Richardson, *The Long Day, the Story of a New York Working Girl,* 258–59.

38. Burgess, *The Heart Line,* 515.

39. Ibid.

40. Donovan, *The Woman Who Waits,* 108.

41. Groth, *Living Downtown,* 115–17.

42. Donovan, *The Woman Who Waits,* 107–8.

43. Logan, *Bring Along Laughter,* 154. Logan uses the name "Slavonian" to denote Serbs, Montenegrins, Croats, and Slovenes.

44. Ibid., 157.

45. Donovan, *The Woman Who Waits,* 110.

46. Ibid., 111.

47. The majority of working women in New York earned below the living wage, making less than eight dollars a week in 1910, when the living wage was about ten dollars. In many jobs, their wages were half those of men working at the same employments. See Peiss, *Cheap Amusements,* 52. Women's wages in San Francisco were similarly low.

48. Richardson, *The Long Day,* 148.

49. Whitaker, "Doing Good in the Cafeteria"; "Picketing Picket is Pinched by Police" *San Francisco Call,* November 18, 1910, 11; *Crocker–Langley San Francisco Directory,* 1911 and 1914.

50. Whitaker, "Doing Good in the Cafeteria."

51. Ibid.

52. Stern and Stern, "Cafeteria," 40.

53. Groth, *Living Downtown,* 115.

54. For example, the decorations in Schroeder's Restaurant include a wall painting of a scantily clad woman riding a champagne bottle.

55. Lewis, *Bay Window Bohemia,* 111.

56. On this phenomenon in New York, see Scobey, "Nymphs and Satyrs."

57. This description of typical cafeterias is based on a survey of period postcards.

58. Kinchin, "Interiors."

59. *Cafeteria, Motor Inn and Other Food Projects,* 1–2.

60. Stern and Stern, "Cafeteria," 42.

61. Ibid. Boos Brothers was a Los Angeles–based chain that began in 1906 (41).

62. Not until later, during Prohibition, did the counter become a more gender-neutral space, perhaps in part because of the changing use of historical bars, which were recast from the centers of male sociability to the center of a healthy heterogeneous sociability in their reuse as soda fountains. (See Levenstein, *Revolution at the Table.*)

63. Sangster, *Good Manners for All Occasions.*

64. Ibid., 40–41.

65. Peiss, *Cheap Amusements,* 28.

66. Haskell Diary, May 21, 1915.

67. Ibid., May 25, 1915.

68. Pierce Diary, March 24, 1915; March 25, 1915; March 28, 1915; April 22, 1915; May 14, 1915; May 18, 1915; May 29, 1915; June 5, 1915; August 2, 1915; August 31, 1915; September 15, 1915; October 13, 1915; November 13, 1915; November 20, 1915; November 21, 1915; November 27, 1915; and November 30, 1915.

69. De Witt, *An Illustrated and Descriptive Souvenir and Guide to San Francisco,* 87.

70. Haskell Diary, Sunday, August 31, 1890.

71. Purdy, *San Francisco,* 151.

72. Haskell Diary, Monday, May 6, 1912: "We had lunch at a cafeteria, the first time I have ever been in one."

73. Ibid., Thursday, July 15, 1915.

74. Pierce Diary, Wednesday, October 13, 1915. That same day she also ate dinner at a cafeteria at the Panama–Pacific International Exposition.

75. Ibid., Wednesday, March 31, 1915; Wednesday, July 14, 1915; Sunday, November 21, 1915; Wednesday, December 1, 1915; Wednesday, December 15, 1915; Tuesday, March 14, 1916; Friday, March 17, 1916; and Wednesday, August 23, 1916, relate eating at a hotel before going to the theater. Thursday, September 9, 1915, and Friday, September 17, 1915, relate going to hotels in the East Bay area with a companion for dinner (once in combination with a drive, once after a walk); Tuesday, June 15, 1915, to St. Francis for lunch; Saturday, June 26, 1915, to St. Francis for tea after motoring through the park. Leigh Diary, dinner at the California Hotel with family three Sundays: January 1, 15, and 29, 1905.

76. Both the Tait-Zinkand and the Portola-Louvre were consolidations of prequake restaurants. Tait's was founded in 1904 and was originally in the Flood Building, in a space that became the Portola-Louvre after the fire. The Louvre was run in the 1890s by Carl Zinkand, who later founded the Café Zinkand, which merged after the earthquake with Tait's. See Kastler, "Portola-Louvre Restaurant"; Jensen, "Tait's"; Edwords, *Bohemian San Francisco*, 26–27, 41–42; and Purdy, *San Francisco*, 148.

77. Austin, *Earth Horizon*, 183.

78. Haskell Diary, Monday, March 17, 1902.

79. Dobie, *San Francisco*, 328.

80. Ibid., 328.

81. Keeler, *San Francisco and Thereabouts*, 46–47.

82. Irwin, "The Adventures of San Francisco," in preliminary notebook, 297, in Inez Haynes Irwin Papers, Schlesinger Library, Radcliffe Institute for Advanced Study, Harvard University.

83. Burgess, *The Heart Line*, 151.

84. Frank Norris, quoted in Lewis, *Bay Window Bohemia*, 95.

85. Burgess, *The Heart Line*, 150. Sanguinetti's was located at 1 Vallejo Street.

86. Edwords, *Bohemian San Francisco*, 23–24.

87. Ibid., 24.

88. Burgess, *The Heart Line*, 503–4.

89. Purdy, *San Francisco*, 150. Lewis, in *Bay Window Bohemia* (104), also complained of the lack of spontaneity in the replacement murals.

90. Lewis, *Bay Window Bohemia*, 104.

91. Purdy, *San Francisco*, 151.

92. Ibid., 151–52.

93. Pierce Diary, Friday, November 26, 1915.

94. Purdy, *San Francisco*, 148.

95. Pierce Diary, Friday, March 17, 1916; Wednesday, March 29, 1916.

96. Groth, *Living Downtown*, 74.

97. Purdy, *San Francisco*, 148.

98. Ibid.

99. Keeler, *San Francisco and Thereabouts*, 46.

100. Ibid.

101. Mercantile Illustrating Co., *San Francisco, the Metropolis of Western America*, 208.

102. Notice of meeting pasted into Leigh Diary, December 8, 1906.

103. Leigh Diary, Saturday, January 14, 1903; Saturday, January 28, 1903; Saturday, January 7, 1905. Pierce Diary, Saturday, March 27, 1915; Friday, November 26, 1915; Sunday, March 19, 1916; Tuesday, March 21, 1916.

104. Mary Pierce's frequency of restaurant visits in 1915–16 is 70 visits over 102 weeks, an average of 0.68 restaurant visits per week; Annie Haskell's frequency of restaurant visits in the same years is 16 visits over 34 weeks in San Francisco, an average of 0.47 restaurant visits per week.

4. Spectacles and Amusements

1. For example, average weekly hours for workers in manufacturing dropped from 60 in 1890 to 59 in 1900, 56.5 in 1910, and 55 in 1915, while hours were much shorter for union workers in manufacturing, which dropped from 54.4 in 1890 to 53 in 1900, 50.1 in 1910, and 48.6 in 1915 (U.S. Bureau of the Census, *Historical Statistics of the United States, Colonial Times to 1970,* "Series D-765-778: Average Hours and Average Earnings in Manufacturing, in Selected Nonmanufacturing Industries, and for 'Lower-Skilled' Labor 1890 to 1926").

2. See Peiss, *Cheap Amusements,* and Nasaw, *Going Out,* for details on the expansion of commercial amusements at the turn of the century.

3. Peiss, *Cheap Amusements;* Nasaw, *Going Out;* Enstad, *Ladies of Labor, Girls of Adventure;* Ewen, "City Lights."

4. Kasson, *Rudeness and Civility,* 218. See also Levine, *Highbrow Lowbrow,* 24.

5. Ryan, *Women in Public,* 79–80.

6. Levine, *Highbrow Lowbrow.*

7. Institute for the Measurement of Worth, "Measuring Worth," www.measuringworth.com/uscompare, accessed October 19, 2010. I am using the equivalents based on the Consumer Price Index, by which $1 in 1900 is worth $26.40 in 2010 dollars. Comparing relative unskilled wages from 1900 and 2010, "Measuring Worth" states that for every $1 paid in 1900, $122 would have been paid in 2008.

8. Berson, *The San Francisco Stage,* 93–94.

9. Number of seats from Union Pacific Railroad Company, *Diagrams, San Francisco Theatres;* seat prices from advertisements in *San Francisco Call, San Francisco Chronicle,* and *San Francisco Examiner.*

10. Norris, *McTeague,* 101.

11. Ibid., 103.

12. Ibid., 98.

13. Peiss, *Cheap Amusements,* 142–43; Nasaw, *Going Out,* 25–26.

14. Peiss, *Cheap Amusements,* 143–44.

15. Nasaw, *Going Out,* 136–38.

16. Orpheum advertisement, *San Francisco Call,* June 1896.

17. Orpheum advertisement, *San Francisco Call,* September 4, 1898, 29.

18. Nasaw, *Going Out,* 147–52; Orpheum advertisements in *San Francisco Call.* The Orpheum once again began showing films, the Orpheum motion pictures, in 1905.

19. Allen, *Vaudeville and Film, 1895–1915,* 192.

20. Enstad, *Ladies of Labor, Girls of Adventure,* 162; Ewen, *Immigrant Women in the Land of Dollars,* 216–17, 221; Ewen, "City Lights," 55, 60; Peiss, *Cheap Amusements,* 146–53.

21. Musser, *The Emergence of Cinema,* 432; Peiss, *Cheap Amusements,* 148–49; Nasaw, *Going Out,* 175.

22. The Haskell Diary mentions going to vaudeville shows at the following theaters—the Orpheum: August 10, 1890; September 21, 1890; August 15, 1903; November 7, 1903; May 10, 1904; August 26, 1909; June 14, 1916; May 25, 1917, usually going in the daytime

and all but one time with her sister Kate; the Wigwam: July 26, 1890; October 8, 1893; May 21, 1909; November 12, 1909; December 23, 1909; December 30, 1909; February 3, 1910, more than once going alone to meet another woman; other places, usually going with Kate: April 7, 1903; June 20, 1915; June 12, 1916; August 18, 1916; September 12, 1916; and "wild melodrama" about the goldfields of Nevada: September 24, 1907.

23. Haskell Diary, February 20, 1890, May 7, 1890, June 10, 1890, June 11, 1890, July 26, 1890, August 10, 1890, September 21, 1890, and September 25, 1890.

24. On May 7, 1890, Haskell wrote: "I don't know as I have enjoyed a play so much since seeing Satanell. Probably one reason was that Burnette was not horrid. He generally takes a book and reads during the play. Burnette is very impossible sometimes."

25. Haskell Diary, February 12, 1910.

26. Pierce Diary, June 5, 1915; Haskell Diary, June 5, 1915.

27. Haskell Diary, May 26, 1911, and February 3, 1910.

28. In their diaries none of the women commonly mentioned what seats they sat in, but when they did, Mary Pierce and Ella Lees Leigh mentioned sitting in box and orchestra seats (Leigh: January 17, 1903; Pierce: May 5, 1915, and August 23, 1916), while Annie Haskell mentioned sitting in the balcony (February 11, 1905; May 26, 1911; June 12, 1912; June 5, 1915) or in the far back of the theater (February 3, 1910).

29. Haskell Diary, Monday, June 12, 1911.

30. Ibid., Tuesday, March 1, 1910.

31. Ibid., Thursday, July 21, 1914; Thursday, September 24, 1908.

32. Of the nine times Mary Pierce specifically mentioned going to a film, six were in the evening, whereas of the thirty-six times Annie Haskell mentioned going to a film, sixteen were in the evening.

33. Feature movies, multiple-reel films that lasted an hour or more, began to be produced in 1912. See Nye, *The Unembarrassed Muse,* 365.

34. *San Francisco Call and Post,* August 18, 1917, 14–15.

35. Nye, *The Unembarrassed Muse,* 366.

36. Advertisements in the *San Francisco Call and Post,* September 5, 1914, 10, list prices at the Tivoli, Portola, and Savoy of ten-cent and twenty-cent evening shows, ten-cent matinees, and at Grauman's Imperial of ten-cent, twenty-cent, and thirty-cent evenings, ten-cent and twenty-cent matinees, and twenty-cent and thirty-cent Sunday evenings. Similar prices are listed in advertisements over the next three years, except for a showing of *Birth of a Nation* at the Savoy in 1916, for which the prices were twenty-five cents, fifty cents, and seventy-five cents, as expensive as legitimate theater and more expensive than vaudeville.

37. De Witt, *An Illustrated and Descriptive Souvenir and Guide to San Francisco,* 42; Haskell Diary, Saturday, September 19, 1903.

38. Haskell Diary, Friday, August 27, 1914.

39. Schivelbusch, *Disenchanted Night,* 148.

40. Southern Pacific Company, *Trips around San Francisco,* 11–12.

41. Davis, *Parades and Power;* Jarman, *Material Conflicts;* Kugelmass and Allen, *Masked Culture;* MacAloon, ed., *Rite, Drama, Festival, Spectacle;* McNamara, *Day of Jubilee;* Manning, ed., *The Celebration of Society;* Ryan, "The American Parade"; Ryan, *Women in Public;*

Slymovics, "New York City's Muslim World Day Parade"; Zandi-Sayek, "Orchestrating Difference, Performing Identity."

42. The *San Francisco Call* showed images of women in its 1897 New Year's coverage and remarked on women's presence in following years. The *San Francisco Chronicle* mentions women celebrating separately on the streets south of Market in 1894 and first mentions women as participants with men, and includes them in illustrations, in 1897. The *San Francisco Examiner* first depicts a woman celebrating in a cartoon-style image in 1896.

43. The *San Francisco Call,* December 25, 1910, 30, estimated 90,000 participants; the *San Francisco Chronicle,* December 25, 1910, 28, reported that Chief Seymour estimated the crowd at 250,000.

44. Bakhtin, *Rabelais and His World,* 255. These characteristics of the carnival are discussed at length by Bakhtin in "Popular-Festive Forms," in *Rabelais and His World,* 196–277.

45. Haskell Diary, January 1, 1906.

46. Ibid., December 31, 1906.

47. Ibid., January 1, 1913.

48. *San Francisco Chronicle,* January 1, 1904, 1; *San Francisco Call,* January 1, 1905, 35.

49. *San Francisco Chronicle,* January 1, 1906, 14; *San Francisco Call,* January 1, 1898, 1.

50. *San Francisco Chronicle,* January 1, 1900.

51. *San Francisco Call,* January 1, 1901, 4; *San Francisco Call,* January 1, 1910, 10.

52. *San Francisco Call,* January 1, 1899.

53. Ibid.

54. *San Francisco Examiner,* January 1, 1901.

55. *San Francisco Call,* January 1, 1901, 4.

56. *San Francisco Call,* January 1, 1905, 35.

57. *San Francisco Chronicle,* January 1, 1912, 1.

58. *San Francisco Call,* January 1, 1905, 35; *San Francisco Call,* January 1, 1906, 13.

59. Haskell Diary, January 1, 1904.

60. "Enthralled by Magic Spell a City Heard a Nightingale Sing," *San Francisco Chronicle,* December 25, 1910, 28. See also the description of the kneeling audience on the platform in "Multitude Bares Heads as First Notes of Sad, Sweet Song, Diva's Christmas Gift to City, Are Heard," *San Francisco Call,* December 25, 1910, 30.

61. See, for example, Farber, "High, Healthy, and Happy"; and Lavenda, "Family and Corporation."

62. *San Francisco Examiner,* July 5, 1890; *San Francisco Call,* July 5, 1894; *San Francisco Examiner,* July 5, 1895; *San Francisco Examiner,* July 5, 1896; *San Francisco Call,* July 5, 1896.

63. Ryan, *Women in Public,* discusses women embodying allegories on pages 44–49 and 52–56; the quotation is from page 46.

64. *San Francisco Call,* September 2, 1902. See also *San Francisco Chronicle,* September 2, 1902. In 1902, as in many years, the parade began at the Ferry Building, marched along Market Street as far as Van Ness, and then doubled back, creating the countermarch. In 1902 the Building Trades Council and the Labor Council marched together, but in several other years, they mounted separate Labor Day parades, which marched in opposite directions along Market Street, reflecting competing union organizations.

65. *San Francisco Examiner,* September 2, 1902, 3.

66. *San Francisco Call,* September 6, 1910, 11.

67. In 1906, the Fourth of July was celebrated with a picnic and address in Golden Gate Park, and the celebration remained there, except in 1913, when the *Call* wrote that the "old custom is revived in parade of Soldiers" (*San Francisco Call,* July 5, 1913, 1).

68. In 1896, the Ladies of the Seven Pines Circle GAR paraded behind several minor political dignitaries and in front of the anti-suffragists (*San Francisco Call,* July 5, 1896, 8), and in 1898 La Estrella Parlor of the Native Daughters of the Golden West paraded (*San Francisco Call,* July 5, 1898, 5).

69. *San Francisco Call,* July 5, 1895, 1. See also *San Francisco Examiner,* July 5, 1895.

70. *San Francisco Call,* July 5, 1896, 8.

71. "Eagle Dons Skirts, Woman Orator Thrills," *San Francisco Call,* July 5, 1912, 1.

72. *San Francisco Call,* September 10, 1890, 1.

73. *San Francisco Call,* September 11, 1900, 2–4.

74. *San Francisco Call,* September 10, 1910, 2; *San Francisco Call,* September 10, 1915, 1–2.

75. *San Francisco Call,* September 10, 1910, 2.

76. Haskell Diary, Saturday, September 10, 1910.

5. Spaces of Suffrage

1. On the public sphere, see Habermas, *The Structural Transformation of the Public Sphere;* Calhoun, ed., *Habermas and the Public Sphere;* Weintraub and Kumar, eds., *Public and Private in Thought and Practice.*

2. Fannie McLean, "Speech to Women's Clubs," in McLean Family Papers, BANC MSS C-B 501, Bancroft Library, University of California, Berkeley.

3. Catt and Shuler, *Woman Suffrage and Politics,* 495–96.

4. In San Francisco, the participating organizations were: the California State Woman Suffrage Association, the College Equal Suffrage League, the Club Women's Franchise League, the Wage Earners' Suffrage League, the Women's Suffrage Party, the Susan B. Anthony Club, the Equal Suffrage League, and the Votes for Women Club of San Francisco. "Battle for Woman Suffrage Now Has Board of Strategy," *San Francisco Call,* August 7, 1911, 5.

5. "Union Men Indorse Suffrage Campaign," *San Francisco Call,* August 28, 1911, 5; "Labor Unions Indorse Plea to Give Vote," *San Francisco Call,* August 18, 1911, 7.

6. "Union Men Indorse Suffrage Campaign," *San Francisco Chronicle,* August 6, 1911.

7. "Labor Unions Indorse Plea to Give Vote."

8. "Equal Suffrage Meets Fate Next Week," *San Francisco Call,* October 3, 1911, 3.

9. "Suffrage Doings," *San Francisco Chronicle,* October 10, 1896, 7.

10. "Women Work for Political Enfranchisement and Men Organize Committee to Assist," *San Francisco Call,* September 30, 1911, 13; "Wage Earners' League to Hold Rally in the Mission," *San Francisco Call,* August 31, 1911, 5; "Battle for Woman Suffrage Now

Has Board of Strategy," *San Francisco Call*, August 7, 1911, 5; "Doings of the Women's Clubs," *San Francisco Chronicle*, September 3, 1911, 25.

11. "Friends of Suffrage," *San Francisco Call*, July 30, 1896; "Miss Anthony Speaks," *San Francisco Call*, May 4, 1896, 14.

12. "Mrs. Julia S. Sanborn Will Work Among Local Colored Folk," *San Francisco Call*, August 24, 1911, 7.

13. College Equal Suffrage League of Northern California, *Winning Equal Suffrage in California*, 86.

14. Ibid., 74.

15. Ibid., 39–40. See "Women's Clubs," *San Francisco Chronicle*, September 17, 1911, 25; "Outdoor Fete to Illustrate Historic Days," *San Francisco Call*, September 18, 1911, 7; "Suffragist Campaigners Plan for Organized District Work," *San Francisco Chronicle*, September 20, 1911, 7; and "Appeals to be Made for Amendment No. 8," *San Francisco Call*, September 21, 1911, 7, on meeting in French on September 21, 1911. See "Club Women Await the Suffrage Issue," *San Francisco Chronicle*, September 24, 1911, on meeting in Swedish Lutheran Church. See "Club Women Plan Campaign Work," *San Francisco Chronicle*, August 27, 1911, 25; "Political Equality to Be Advocated at North Beach Rally," *San Francisco Call*, September 14, 1911, 7; "Women Seek Votes in Italian Quarter," *San Francisco Examiner*, September 15, 1911, 4; and "Rallies Held Under the Auspices of Franchise League," *San Francisco Chronicle*, September 10, 1911, 25, on meetings in Italian.

16. "Mrs. Foltz on Suffrage," *San Francisco Call*, April 1, 1896, 11.

17. Haskell Diary, July 31, 1896.

18. From multiple newspaper clippings in Mary McHenry Keith Scrapbook, Keith Family Papers, Bancroft Library, University of California, Berkeley.

19. I refer to these spaces as semiprivate because access to them has been strongly limited and they have been privately controlled. They are symbolically part of the public realm, however, because the private realm is equated most often with the domestic. Franck and Paxson, in "Women and Urban Public Space," provide a useful model of "public," which includes question of access, ownership, and power, going beyond public as the opposite of domestic.

20. "Looking Forward to Sure Victory," clipping from a San Francisco paper, November 4, 1896, covering November postelection rally, at Metropolitan Temple, in Mary McHenry Keith Scrapbook.

21. Edelman, "'A Red Hot Suffrage Campaign,'" 81–83.

22. The "municipal housekeeping" movement was quite widespread in the late nineteenth and early twentieth centuries. Women's clubs in cities throughout the United States (largely white and middle- to upper-middle-class) organized downtown cleanups, donated trash bins to relieve the problem of litter and teach citizens to keep the city clean, pushed for and often organized street cleaning, beautified cities through street furnishings and other measures, and educated decision makers and others by sponsoring lectures and plans by urban planning experts. This practical work was tied always to the notion of morality, and the citizens of the cities were to become both healthier and better citizens through the influence of a cleaner environment. Many women moved from voluntary

positions within clubs to professional positions within city government, focusing primarily on sanitation. See especially Beard, *Women's Work in Municipalities*. Studies examining the role of municipal housekeeping in turn-of-the-century cities include Deutsch, *Women and the City*; Enstam, *Women and the Creation of Urban Life*; Flanagan, *Seeing with Their Hearts*; Isenberg, *Downtown America*, especially chapter 1, "The City Beautiful or Beautiful Mess? The Gendered Origins of a Civic Ideal"; and Spain, *How Women Saved the City*. On sanitation and municipal housekeeping, see Hoy, "'Municipal Housekeeping'"; and Platt, "Visible Smoke: Pollution and Gender Politics in Chicago," in *Shock Cities*, 468–92.

23. "Mrs. Foltz on Suffrage," *San Francisco Call*, April 1, 1896, 11.

24. "Suffragists Plan for Housewarming: Equality Tea to be Dispensed at New Headquarters of the League," *San Francisco Examiner*, August 7, 1911, 5.

25. "Friends of Suffrage," *San Francisco Call*, July 30, 1896, 7.

26. Kwolek-Folland, *Engendering Business*, 116–19.

27. Solomons, *How We Won the Vote in California*, 70.

28. "Pink Tea in Extensive Use for Winning Over Antis," *San Francisco Chronicle*, August 18, 1911, 7.

29. In 1911 all of the three major papers, the *San Francisco Call*, the *San Francisco Chronicle*, and the *San Francisco Examiner*, segregated the vast majority of their suffrage coverage to a page covering items of interest to women, particularly society news. The *Examiner* also regularly ran pro-suffrage arguments in articles labeled as "submitted by the publicity committee of the State Equal Suffrage Association." The coverage in the *Call* was quite extensive and often included photographs. The coverage in the *Examiner* was somewhat less extensive but also often included photographs. Both of these papers supported the 1911 woman suffrage amendment. In contrast, the *Chronicle* printed a number of mildly anti-suffrage columns and editorials, though it did not explicitly come out either against or for the amendment. This was in keeping with the positions of these three papers in 1896, when the *Call* was pro-suffrage, the *Examiner* was neutral, and the *Chronicle* was anti-suffrage. The *Chronicle* did not include photographs of suffragists in 1911 and nearly always kept all of its coverage within a column on women's clubs, so that suffrage activities and the meetings of the California Club or the Women's Outdoor Club were treated as equivalent and often shared space in the same column.

30. "Encouraging Reports Sent in by Workers," *San Francisco Call*, August 22, 1911, 7.

31. "Society Women Over Tea Table Aid Suffrage," *San Francisco Call*, August 10, 1911, 7; "Suffrage Leagues of City Continue Aggressive Campaign," *San Francisco Call*, August 25, 1911, 7.

32. "Equality Tea Will Take Place in Carnegie Library at Richmond," *San Francisco Call*, August 27, 1911, 7.

33. "Equality Beverage to Coax Votes at the St. Francis," *San Francisco Call*, August 11, 1911; "Suffragists Plan for Housewarming: Equality Tea to be Dispensed at New Headquarters of the League," *San Francisco Examiner*, August 7, 1911.

34. "Two Mayors to Speak on Votes for Women" *San Francisco Call*, August 30, 1911; "Lectures and Personal Appeals Used to Win Support for Clubs," *San Francisco Call*, August 14, 1911, 5.

35. "Women Ready to Serve in Aid of 'Cause,'" *San Francisco Call*, October 10, 1911, 7; "Open Houses Arranged for Poll Pickets," *San Francisco Call*, October 9, 1911, 5; "Open House to be Kept For Women Busy at the Polls," *San Francisco Call*, October 8, 1911, 33. See also "Suffragists Plan For Election Day," *San Francisco Chronicle*, October 1, 1911, 47; "Wanted, 1068 Young and Beautiful Women at the Polls," *San Francisco Chronicle*, October 6, 1911, 7; and "Women's Courtesy Requested," *San Francisco Examiner*, October 7, 1911, 3.

36. "Women are Organizing," *San Francisco Call*, July 7, 1896, 16; "Equal Suffrage and Its Friends," *San Francisco Call*, July 9, 1896, 14; "Women in the Precincts," *San Francisco Call*, July 11, 1896; "Women in Precincts," *San Francisco Call*, August 7, 1896, 16.

37. "Looking Forward to Sure Victory," clipping from a San Francisco paper, November 4, 1896, on November postelection suffrage rally at Metropolitan Temple; in Mary McHenry Keith scrapbook.

38. She began her door-to-door canvassing on July 29, 1896, and continued until the amendment's defeat on November 3.

39. Haskell Diary, August 3, 1896.

40. Ibid., August 28, 1896.

41. "Campaign Carried to Voters' Homes," *San Francisco Call*, August 19, 1911, 13.

42. "Mrs. Foltz on Suffrage," *San Francisco Call*, April 1, 1896, 11.

43. "Will Ratify Their Planks," *San Francisco Call*, June 20, 1896, 9.

44. "Food for Mind and Body," *San Francisco Call*, July 25, 1896, 6.

45. "Boston Tea Party Is Far Eclipsed by California Women," *San Francisco Call*, August 11, 1911, 7.

46. Ibid.

47. Ibid.

48. "Mrs. H. Hall Serving Tea at Industrial Fair," *San Francisco Call*, August 19, 1911, 13; "League of Club Women to Give Big Card Party," *San Francisco Call*, September 25, 1911, 7; Solomons, *How We Won the Vote in California*, 54.

49. "Emancipated Woman's Superior Fascinations Shown by Novel," *San Francisco Call*, September 21, 1911, 7.

50. Solomons, *How We Won the Vote in California*, 55.

51. "Yes, the Lady with the Postals Wants Both Coin and Vote," *San Francisco Call*, October 5, 1911, 7.

52. "Final Big Rally for Suffrage To-night: Some of the Best Speakers in the Fight to be Heard in Valencia Theater. To-Day Postal Card Day: Girls will be Stationed all over City Selling Copies of Amendment 8," *San Francisco Examiner*, October 5, 1911, 3. The other stores that provided rest stations, according to this article, were Plum's, DN&E Walters Company, and Deremer & Company.

53. College Equal Suffrage League, *Winning Equal Suffrage in California*, 80.

54. Ibid., 33.

55. "Women's Clubs," *San Francisco Chronicle*, August 13, 1911.

56. "Suffrage Leaders Appeal to Merchants to make Display," *San Francisco Call*, August 15, 1911, 5; Fannie McLean, "Campaign of Ed," essay manuscript, McLean Family Papers.

57. College Equal Suffrage League, *Winning Equal Suffrage in California*, 46.

58. "Women Capture a Stronghold," *San Francisco Call*, October 7, 1911, 26.

59. McLean, "Campaign of Ed."

60. DuBois, "Votes for Women."

61. Solomons, *How We Won the Vote in California*, 40.

62. "Women Freely Give Money for Ballot Battle," *San Francisco Call*, August 20, 1911, 7.

63. "Mrs. Maud Wood Park Compares Short Haired Enthusiasts and Dainty Advocates," clipping in Fannie McLean Scrapbook.

64. "Workers of Washington and California Map Out Vigorous Campaign for This Fall," *San Francisco Call*, August 15, 1911, 3; see also Solomons, *How We Won the Vote in California*, 55; "Fifty Ushers to Disprove That Suffragists Are Unbeautiful," *San Francisco Chronicle*, October 5, 1911, 7; "Wanted, 1068 Young and Beautiful Women at the Polls," *San Francisco Chronicle*, October 6, 1911, 7; "A New Use for Beauty: Attractive Young Women as Election Watchers to Aid Suffrage," *San Francisco Chronicle*, October 7, 1911, 6; "Dowdy Suffragists No Longer De Rigueur," *San Francisco Examiner*, September 26, 1911, 1.

65. "Fifty Ushers to Disprove That Suffragists Are Unbeautiful," *San Francisco Chronicle*, October 5, 1911, 7.

66. "Suffrage Cause Is Boosted at Three Rallies," *San Francisco Examiner*, September 30, 1911, 8.

67. College Equal Suffrage League, *Winning Equal Suffrage in California*, 46.

68. Ibid., 49.

69. Leach, "Transformations in a Culture of Consumption," 323.

70. The California campaign was the first to use window displays to this extent, although British suffragettes opened a suffrage shop in London in 1910 and decorated their window with suffrage posters and books; see McQuiston, *Suffragists to She-Devils*, 40. Alice Park, a Palo Alto suffragist who was instrumental in the use of posters, window displays, and the color yellow in both the California campaign and other state campaigns, engaged shop windows in Palo Alto in the years before 1911 with a suffrage bulletin board that would move among different prominent businesses' front windows on a monthly basis (see Alice Park Papers, Huntington Library; and "A Bright Idea," *Woman's Journal*, September 25, 1909, 155). This borrowing of businesses' windows for a suffrage message was probably the most immediate precursor of the 1911 shop window campaign. New York suffragists, whose strategies were the most similar to California suffragists in their use of advertising and spectacle, used show windows later in the 1910s.

71. "Yellow Glories of Golden State Told to Anti-Suffragists," in *Clippings*, vol. 18, 31, Susan B. Anthony Memorial Collection, Huntington Library.

72. Alice Park, Alice Park Papers, PK 323, box 2, Huntington Library.

73. Finnegan, *Selling Suffrage*, 111–16; College Equal Suffrage League, *Winning Equal Suffrage in California*, 49. When yellow was first used as a suffrage color, in Kansas, it was called the "sunflower badge" ("Sunflower Badge for Suffrage," *Woman's Journal*, November 26, 1887, 1). Following this, several articles in the *Woman's Journal* mentioned yellow as a suffrage color (Virginia D. Young, "Yellow Ribbon in South Carolina's Fourth Estate,"

Woman's Journal, July 23, 1892, 236; "A Yellow, White and Purple Bow-Knot," *Woman's Journal,* October 8, 1892, 324; "Sunflower Lunch in Orange, New Jersey," *Woman's Journal,* May 12, 1894, 146; "Show the Yellow," *Woman's Journal,* May 19, 1894, 156; "New Suffrage Post Cards," *Woman's Journal,* January 9, 1909, 5; "'Votes for Women' Flags," *Woman's Journal,* May 8, 1909, 74). Starting in 1908, *Woman's Journal* also contained several mentions of the use of yellow as a suffrage color in California, all attributable to Alice Park. In 1906 and 1907, a San Francisco–based suffrage journal called the *Yellow Ribbon* was published as the official organ of West Coast suffragists.

74. College Equal Suffrage League, *Winning Equal Suffrage in California,* 46.

75. "Why, Ladies! Anti-Suffrage Cards Torn? Too 'Practical' Methods are Complained of by Women Who Don't Want Vote, And Boycott Used, Too! Shopmen and Even Bankers Told Not to Exhibit Banners or They'll Lose Patrons," *San Francisco Examiner,* August 29, 1911, 5.

76. "Suffragists Seek Votes by Distribution of Literature," *San Francisco Chronicle,* September 30, 1911.

77. "Apron Sale," *Dry Goods Reporter,* July 4, 1903, 69.

78. College Equal Suffrage League, *Winning Equal Suffrage in California,* 39.

79. 1911 letter from M. J. Bearby to Alice Park about the California campaign, PK133, box 3, Alice Park Papers, Huntington Library. The wording on grocery bags distributed by the College Equal Suffrage League read "FOR HOME AND FAMILY VOTE FOR WOMAN'S SUFFRAGE, Fourth Place on Ballot at Next Tuesday's Election. It means Clean Streets, Clean Milk, Pure Food, Playgrounds, Better Schools" (College Equal Suffrage League, *Winning Equal Suffrage in California,* 130).

80. "30,000 Paper Bags," *Woman's Journal,* July 30, 1910, 121.

81. Ibid.

82. "Suffragists Seek Votes by Distribution of Literature," *San Francisco Chronicle,* September 30, 1911.

83. "Equality Beverage to Coax Votes at St. Francis," *San Francisco Call,* August 18, 1911, 7.

84. "Boston Tea Party Is Far Eclipsed by California Women."

85. Ibid.

86. "Equality Beverage to Coax Votes at St. Francis."

87. "Boston Tea Party Is Far Eclipsed by California Women."

88. Ibid.

89. Caroline Singer, "What Working Girls Do With Their 60 Minutes at Noon: Imbibe Votes for Women Arguments as Side-Dish to 'Just Home Cooking,'" clipping in Selina Solomons Papers, Bancroft Library, University of California, Berkeley.

90. Ibid.

91. "A Business Woman's Club," *Woman's Journal,* April 6, 1901, 106; "College Women's Lunch Room," *Woman's Journal,* May 16, 1903, 151; "A Model Eating House," *Woman's Journal,* February 14, 1903, 52.

92. "A Model Eating House."

93. 1911 letter from M. J. Bearby to Alice Park about the California campaign, Alice Park Papers.

94. "Women Freely Give Money for Ballot Battle," *San Francisco Call*, August 20, 1911, 7.

95. College Equal Suffrage League, *Winning Equal Suffrage in California*, 84.

96. "College Equal Suffrage and Clubwoman's Leagues Prosecuting Campaign with Vigor," *San Francisco Call*, September 16, 1911, 7.

97. College Equal Suffrage League, *Winning Equal Suffrage in California*, 83. Large signs were also placed at the baseball fields in both Oakland and San Francisco (ibid., 84).

98. Solomons, *How We Won the Vote in California*, 41.

99. College Equal Suffrage League, *Winning Equal Suffrage in California*, 88.

100. Ibid., 88–89.

101. Ibid., 84–85.

102. "Neatly Packed Lunches Wanted for Watchers at the Polls," *San Francisco Chronicle*, October 10, 1911, 7; "Speakers for the League Make Tour of City in Automobiles," *San Francisco Chronicle*, October 7, 1911, 7.

103. "The Suffrage Campaign Continues to Show New Features," *San Francisco Chronicle*, September 7, 1911, 7; "Street Meetings Held by the Equal Suffrage League," *San Francisco Chronicle*, September 12, 1911, 7; "Political Equality to be Advocated at North Beach Rally," *San Francisco Call*, September 14, 1911, 7; "Street Meetings Said to Be Growing in Interest," *San Francisco Chronicle*, September 14, 1911, 7; "Meetings on the Street to Help Cause of Suffrage," *San Francisco Chronicle*, September 15, 1911, 7; "Women Work for Political Enfranchisement" *San Francisco Call*, September 30, 1911; "Big Suffrage Event on Thursday at Dreamland Rink," *San Francisco Chronicle*, October 3, 1911, 7; "Women Make Plea for the Ballot," *San Francisco Chronicle*, October 5, 1911, 4; "Suffrage Doctrine Told Crowds in Union Square Park," *San Francisco Chronicle*, October 6, 1911, 7; "Women Closing Campaign With Whirl," *San Francisco Call*, October 5, 1911, 4; "Speakers for the League Make Tour of City in Automobiles," *San Francisco Chronicle*, October 7, 1911, 7; "Street Meetings Will Be Held Today and Tonight," *San Francisco Chronicle*, October 9, 1911, 7.

104. Austin, *The Ford*, 184.

105. "Suffrage Doctrine Told Crowds in Union Square Park," *San Francisco Chronicle*, October 6, 1911, 7.

106. "Nordica's Voice Rings in Songs for Women" *San Francisco Examiner*, October 10, 1911, 1.

107. "Diva Sings for Suffrage," *San Francisco Call*, October 10, 1911, 1.

108. "Meetings on the Street to Help Cause of Suffrage" *San Francisco Chronicle*, September 15, 1911, 7.

109. "The Suffrage Campaign Continues to Show New Features," *San Francisco Chronicle*, September 7, 1911, 7; "Street Meetings Held by the Equal Suffrage League," *San Francisco Chronicle*, September 12, 1911, 7.

110. "Meetings on the Street to Help Cause of Suffrage," *San Francisco Chronicle*, September 15, 1911, 7.

111. "Women Closing Campaign With Whirl," *San Francisco Call*, October 5, 1911, 4.

112. College Equal Suffrage League, *Winning Equal Suffrage in California*, 63–72, includes a lengthy report on the Blue Liner, campaigning car.

113. Ibid., 61.

114. "Mrs. Jeannette Rankin Arrives Here From New York," *San Francisco Chronicle*, September 1, 1911, 7.

115. "Meetings on the Street to Help Cause of Suffrage," *San Francisco Chronicle*, September 15, 1911, 7.

116. "How Suffragists Spent the Day," *San Francisco Call*, November 11, 1896.

117. Alice Park, PK 132, box 3, Alice Park Collection, Huntington Library.

118. "Women Got Only Courtesy," *San Francisco Call*, October 11, 1911, 2.

119. "To Aid the Suffrage Cause," *San Francisco Chronicle*, October 7, 1896.

120. Ibid.

121. "Suffrage Performance Promises to be a Big Success," *San Francisco Call*, August 21, 1911, 5; "Club Notes," *San Francisco Examiner*, September 2, 1911, 9; "Singer to Give Concert Money Toward Cause," *San Francisco Call*, September 5, 1911, 7; "Suffrage to Be Aided by Dramatic Readings," *San Francisco Examiner*, September 5, 1911, 9; "League Gives a Concert," *San Francisco Chronicle*, September 6, 1911, 7; "Benefit Entertainment To Aid the College League Work," *San Francisco Call*, September 8, 1911, 7; "Women Will Give Their Services to Aid Ballot Battle," *San Francisco Call*, September 11, 1911, 7; "Society Will Hear Reader's Two Programs," *San Francisco Call*, September 12, 1911; "A Dramatic Reading," *San Francisco Chronicle*, September 12, 1911.

122. "Singer to Give Concert Money Toward Cause."

123. Levine, *Highbrow Lowbrow*, 134.

124. "Aid from Boys of Australia Given Women; New York Suffrage Worker to Dance on Stage of Valencia Theater," *San Francisco Call*, September 28, 1911, 7.

125. Ibid.

126. "Singer to Give Concert Money Toward Cause."

127. "Meeting Against Votes for Women at Valencia Theater," *San Francisco Chronicle*, October 4, 1911, 7; "Big Crowd Hears Anti-Suffragists," *San Francisco Chronicle*, October 5, 1911, 4; "Religious Drama of the Time of Nero to be Staged at the Valencia Theater," *San Francisco Chronicle*, October 1, 1911, 38.

128. "Miss Lambert's Play Soon to be Produced," *San Francisco Call*, September 27, 1911, 7; "Oakland Suffragists See Play Senator Won," *San Francisco Call*, October 4, 1911, 7; "Oakland Woman to Stage Suffrage Play," *San Francisco Call*, September 22, 1911, 7; "Suffrage Playlet to Get Funds and Votes for the Cause," *San Francisco Call*, August 13, 1911, 31; "Suffragists Win Applause in Play," *San Francisco Call*, October 4, 1911, 7; "Suffrage Drama Is Written to Assist Cause of Women," *San Francisco Call*, August 12, 1911, 13; "Anti-Suffrage Aunty 'Antes' Vote in Comedy," *San Francisco Call*, September 25, 1911, 7; "Suffragists Mingle Entertainment with Business," *San Francisco Chronicle*, August 27, 1911, 25.

129. McLean, "Campaign of Ed."

130. "Converts to Cause Made at a Studio 'Tea,'" *San Francisco Call*, October 1, 1911, 47.

131. "September 1 is Set as Date of Statewide Rally for Suffrage," *San Francisco Call*, August 29, 1911, 7.

132. "Suffrage Party to Show Pictures at Princess Theater," *San Francisco Call*, September 2, 1911, 13.

133. College Equal Suffrage League, *Winning Equal Suffrage in California*, 96.

134. "Theaters to Display Suffragist Pictures," *San Francisco Call*, August 25, 1911, 7.

135. "Suffrage Auto 'Blue Liner' Will Tour State with Women Making Addresses," *San Francisco Call*, August 16, 1911, 7.

136. "Five Orators to Close Long Ballot Fight," *San Francisco Call*, October 10, 1911, 13.

137. "Suffrage Pageant and Picnic Planned at Piedmont Park," *San Francisco Call*, September 15, 1911, 7.

138. "Suffragists Try Vaudeville as Means of Conversion to Their Cause," *San Francisco Chronicle*, August 30, 1911, 7.

139. "Vaudeville and Street Speaking as Means to the End," *San Francisco Chronicle*, September 2, 1911, 7. This performance was also covered briefly in "Club Notes," *San Francisco Examiner*, September 2, 1911, 9.

140. Peiss, *Cheap Amusements*, 149; Nasaw, *Going Out*, 163–64.

141. "Presence of Their Leader Signal for Big Turnout by Labor," *San Francisco Call*, September 5, 1911, 2.

142. College Equal Suffrage League, *Winning Equal Suffrage in California*, 97.

BIBLIOGRAPHY

Abelson, Elaine S. *When Ladies Go A-Thieving: Middle-Class Shoplifters in the Victorian Department Store.* New York: Oxford University Press, 1989.

Agrest, Diana, Patricia Conway, and Leslie Weisman. *The Sex of Architecture.* New York: Harry N. Abrams, 1996.

Ainley, Rosa. *New Frontiers of Space, Bodies, and Gender.* London: Routledge, 1998.

Allen, Robert Clyde. *Vaudeville and Film, 1895–1915: A Study in Media Interaction.* New York: Arno Press, 1980.

Altman, Irwin, and Ervin H. Zube. *Public Places and Spaces.* New York: Plenum Press, 1989.

Ames, Kenneth L. *Death in the Dining Room and Other Tales of Victorian Culture.* Philadelphia: Temple University Press, 1992.

Andrew, Caroline, Fran Klodawsky, and Colleen Lundy. "Women's Safety and the Politics of Transformation." *Women and Environments* 14, no. 1 (1994): 23–26.

Andrew, Caroline, and Beth Moore Milroy, eds., *Life Spaces: Gender, Household, Employment.* Vancouver: University of British Columbia Press, 1988.

Anthony, Susan B., and Ida Husted Harper. *The History of Woman Suffrage.* Rochester, N.Y.: Susan B. Anthony, 1902.

Appleton's General Guide to the United States and Canada. New York: Appleton & Company, 1897.

Ardener, Shirley, ed. *Women and Space: Ground Rules and Social Maps.* Rev. ed. Providence, R.I.: Berg, 1993.

Arendt, Hannah. *The Human Condition.* Charles R. Walgreen Foundation Lectures. Chicago: University of Chicago Press, 1958.

Artley, Alexandra. *The Golden Age of Shop Design: European Shop Interiors, 1880–1939.* London: Architectural Press, 1975.

The Art of Decorating: Show Windows and Interiors. Chicago: Merchants Record Company, 1906–9.

Atherton, Gertrude Franklin Horn. *My San Francisco, a Wayward Biography.* Indianapolis: Bobbs-Merrill Company, 1946.

Auslander, Leora. *Taste and Power.* Berkeley: University of California Press, 1996.

Auster, Albert. *Actresses and Suffragists: Women in the American Theater, 1890–1920.* New York: Praeger, 1984.

Austin, Bruce A. *Immediate Seating: A Look at Movie Audiences.* Belmont, Calif.: Wadsworth Publishing Company, 1989.

Austin, Mary Hunter. *Earth Horizon, Autobiography.* Boston: Houghton Mifflin Company, 1932.

———. *The Ford.* Berkeley: University of California Press, 1997.

Averbach, Alvin. "San Francisco's South of Market District, 1850–1950: The Emergence of a Skid Row." *California Historical Quarterly* 52, no. 3 (1973): 196–223.

Bakhtin, Mikhail. *Rabelais and His World.* Translated by Helene Iswolsky. Bloomington: Indiana University Press, 1968.

Barber, Bernard. "Stratification, Social: Introduction." In *International Encyclopedia of the Social Sciences,* vol. 2, ed. David L. Sills, 288–96. New York: Macmillan Company and Free Press, 1968.

Barth, Gunther. *City People: The Rise of Modern City Culture in Nineteenth-Century America.* New York: Oxford University Press, 1980.

Baudelaire, Charles. *The Painter of Modern Life and Other Essays.* Translated and edited by Jonathan Mayne. London: Phaidon, 1964.

Bean, Walton. *Boss Ruef's San Francisco: The Story of the Union Labor Party, Big Business, and the Graft Prosecution.* Berkeley: University of California Press, 1952.

Beard, Mary Ritter. *Women's Work in Municipalities.* New York: D. Appleton & Company, 1915.

Beebe, Lucius Morris, and Charles Clegg. *Cable Car Carnival.* Oakland, Calif.: G. Hardy, 1951.

———. *San Francisco's Golden Era: A Picture Story of San Francisco before the Fire.* Berkeley: Howell-North, 1960.

Beeching, C. L. T. *Salesmanship for the Grocer and Provision Dealer.* London: Institute of Certificated Grocers, 1924.

Bender, Barbara, ed. *Landscape: Politics and Perspectives.* Providence, R.I.: Berg, 1993.

Bendix, Reinhard, and Seymour Martin Lipset, eds. *Class, Status, and Power: A Reader in Social Stratification.* Glencoe, Ill.: Free Press, 1953.

Benjamin, Walter. "Paris, Capital of the Nineteenth Century." *Reflections: Esssays, Aphorisms,*

Autobiographical Writings. Edited by Peter Demetz. New York: Harcourt Brace Jovanovich, 1978.

Benson, Susan Porter. *Counter Cultures: Saleswomen, Managers, and Customers in American Department Stores, 1890–1940.* Urbana: University of Illinois Press, 1986.

———. "Palace of Consumption and Machine for Selling: The American Department Store, 1880–1940." *Radical History Review* 21 (Fall 1979): 199–221.

Berger, Frances de Talavera, and John Parke Custis. *Sumptuous Dining in Gaslight San Francisco, 1875–1915: Lost Recipes, Culinary Secrets, Flamboyant People, and Fabled Saloons and Restaurants from a Golden Era.* Garden City, N.Y.: Doubleday, 1985.

Berkeley, Ellen Perry, and Matilda McQuaid. *Architecture: A Place for Women.* Washington, D.C.: Smithsonian Institution Press, 1989.

Bernhardi, Robert. *Great Buildings of San Francisco: A Photographic Guide.* New York: Dover Publications, 1980.

Berson, Misha. *The San Francisco Stage: From Golden Spike to Great Earthquake, 1869–1906.* Series 4. San Francisco: San Francisco Performing Arts Library and Museum, 1992.

Blumin, Stuart M. *The Emergence of the Middle Class: Social Experience in the American City, 1760–1900.* Cambridge, U.K.: Cambridge University Press, 1989.

Blunt, Alison, and Gillian Rose. *Writing Women and Space: Colonial and Postcolonial Geographies.* New York: Guilford Press, 1994.

Bourdieu, Pierre. *Distinction.* Translated by Richard Nice. London: Routledge and Kegan Paul, 1984.

Bowden, Martyn John. "The Dynamics of City Growth: An Historical Geography of the San Francisco Central District, 1850–1931." Ph.D. dissertation, University of California, Berkeley, 1967.

Bowlby, Rachel. *Just Looking: Consumer Culture in Dreiser, Gissing, and Zola.* New York: Methuen, 1985.

Boyer, M. Christine. *Dreaming the Rational City: The Myth of American City Planning.* Cambridge, Mass.: MIT Press, 1983.

Brandimarte, Cynthia. "'To Make the Whole World Homelike': Gender, Space, and America's Tea Room Movement." *Winterthur Portfolio* 30, no. 1 (Spring 1995): 1–19.

Breen, Richard, and David B. Rottman. *Class Stratification: A Comparative Perspective.* New York: Harvester Wheatsheaf, 1995.

Bronner, Simon J., ed. *Consuming Visions: Accumulation and Display of Goods in America, 1880–1920.* Winterthur, Del.: Henry du Pont Winterthur Museum, 1989.

Broussard, Albert S. *Black San Francisco: the Struggle for Racial Equality in the West, 1900–1954.* Lawrence: University Press of Kansas, 1993.

Brucken, Caroline. "In The Public Eye: Women and the American Luxury Hotel." *Winterthur Portfolio* 31, no. 4 (Winter 1996): 203–20.

Bunce, Mrs. Oliver Bell. *What to Do: A Companion to Don't.* New York: D. Appleton & Company, 1892.

Bunkers, Suzanne L., and Cynthia Anne Huff. *Inscribing the Daily: Critical Essays on Women's Diaries.* Amherst: University of Massachusetts Press, 1996.

Burgess, Gelett. *The Heart Line; a Drama of San Francisco.* Indianapolis: Bobbs-Merrill, 1907.

Bushman, Richard L. *The Refinement of America: Persons, Houses, Cities.* New York: Knopf, 1992.

Butsch, Richard. *For Fun and Profit: The Transformation of Leisure into Consumption.* Philadelphia: Temple University Press, 1990.

Cafeteria, Motor Inn and Other Food Projects. Scranton, Pa.: Woman's Institute of Domestic Arts and Sciences, 1932.

California Mid Winter Fair 1894. Fair guidebook. Collections of the Bancroft Library, University of California, Berkeley.

California Woman Suffrage Association. *Constitution and By-Laws of the California Woman Suffrage Association.* San Francisco: Wale Printing Company, 1902.

Calhoun, Craig J., ed. *Habermas and the Public Sphere.* Cambridge, Mass.: MIT Press, 1992.

Cameron, James. *Guide to San Francisco and Map, 1908.* San Francisco: James Cameron, 1908.

Carol, Hans. "The Hierarchy of Central Business Functions within the City." *Annals of the Association of American Geographers* 50, no. 4 (1960): 419–38.

Carter, Thomas, and Elizabeth C. Cromley. *Invitation to Vernacular Architecture: A Guide to the Study of Ordinary Buildings and Landscapes.* Knoxville: University of Tennessee Press, 2005.

Catt, Carrie Chapman, and Nettie Rogers Shuler. *Woman Suffrage and Politics.* Seattle: University of Washington Press, 1923.

Censor. *Don't: A Manual of Mistakes and Improprieties more or less prevalent in Conduct and Speech.* New York: D. Appleton & Company, 1883.

Chamberlain, Esther, and Lucia Chamberlain. *The Coast of Chance.* Indianapolis: Bobbs-Merrill Company, 1908.

Charvat, Frank J. *Supermarketing.* New York: Macmillan, 1961.

Chase, John, Margaret Crawford, and John Kaliski. *Everyday Urbanism.* New York: Monacelli Press, 1999.

Chauncey, George. *Gay New York: Gender, Urban Culture, and the Makings of the Gay Male World, 1890–1940.* New York: Basic Books, 1994.

Clapp, Eleanor B. *Social Usage and Etiquette: A Book of Manners for Every-Day Use.* New York: Home Circle Library, 1910.

Clayton, John. *Gumps since 1861: A San Francisco Legend.* San Francisco: Chronicle Books, 1990.

Coleman, Debra, Elizabeth Danze, and Carol Henderson. *Architecture and Feminism.* New York: Princeton Architectural Press, 1996.

College Equal Suffrage League of Northern California. *Winning Equal Suffrage in California: Reports of Committees of the College Equal Suffrage League of Northern California in the Campaign of 1911.* San Francisco: National College Equal Suffrage League, 1913.

Colomina, Beatriz, and Jennifer Bloomer. *Sexuality and Space.* New York: Princeton Architectural Press, 1992.

Columbia Theatre; Souvenir Commemorating the Opening of the Columbia Theatre. San Francisco: Sterett Show Printing Company, 1895.

Conzen, Michael P., ed. *The Making of the American Landscape*. Boston: Unwin Hyman, 1990.

Cooke, Maud C. *Social Etiquette, or Manners and Customs of Polite Society*. Boston: Geo. M. Smith & Company, 1896.

Cosgrove, Denis E. *Social Formation and Symbolic Landscape*. London: Croom Helm, 1984.

Cosgrove, Denis E., and Stephen Daniels, eds. *The Iconography of Landscape: Essays on the Symbolic Representation, Design, and Use of Past Environments*. Cambridge, U.K.: Cambridge University Press, 1988.

Cranz, Galen. *The Politics of Park Design: A History of Urban Parks in America*. Cambridge, Mass.: MIT Press, 1982.

Cromley, Elizabeth C., and Carter L. Hudgins, eds. *Gender, Class, and Shelter, Perspectives in Vernacular Architecture, 5*. Knoxville: University of Tennessee Press, 1995.

Crossick, Geoffrey, and Serge Jaumain, eds. *Cathedrals of Consumption: The European Department Store, 1850–1939*. Aldershot, U.K.: Ashgate, 1999.

Dale, Daphne. *Our Manners and Social Customs: A Practical Guide to Deportment, Easy Manners, and Social Etiquette*. Chicago: Elliott & Beezley, 1892.

Daniels, Douglas Henry. *Pioneer Urbanites: A Social and Cultural History of Black San Francisco*. Berkeley: University of California Press, 1990.

Davidoff, Leonore, and Catherine Hall. *Family Fortunes: Men and Women of the English Middle Class, 1780–1850*. Chicago: University of Chicago Press, 1987.

Davis, Reda. *California Women: A Guide to Their Politics, 1885–1911*. San Francisco: California Scene, 1967.

Davis, Susan G. *Parades and Power: Street Theatre in Nineteenth-Century Philadelphia*. Philadelphia: Temple University Press, 1986.

de Certeau, Michel. *The Practice of Everyday Life*. Berkeley: University of California Press, 1984.

de Certeau, Michel, Luce Giard, and Pierre Mayol. *The Practice of Everyday Life*, vol. 2, *Living and Cooking*. Minneapolis: University of Minnesota Press, 1998.

De Ford, Miriam Allen. *They Were San Franciscans*. Caldwell, Idaho: Caxton, 1941.

De Grazia, Victoria, and Ellen Furlough, eds. *The Sex of Things: Gender and Consumption in Historical Perspective*. Berkeley: University of California Press, 1996.

Deitrick, Elizabeth Platt. *Best Bits of the Exposition and San Francisco*. San Francisco: Galen Publishing Company, 1915.

Derks, Scott. *The Value of a Dollar: Prices and Incomes in the United States, 1860–1999*. Lakeville, Conn.: Grey House Publishing, 1999.

Desepte, Warren Gunther. *The Early Days of Grocery Clerk Unionism: An Interview*. Berkeley: Institute of Industrial Relations, Oral History Project of the University of California, 1958.

Deutsch, Sarah. *Women and the City: Gender, Space, and Power in Boston, 1870–1940*. New York: Oxford University Press, 2000.

De Witt, Frederic M. *An Illustrated and Descriptive Souvenir and Guide to San Francisco: A New Handbook for Strangers and Tourists, with a Short Historical Sketch and a Bird's-Eye*

View of the Business Center of the City. 4th ed., rev. and corrected. San Francisco: M. De Witt, 1902.

Dickson, Samuel. *San Francisco Kaleidoscope.* Stanford, Calif.: Stanford University Press, 1949.

Dipman, Carl William. *The Modern Grocery Store.* New York: Progressive Grocer, 1931.

Dobie, Charles Caldwell. *San Francisco; a Pageant.* New York: D. Appleton–Century Company, 1933.

Dodd, Jack L., and Hazel Blair Dodd. *Bohemian Eats of San Francisco.* San Francisco, 1925.

Domosh, Mona. "Those 'Gorgeous Incongruities': Polite Politics and Public Space on the Streets of Nineteenth-Century New York City." *Annals of the Association of American Geographers* 88, no. 2 (June 1998): 209–26.

Donovan, Frances R. *The Saleslady.* Chicago: University of Chicago Press, 1929.

———. *The Woman Who Waits.* Boston: R. G. Badger, 1920.

Down Town Association. *For the Good of San Francisco: 20 Years of Civic Service by the Down Town Association.* San Francisco: Down Town Association, 1927.

Doxey, William. *Doxey's Guide to San Francisco and the Pleasure Resorts of California.* San Francisco: W. Doxey, 1897.

DuBois, Ellen Carol. *Feminism and Suffrage: The Emergence of an Independent Women's Movement in America, 1848–1869.* Ithaca, N.Y.: Cornell University Press, 1978.

———. "Votes for Women." Lecture presented at San Francisco Public Library, April 17, 1997.

DuBois, Ellen, and Karen Kearns. *Votes for Women: A 75th Anniversary Album.* San Marino, Calif.: Huntington Library, 1995.

Duncan, James S. "The Superorganic in American Cultural Geography." *Annals of the Association of American Geographers* 70 (1980): 181–98.

Duncan, Nancy. *BodySpace: Destabilising Geographies of Gender and Sexuality.* London: Routledge, 1996.

Dunn, J. Allan. *Care-Free San Francisco.* San Francisco: A. M. Robertson, 1913.

Durning, Louise, and Richard Wrigley, eds. *Gender and Architecture.* New York: Wiley, 2000.

Edelman, Susan Scheiber. "'A Red Hot Suffrage Campaign': The Woman Suffrage Cause in California, 1896." *California Supreme Court Historical Society Yearbook* 2 (1995): 49–131.

Edgar, Albert E. *How to Advertise a Retail Store.* 2nd ed. Deposit, N.Y.: Outing Press, 1909.

Edgell, Stephen. *Class.* London: Routledge, 1993.

Edwords, Clarence E. *Bohemian San Francisco: Its Restaurants and Their Most Famous Recipes.* San Francisco: P. Elder and Company, 1914.

Eighteen Distinguished Authors. *Correct Social Usage.* New York: New York Society of Self-Culture, 1907.

Elliott, R. N. *Tea Room and Cafeteria Management.* Boston: Little, Brown and Company, 1926.

Englander, Susan. *Class Coalition and Class Conflict in the California Woman Suffrage Movement 1907–1912.* Lewiston, N.Y.: Mellen Research University Press, 1992.

Enstad, Nan. *Ladies of Labor, Girls of Adventure: Working Women, Popular Culture, and*

Labor Politics at the Turn of the Twentieth Century. New York: Columbia University Press, 1999.

Enstam, Elizabeth York. *Women and the Creation of Urban Life: Dallas, Texas, 1843–1920.* College Station: Texas A&M University Press, 1998.

Establishing a Food Business. Scranton, Pa.: Woman's Institute of Domestic Arts and Sciences, 1932.

Estavan, Lawrence, and Mary Wickizer Burgess. *The Italian Theatre in San Francisco.* 1st rev. ed. San Bernardino, Calif.: Borgo Press, 1991.

Everett, Marshall. *The Etiquette of Today.* N.p.: Henry Neil, 1902.

Evers, Cecil C. *The Commercial Problem in Buildings.* New York: Record and Guide Company, 1914.

Ewen, Elizabeth. "City Lights: Immigrant Women and the Rise of the Movies." In *Women and the American City,* ed. Catherine R. Stimpson, Elsa Sixler, Martha J. Nelson, and Kathryn B. Yatrakis, 42–63. Chicago: University of Chicago Press, 1980.

———. *Immigrant Women in the Land of Dollars: Life and Culture on the Lower East Side, 1890–1925.* New York: Monthly Review Press, 1985.

Falk, Pasi, and Colin Campbell, eds. *The Shopping Experience.* London: Sage Publications, 1997.

Farber, Carole. "High, Healthy, and Happy: Ontario Mythology on Parade." In *The Celebration of Society: Perspectives on Contemporary Cultural Performance,* ed. Frank E. Manning, 33–50. Bowling Green, Ohio: Bowling Green University Popular Press, 1983.

Farrington, Frank. *Store Management-Complete.* Chicago: Byxbee Publishing Company, 1911.

Findlay, Paul. *Paul Findlay's Book for Grocers: A Ready Reference Book Which Covers the Fundamental Principles and Practice of Successful Retail Grocery Merchandising.* San Francisco, 1924.

Finkelstein, Joanne. *Dining Out.* New York: New York University Press, 1989.

Finnegan, Margaret. *Selling Suffrage: Consumer Culture and Votes for Women.* New York: Columbia University Press, 1999.

Fischer, Claude S. *The Urban Experience.* New York: Harcourt Brace Jovanovich, 1976.

Fisk, James W. *Retail Selling: A Guide to the Best Modern Practice.* New York: Harper & Brothers Publishers, 1916.

Flanagan, Maureen. *Seeing with Their Hearts: Chicago Women and the Vision of the Good City, 1871–1933.* Princeton, N.J.: Princeton University Press, 2002.

Flexner, Eleanor, and Ellen Fitzpatrick. *Century of Struggle: The Woman's Rights Movement in the United States.* Cambridge, Mass.: Belknap Press of Harvard University Press, 1996.

Foote, Kenneth E. *Shadowed Ground: America's Landscapes of Violence and Tragedy.* Austin: University of Texas Press, 1997.

Forbes, Kathryn (pseud. Kathryn McLean). *Mama's Bank Account.* New York: Harcourt Brace and Company, 1943.

Franck, Karen A., and Lynn Paxson. "Women and Urban Public Space: Research, Design, and Policy Issues." In *Public Places and Spaces,* ed. Irwin Altman and Ervin Zube, 121–46. New York: Plenum Press, 1989.

Frederick, Christine. *Household Engineering; Scientific Management in the Home. A correspondence course on the application of the principles of efficiency engineering and scientific management to the everyday tasks of housekeeping.* Chicago: American School of Home Economics, 1919.

———. *The New Housekeeping; Efficiency Studies in Home Management.* Garden City, N.Y.: Doubleday Page & Company, 1913.

Freeman, Sarah. *Mutton and Oysters: Food, Cooking and Eating in Victorian Times.* London: Victor Gollancz Ltd., 1989.

Friedan, Betty. *The Feminine Mystique.* New York: W. W. Norton, 1963.

Friedberg, Anne. *Window Shopping: Cinema and the Postmodern.* Berkeley: University of California Press, 1993.

Fussell, Paul. *Class: A Guide through the American Status System.* New York: Summit Books, 1983.

Gagey, Edmond McAdoo. *The San Francisco Stage, a History.* New York: Columbia University Press, 1950.

Gardner, Carol Brooks. *Passing By: Gender and Public Harassment.* Berkeley: University of California Press, 1995.

Gero, Joan M., and Margaret Wright Conkey. *Engendering Archaeology: Women and Prehistory.* Oxford, U.K.: B. Blackwell, 1991.

Gibson, Campbell. "Population of the 100 Largest Cities and Other Urban Places in the United States: 1790 to 1990." Population Division Working Paper no. 27, U.S. Bureau of the Census, Washington, D.C., June 1998.

Gilchrist, Roberta. *Gender and Material Culture: The Archaeology of Religious Women.* London: Routledge, 1994.

Glassie, Henry. *Vernacular Architecture.* Bloomington: Indiana University Press, 2000.

Glazer, Nathan, and Mark Lilla, eds. *The Public Face of Architecture: Civic Culture and Public Spaces.* New York: Free Press, 1987.

Gluck, Sherna Berger. *From Parlor to Prison: Five American Suffragists Talk about Their Lives.* New York: Octagon Books, 1976.

Goldberg Bowen and Company, 1925 Catalog. Collections of the Bancroft Library, University of California, Berkeley.

Goodrich, Mary. *The Palace Hotel.* San Francisco, 1930.

Greed, Clara. *Women and Planning: Creating Gendered Realities.* London: Routledge, 1994.

Green, W. C. *A Dictionary of Etiquette: A Guide to Polite Usage for All Social Functions.* New York: Brentano's, 1904.

Greene, James Henry. *Principles and Methods of Retailing.* 1st ed. New York: McGraw-Hill, 1924.

Grier, Katherine C. *Culture and Comfort: People, Parlors, and Upholstery, 1850–1930.* Rochester, N.Y.: Strong Museum, 1988.

Groth, Paul Erling. "Frameworks for Cultural Landscape Study." In *Understanding Ordinary Landscapes,* ed. Paul Erling Groth and Todd W. Bressi, 1–21. New Haven, Conn.: Yale University Press, 1997.

————. *Living Downtown: The History of Residential Hotels in the United States.* Berkeley: University of California Press, 1994.

Groth, Paul Erling, and Todd W. Bressi, eds. *Understanding Ordinary Landscapes.* New Haven, Conn.: Yale University Press, 1997.

Groth, Paul Erling, and Chris Wilson, eds. *Everyday America: Cultural Landscape Studies after J. B. Jackson.* Berkeley: University of California Press, 2003.

Gullett, Gayle. *Becoming Citizens: The Emergence and Development of the California Women's Movement, 1880–1911.* Urbana: University of Illinois Press, 2000.

Haarsager, Sandra. *Organized Womanhood: Cultural Politics in the Pacific Northwest, 1840–1920.* Norman: University of Oklahoma Press, 1997.

Habermas, Jürgen. *The Structural Transformation of the Public Sphere: An Inquiry into a Category of Bourgeois Society.* Cambridge, Mass.: MIT Press, 1989.

Hahn, Lew, and Percival White. *The Merchants' Manual.* 1st ed. New York: McGraw-Hill Book Company and National Retail Dry Goods Association, 1924.

Hall, Florence Howe. *Social Customs.* Boston: Dana Estes & Company, 1911.

Hall, John R., ed. *Reworking Class.* Ithaca, N.Y.: Cornell University Press, 1997.

Halttunen, Karen. *Confidence Men and Painted Women: A Study of Middle-Class Culture in America, 1830–1870.* New Haven, Conn.: Yale University Press, 1982.

Harlan, George H. *San Francisco Bay Ferryboats.* Berkeley: Howell-North Books, 1967.

Harland, Marion, and Virginia Van de Water. *Everyday Etiquette: A Practical Manual of Social Usages.* Indianapolis: Bobbs-Merrill Company, 1905.

Harris, Steven, and Deborah Berke, eds. *Architecture of the Everyday.* New York: Princeton Architectural Press, 1997.

Hartley, Florence. *The Ladies' Book of Etiquette and Manual of Politeness.* Boston: DeWolfe, Fiske & Company, 1879.

Hayden, Dolores. *The Grand Domestic Revolution: A History of Feminist Designs for American Homes, Neighborhoods, and Cities.* Cambridge, Mass.: MIT Press, 1981.

————. *Redesigning the American Dream: The Future of Housing, Work, and Family Life.* New York: W. W. Norton, 1984.

Hayward, Walter S. *The Retail Handbook.* New York: McGraw-Hill, 1924.

Helly, Dorothy O., and Susan Reverby, eds. *Gendered Domains: Rethinking Public and Private in Women's History: Essays from the 7th Berkshire Conference on the History of Women.* Ithaca, N.Y.: Cornell University Press, 1992.

Heresies Collective. *Making Room: Women and Architecture.* New York: Heresies Collective, 1981.

Hersey, Heloise Edwina. *To Girls: A Budget of Letters.* Boston: Small, Maynard & Company, 1901.

Hess, Max, Jr. *Every Dollar Counts: The Story of the American Department Store.* New York: Fairchild Publications, 1952.

Hodge, Robert W., and Paul M. Siegel. "Stratification, Social: The Measurement of Social Class." In *International Encyclopedia of the Social Sciences,* vol. 2, ed. David L. Sills, 316–25. New York: Macmillan Company and Free Press, 1968.

Holt, Emily. *Encyclopaedia of Etiquette.* New York: Nelson Doubleday, 1901.

Holub, Robert C. *Jürgen Habermas: Critic in the Public Sphere.* London: Routledge, 1991.

Hooker, Richard James. *Food and Drink in America: A History.* Indianapolis: Bobbs-Merrill, 1981.

Horowitz, Roger, and Arwen Mohun, eds. *His and Hers: Gender, Consumption, and Technology.* Charlottesville: University Press of Virginia, 1998.

Hotel Fairmont, San Francisco. Brochure. Chicago: Norman Pierce Company. Collections of Bancroft Library, University of California, Berkeley.

The Hotel Monthly. *Ideas for Refreshment Rooms: Hotel, Restaurant, Lunch Room, Tea Room, Coffee Shop, Cafeteria, Dining Car, Industrial Plant, School, Club, Soda Fountain; a Ready Reference to Catering Methods, Covering a Wide Range of Practice.* Chicago: Hotel Monthly Press, 1923.

How to Advertise to Men. Chicago: System Company, 1912.

Hoy, Suellen M. "'Municipal Housekeeping': The Role of Women in Improving Urban Sanitation Practices, 1880–1917." In *Pollution and Reform in American Cities, 1870–1930,* ed. Martin Melosi, 173–98. Austin: University of Texas Press, 1980.

Hunt, Lynn Avery, and Aletta Biersack, eds. *The New Cultural History.* Berkeley: University of California Press, 1989.

Hurd, Richard M. *Principals of City Land Values.* New York: Record and Guide, 1911.

Isenberg, Alison. *Downtown America: A History of the Place and the People Who Made It.* Chicago: University of Chicago Press, 2004.

Issel, William, and Robert W. Cherny. *San Francisco, 1865–1932: Politics, Power, and Urban Development.* Berkeley: University of California Press, 1986.

Jackson, John Brinckerhoff. *Discovering the Vernacular Landscape.* New Haven, Conn.: Yale University Press, 1984.

Jackson, Joseph Henry, ed. *The Western Gate: A San Francisco Reader.* New York: Farrar, Straus and Young, 1952.

Jackson, Peter. *Maps of Meaning: An Introduction to Cultural Geography.* London: Unwin Hyman, 1989.

Janson, Joyce. *San Francisco's Cable Cars: Riding the Rope through Past and Present.* San Francisco: Woodford Press, 1995.

Jarman, Neil. *Material Conflicts: Parades and Visual Displays in Northern Ireland.* Oxford: Berg, 1997.

Jensen, Carol A. "Tait's." *San Francisco Bay Area Post Card Club Newsletter* 23, no. 3 (March 2008): 10–13.

Johnson, William Martin. *Inside of A Hundred Homes.* Philadelphia: Curtis Publishing Company, 1897.

Junior League of San Francisco. *Here Today: San Francisco's Architectural Heritage.* San Francisco: Chronicle Books, 1968.

Kahn, Judd. *Imperial San Francisco: Politics and Planning in an American City, 1897–1906.* Lincoln: University of Nebraska Press, 1979.

Kasinitz, Philip, ed. *Metropolis: Center and Symbol of our Times.* New York: New York University Press, 1995.

Kasson, John F. *Rudeness and Civility: Manners in Nineteenth-Century Urban America.* New York: Hill and Wang, 1990.

Kastler, Deanna L. "Portola Lourvre Restaurant." *San Francisco Bay Area Post Card Club Newsletter* 23, no. 1 (January 2008): 6–9.

Kazin, Michael. *Barons of Labor: The San Francisco Building Trades and Union Power in the Progressive Era.* Urbana: University of Illinois Press, 1987.

Keeler, Charles. *San Francisco and Thereabouts.* San Francisco: California Promotion Committee, 1903.

Keith, Mary. *Address Delivered at the California State Suffrage Association Annual Convention, San Francisco, October 25, 1902.* Berkeley, Calif.: Press of Berkeley Daily Gazette, 1902.

Kidd, Alan J., and David Nicholls, eds. *Gender, Civic Culture and Consumerism: Middle-Class Identity in Britain, 1800–1940.* Manchester, U.K.: Manchester University Press, 1999.

Kinchin, Juliet. "Interiors: Nineteenth-Century Essays on the 'Masculine' and 'Feminine' Room." In *The Gendered Object,* ed. Pat Kirkham, 12–29. Manchester, U.K.: Manchester University Press, 1996.

Kingsland, Mrs. Burton (Florence). *The Book of Good Manners: "Etiquette for all Occasions."* Garden City, N.Y.: Doubleday, Page & Company, 1910.

Kirkham, Pat, ed. *The Gendered Object.* Manchester, U.K.: Manchester University Press, 1996.

Koslofsky, Craig. "Embracing the Night: Street Lighting in Early Modern Europe." Paper delivered at American Historical Association Meeting, Chicago, January 2000.

Kugelmass, Jack, and Mariette Pathy Allen. *Masked Culture: The Greenwich Village Halloween Parade.* New York: Columbia University Press, 1994.

Kwolek-Folland, Angel. *Engendering Business: Men and Women in the Corporate Office, 1870–1930.* Baltimore: Johns Hopkins University Press, 1994.

Laermans, Rudi. "Learning to Consume: Early Department Stores and the Shaping of the Modern Consumer Culture (1860–1914)." *Theory, Culture and Society* 10 (1993): 79–102.

Landes, Joan B. *Women and the Public Sphere in the Age of the French Revolution.* Ithaca, N.Y.: Cornell University Press, 1988.

Lavenda, Robert H. "Family and Corporation: Celebration in Central Minnesota." In *The Celebration of Society: Perspectives on Contemporary Cultural Performance,* ed. Frank E. Manning, 51–64. Bowling Green, Ohio: Bowling Green University Popular Press, 1983.

Leach, Belinda, Ellen Lesiuk, and Penny E. Morton. "Perceptions of Fear in the Urban Environment." *Women and Environments* 8, no. 2 (1986): 10–12.

Leach, William. *Consuming Visions: Accumulation and Display of Goods in America, 1880–1920.* Edited by Simon J. Bronner. Winterthur, Del.: Henry du Pont Winterthur Museum, 1989.

———. *Land of Desire: Merchants, Power, and the Rise of a New American Culture.* New York: Pantheon Books, 1993.

———. "Transformations in a Culture of Consumption: Women and Department Stores, 1890–1925." *Journal of American History* 71, no. 2 (1984): 319–42.

Lefebvre, Henri. *Everyday Life in the Modern World.* New Brunswick, N.J.: Transaction Books, 1984.

———. *The Production of Space.* Oxford, U.K.: Blackwell, 1991.

Leighly, John, ed. *Land and Life: A Selection from the Writings of Carl Sauer.* Berkeley: University of California Press, 1963.

Leslie, Eliza. *The Behavior Book: A Manual for Ladies.* Philadelphia: Willis P. Hazard, 1855.

Levenstein, Harvey A. *Revolution at the Table: The Transformation of the American Diet.* New York: Oxford University Press, 1988.

Levine, Laurence. *Highbrow Lowbrow.* Cambridge, Mass.: Harvard University Press, 1988.

Levy, Harriet Lane. *920 O'Farrell Street: A Jewish Girlhood in Old San Francisco.* Garden City, N.Y.: Doubleday, 1947.

Lewis, Oscar. *Bay Window Bohemia; an Account of the Brilliant Artistic World of Gaslit San Francisco.* Garden City, N.Y.: Doubleday, 1956.

Light, Andrew, and Jonathan M. Smith, eds. *Philosophy and Geography II: The Production of Public Space.* Lanham, Md.: Rowman & Littlefield Publishers, 1998.

Lipset, Seymour. "Stratification, Social: Social Class." In *International Encyclopedia of the Social Sciences,* vol. 2, ed. David L. Sills, 296–316. New York: Macmillan Company and Free Press, 1968.

Lloyd, B. E. *Lights and Shades in San Francisco.* San Francisco: A. L. Bancroft, 1876.

Logan, Milla Zenovich. *Bring Along Laughter.* New York: Random House, 1947.

London, Jack. *Martin Eden.* New York: Macmillan, 1908.

Longstreth, Richard W. *The Buildings of Main Street: A Guide to American Commercial Architecture.* Walnut Creek, Calif.: AltaMira Press, 2000.

———. *City Center to Regional Mall: Architecture, the Automobile, and Retailing in Los Angeles, 1920–1950.* Cambridge, Mass.: MIT Press, 1997.

———. *The Drive-in, the Supermarket, and the Transformation of Commercial Space in Los Angeles, 1914–1941.* Cambridge, Mass.: MIT Press, 1999.

Lortie, Francis N. *San Francisco's Black Community, 1870–1890: Dilemmas in the Struggle for Equality; a Thesis.* San Francisco: R and E Research Associates, 1970.

Louis, S. L. *Decorum: A Practical Treatise on Etiquette and Dress of the Best American Society.* New York: Union Publishing House, 1881.

Lumsden, Linda J. *Rampant Women: Suffragists and the Right of Assembly.* Knoxville: University of Tennessee Press, 1997.

Lynch, Kevin. *The Image of the City.* Cambridge, Mass.: Technology Press, 1960.

MacAloon, John J. *Rite, Drama, Festival, Spectacle: Rehearsals toward a Theory of Cultural Performance.* Philadelphia: Institute for the Study of Human Issues, 1984.

MacLean, Annie Marion. *Wage-Earning Women.* New York: Macmillan Company, 1910.

———. *Women Workers and Society.* Chicago: A. C. McClurg, 1916.

Madden, Janice. "Why Women Work Closer to Home." *Urban Studies* 18, no. 2 (1981): 181–94.

Manning, Frank E., ed. *The Celebration of Society: Perspectives on Contemporary Cultural Performance.* Bowling Green, Ohio: Bowling Green University Popular Press, 1983.

Marcus, Leonard S. *The American Store Window.* New York: Whitney Library of Design, 1978.

Martinez, Katharine, and Kenneth L. Ames, eds. *The Material Culture of Gender, the Gender of Material Culture.* Winterthur, Del.: Henry du Pont Winterthur Museum, 1997.

Massey, Doreen. *Space, Place, and Gender.* Minneapolis: University of Minnesota Press, 1994.

Master Grocer. Catalog–magazine of Goldberg, Bowen & Company. February 1906.

Matrix Book Group. *Making Space: Women and the Man-Made Environment.* London: Pluto Press, 1984.

Mayo, James M. *The American Grocery Store: The Business Evolution of an Architectural Space.* Westport, Conn.: Greenwood Press, 1993.

Mazey, Mary Ellen, and David R. Lee, eds. *Her Space, Her Place: A Geography of Women.* Washington, D.C.: Association of American Geographers, 1983.

McCarthy, Mary Eunice. *Meet Kitty.* New York: Thomas Y. Crowell Company, 1957.

McDougall, Ruth Bransten. *Under Mannie's Hat.* San Francisco: Hesperian Press, 1964.

McDowell, Linda. "Towards an Understanding of the Gender Division of Urban Space." *Environment and Planning D: Society and Space* 1 (1983): 59–72.

McIntosh, Elaine N. *American Food Habits in Historical Perspective.* Westport, Conn.: Praeger, 1995.

McLean, Fannie W. *Why the Teacher Should Be a Suffragist.* San Francisco: College Equal Suffrage League, c. 1911.

McMurray, William. *Hotel St. Francis, San Francisco, California.* San Francisco: Promotion Bureau, Hotel St. Francis, 1904.

McNamara, Brooks. *Day of Jubilee: The Great Age of Public Celebrations in New York, 1788–1909.* New Brunswick, N.J.: Rutgers University Press, 1997.

McQuiston, Liz. *Suffragists to She-Devils.* London: Phaidon Press, 1997.

Meinig, D. W., and John Brinckerhoff Jackson, eds. *The Interpretation of Ordinary Landscapes: Geographical Essays.* New York: Oxford University Press, 1979.

Melosh, Barbara. *Gender and American History since 1890.* London: Routledge, 1993.

Mercantile Illustrating Company. *San Francisco, the Metropolis of Western America: Her Phenomenal Progress, Incomparable Industries and Remarkable Resources.* San Francisco: Mercantile Illustrating Company, 1899.

Meyerowitz, Joanne J. *Women Adrift: Independent Wage Earners in Chicago, 1880–1930.* Chicago: University of Chicago Press, 1988.

Middleton, William D. *The Time of the Trolley.* San Marino, Calif.: Golden West Books, 1987.

Miller, Michael Barry. *The Bon Marché: Bourgeois Culture and the Department Store.* Princeton, N.J.: Princeton University Press, 1981.

Mitchell, W. J. Thomas. *Landscape and Power.* Chicago: University of Chicago Press, 1994.

Modern San Francisco and the Men of Today, 1905–1906. San Francisco: Western Press Association, 1905.

Mohl, Raymond A. *The Making of Urban America.* Wilmington, Del.: Scholarly Resources, 1988.

Montgomery, Maureen E. *Displaying Women: Spectacles of Leisure in Edith Wharton's New York*. New York: Routledge, 1998.

Morgan, Roland. *San Francisco Then and Now*. San Francisco: Bodima Books, 1978.

Moskowitz, Marina. *Standard of Living: The Measure of the Middle Class in Modern America*. Baltimore: Johns Hopkins University Press, 2004.

Mueller, Willard Fritz, and Leon Garoian. *Changes in the Market Structure of Grocery Retailing*. Madison: Agricultural Experiment Station, University of Wisconsin, 1961.

Murphy, Raymond, J. E. Vance Jr., and Bart J. Epstein. *Central Business District Studies*. Worcester, Mass.: Clark University, 1955.

Muscatine, Doris. *A Cook's Tour of San Francisco: The Best Restaurants and Their Recipes*. New York: Charles Scribner's Sons, 1963.

Musser, Charles. *The Emergence of Cinema: The American Screen to 1907*. New York: Scribner, 1990.

Nasaw, David. *Going Out: The Rise and Fall of Public Amusements*. New York: Basic Books, 1993.

National American Woman Suffrage Association. *Victory, How Women Won It; a Centennial Symposium, 1840–1940*. New York: H. W. Wilson Company, 1940.

Nava, Mica. "Modernity's Disavowal: Women, the City and the Department Store." In *The Shopping Experience*, ed. Pasi Falk and Colin Campbell, 56–91. London: Sage Publications, 1997.

Nelson, Sarah M. *Gender in Archaeology: Analyzing Power and Prestige*. Walnut Creek, Calif.: AltaMira Press, 1997.

Neville, Mrs. Amelia. *The Fantastic City, Memoirs of the Social and Romantic Life of Old San Francisco*. Boston: Houghton Mifflin Company, 1932.

Nord, Deborah Epstein. *Walking the Victorian Streets: Women, Representation, and the City*. Ithaca, N.Y.: Cornell University Press, 1995.

Norris, Frank. *Frank Norris of "the Wave": Stories and Sketches from the San Francisco Weekly, 1893 to 1897*. San Francisco: Westgate Press, 1931.

———. *McTeague: A Story of San Francisco*. 1899; reprinted, New York: Penguin Books, 1982.

Norton, William. *Explorations in the Meaning of Landscape: A Cultural Geography*. New York: Greenwood, 1989.

Novell, Irena. *Our City: The Jews of San Francisco*. San Diego: Howell-North Books, 1981.

Nye, Russel Blaine. *The Unembarrassed Muse: The Popular Arts in America*. New York: Dial Press, 1970.

Nystrom, Paul Henry. *Retail Selling and Store Management*. New York: D. Appleton & Company, 1916.

Official Guide and Instructions for Delegates, Epworth League Convention, 1901. San Francisco: The League, 1901.

Official Guide, Panama-Pacific International Exposition. San Francisco: Wahlgreen Company, 1915.

Ogborn, Miles. *Spaces of Modernity: London's Geographies, 1680–1780*. New York: Guilford Press, 1998.

Olmsted, Nancy. "Ferryboats, a San Francisco Tradition." *Sea Letter of the National Maritime Museum* (1990): 2–3.

———. *The Ferry Building: Witness to a Century of Change, 1898–1998*. San Francisco: Port of San Francisco, and Berkeley: Heyday Books, 1998.

O'Shaughnessy, M. M. *Street Railway Transportation Requirements of San Francisco*. San Francisco: City and County of San Francisco, Department of Public Works, Department of Engineering, 1929.

Ottes, L., E. Poventud, M. van Schelenden, and G. Segond von Banchet, eds. *Gender and the Built Environment: Emancipation in Planning, Housing, and Mobility in Europe*. Assen, the Netherlands: Van Gorcum, 1995.

Palace Hotel, San Francisco. N.d. Collections of Bancroft Library, pF869.53.7.P164.53, University of California, Berkeley.

Pascoe, Peggy. *Relations of Rescue: The Search for Female Moral Authority in the American West, 1874–1939*. New York: Oxford University Press, 1990.

Peiss, Kathy Lee. *Cheap Amusements: Working Women and Leisure in Turn-of-the-Century New York*. Philadelphia: Temple University Press, 1986.

Pennell, Joseph. *San Francisco: The City of the Golden Gate*. London: T. N. Foulis, 1913.

Perles, Anthony. *The People's Railway: The History of the Municipal Railway of San Francisco*. Glendale, Calif.: Interurban Press, 1981.

Personal Narratives Group, ed. *Interpreting Women's Lives*. Bloomington: Indiana University Press, 1989.

Picken, James Hamilton. *Principles of Window Display*. Chicago: A. W. Shaw and Company, 1927.

Pillsbury, Richard. *From Boarding House to Bistro: The American Restaurant Then and Now*. Boston: Unwin Hyman, 1990.

Planer, E. T. *Guide to Some Representative San Francisco, Oakland, Berkeley Restaurants*. 1940. Collections of Bancroft Library, F869.53.7.P5, University of California, Berkeley.

Platt, Harold. *Shock Cities: The Environmental Transformation and Reform of Manchester and Chicago*. Chicago: University of Chicago Press, 2005.

Pollock, Griselda. *Vision and Difference: Femininity, Feminism, and Histories of Art*. London: Routledge, 1988.

Post, Emily. *Etiquette in Society, in Business, in Politics and at Home*. New York: Funk and Wagnalls Company, 1922.

Post Street Improvement Club. *A Brief Outline of Interesting Jaunts in and About San Francisco: And, also, a Statement Relative to Post Street as a Shopping Thoroughfare*. San Francisco: Post Street Improvement Club, n.d. (c. 1905).

Pratt, Geraldine. "Feminist Analyses of the Restructuring of Urban Life." *Urban Geography* 11 (1990): 594–605.

Pred, Allan. "In Other Wor(l)ds: Fragmented and Integrated Observations on Gendered Languages, Gendered Spaces and Local Transformation." *Antipode* 22, no. 1 (1990): 33–52.

"Public Transportation for Women in London." *Women and Environments* 7, no. 2 (1985): 7.

Purdy, Helen Throop. *San Francisco: As It Was, As It Is, and How to See It.* San Francisco: P. Elder, 1912.

Rannells, John. *The Core of the City.* New York: Columbia University Press, 1956.

Reekie, Gail. *Temptations: Sex, Selling, and the Department Store.* St. Leonards, Australia: Allen & Unwin, 1993.

Rendell, Jane, Barbara Penner, and Iain Borden. *Gender Space Architecture: An Interdisciplinary Introduction.* London: Routledge, 2000.

Richards, Lenore, and Nola Treat. *Tea-Room Recipes, a Book for Home Makers and Tea-Room Managers.* Boston: Little, Brown and Company, 1925.

Richardson, Dorothy. *The Long Day, the Story of a New York Working Girl.* New York: Century Company, 1905.

Richter, Amy G. *Home on the Rails: Women, the Railroad, and the Rise of Public Domesticity.* Chapel Hill: University of North Carolina Press, 2005.

Roberts, Helen L. *Putnam's Handbook of Etiquette.* New York: G. P. Putnam's Sons, 1913.

Rodes, Donald Waller. "The California Woman Suffrage Campaign of 1911." Master's thesis, California State University, Hayward, 1974.

Root, Waverley, and Richard de Rochemont. *Eating in America: A History.* New York: Ecco Press, 1976.

Rosenzweig, Roy. *Eight Hours for What We Will: Workers and Leisure in an Industrial City, 1870–1920.* Cambridge, U.K.: Cambridge University Press, 1983.

Rowntree, Lester. "Cultural/Humanistic Geography." *Progress in Human Geography* 10, no. 4 (1986): 580–86.

Rüedi, Katerina, Sarah Wigglesworth, and Duncan McCorquodale. *Desiring Practices: Architecture, Gender, and the Interdisciplinary.* London: Black Dog Publishing, 1996.

Ryan, Jenny. "Women, Modernity and the City." *Theory, Culture and Society* 11 (1994): 35–63.

Ryan, Mary P. "The American Parade: Representations of the Nineteenth Century Social Order." In *The New Cultural History,* ed. Lynn Hunt, 131–54. Berkeley: University of California Press, 1989.

———. *Civic Wars: Democracy and Public Life in the American City during the Nineteenth Century.* Berkeley: University of California Press, 1997.

———. *Cradle of the Middle Class.* Cambridge, U.K.: Cambridge University Press, 1981.

———. *Women in Public: Between Banners and Ballots, 1825–1880.* Baltimore: Johns Hopkins University Press, 1990.

Ryder, David Warren. *The Story of Sherman, Clay & Co.* San Francisco: Neal, Stratford, and Kerr, 1947.

San Francisco. Chicago: Passenger Department, Santa Fe Route, 1901.

San Francisco Board of Supervisors. *San Francisco Municipal Reports,* Fiscal Year 1904–5. San Francisco, 1905.

San Francisco, California: Guide to Points of Interest. San Francisco: St. Dunstan's Hotel, c. 1905.

San Francisco Chamber of Commerce. *San Francisco: The Financial, Commercial and Industrial Metropolis of the Pacific Coast.* San Francisco: H. S. Crocker Company, 1915.

San Francisco Department of City Planning. *Local Shopping Districts in San Francisco: Their Development and Future Development.* San Francisco: Department of City Planning, 1952.

San Francisco Map and Directory, Hotel Manx. San Francisco: Hotel Manx, 1915.

San Francisco since 1872: A Pictorial History of Seven Decades. San Francisco: Ray Oil Burner Company, 1946.

San Francisco, The Metropolis of Western America: Her Phenomenal Progress, Incomparable Industries and Remarkable Resources. San Francisco: Mercantile Illustrating Company, 1899.

San Francisco: The Queen City. San Francisco: Pacific Novelty Company, 1914.

Sangster, Margaret E. (Mrs.). *Good Manners for All Occasions: A Practical Manual.* New York: Christian Herald, 1904.

Schein, Richard H. "The Place of Landscape: A Conceptual Framework for Interpreting an American Scene." *Annals of the Association of American Geographers* 87, no. 4 (1997): 660–80.

Schivelbusch, Wolfgang. *Disenchanted Night: The Industrialization of Light in the Nineteenth Century.* Berkeley: University of California Press, 1988.

Schlereth, Thomas J. *Victorian America: Transformations in Everyday Life, 1876–1915.* New York: HarperCollins Publishers, 1991.

Schlesinger, Arthur Meier. *Learning How to Behave: A Historical Study of American Etiquette Books.* New York: Macmillan, 1947.

Schwartz, Vanessa R. *Spectacular Realities: Early Mass Culture in Fin-de-Siècle Paris.* Berkeley: University of California Press, 1998.

Scobey, David. "Nymphs and Satyrs: Sex and the Bourgeois Public Sphere in Victorian New York." *Winterthur Portfolio* 37, no. 1 (2002): 43–66.

Scott, Joan Wallach. *Gender and the Politics of History.* New York: Columbia University Press, 1988.

Seeing San Francisco. San Francisco: United Railroads of San Francisco, 1909.

Sennett, Richard, ed. *Classic Essays on the Culture of Cities.* New York: Appleton-Century-Crofts, 1969.

Sewell, Jessica. "Tea and Suffrage." *Food, Culture, and Society* 11, no. 4 (October 2008): 487–508.

Sherwood, Mrs. John. *Manners and Social Usages.* New York: Harper and Brothers, 1887.

Shumate, Albert. *Rincon Hill and South Park: San Francisco's Early Fashionable Neighborhood.* Sausalito, Calif.: Windgate Press, 1988.

Sibley, David. *Geographies of Exclusion: Society and Difference in the West.* London: Routledge, 1995.

Sight Seeing Suggestions. San Francisco: Palace Hotel and Norman Pierce Company.

Silverman, Ruth. *San Francisco Observed: A Photographic Portfolio from 1850 to the Present.* San Francisco: Chronicle Books, 1986.

"Six Months of Woman Suffrage in California." *West Coast Magazine* 12, no. 4 (1912): 419–39.

Slymovics, S. "New York City's Muslim World Day Parade." In *Nation and Migration: The*

Politics of Space in the South Asian Diaspora, ed. P. van der Veer, 157–77. Philadelphia: University of Pennsylvania Press, 1995.

Smallwood, Charles. *The White Front Cars of San Francisco.* Interurbans Special 44. Glendale, Calif.: Interurbans, 1978.

Smith, Dorothy E. *The Everyday World as Problematic: A Feminist Sociology.* Boston: Northeastern University Press, 1987.

Solomons, Selina. *How We Won the Vote in California.* San Francisco: New Woman Press, n.d. (c. 1912–13).

Southern Pacific Company. *Trips around San Francisco.* N.p.: Southern Pacific Company, 1917.

Souvenir of the Baldwin Hotel, San Francisco. San Francisco: Crocker and Company Print Company, c. 1887.

Souvenir of the Palace Hotel, San Francisco. San Francisco: Crocker and Company, 1891.

Spain, Daphne. *Gendered Spaces.* Chapel Hill: University of North Carolina Press, 1991.

———. *How Women Saved the City.* Minneapolis: University of Minnesota Press, 2001.

Sparke, Penny. *As Long as It's Pink: The Sexual Politics of Taste.* London: Pandora, 1995.

Speck, John H. "Real Estate." *San Francisco: The Metropolis of the West.* San Francisco: Western Press Association, 1910.

Stamp, Shelley. *Movie-Struck Girls: Women and Motion Picture Culture after the Nickelodeon.* Princeton, N.J.: Princeton University Press, 2000.

Stansell, Christine. *City of Women: Sex and Class in New York, 1789–1860.* Urbana: University of Illinois Press, 1987.

Starrett, Helen Ekin. *The Charm of Fine Manners.* Philadelphia: J. J. Lippincott Company, 1907.

Steele, James King. *Fairmont, San Francisco.* San Francisco: Britton & Ray, n.d.

Stern, Jane, and Michael Stern. "Cafeteria." *New Yorker,* August 1, 1988, 37–54.

Stewart, David Ogden. *Perfect Behavior: A Parody Outline of Etiquette.* New York: George H. Doran Company, 1922.

Stilgoe, John R. *Common Landscapes of America, 1580 to 1845.* New Haven, Conn.: Yale University Press, 1982.

Stimpson, Catherine R., Elsa Sixler, Martha J. Nelson, and Kathryn B. Yatrakis, eds. *Women and the American City.* Chicago: University of Chicago Press, 1980.

The Story of Roos Brothers, Outfitters since 1865. San Francisco: Roos Brothers, 1945.

Swett, Ira L., ed. *Market Street Railway Revisited: The Best of the "Inside Track."* Interurbans Special. South Gate, Calif.: Interurbans, 1972.

Taber, Louise E. *The Flame.* New York: Alice Harriman Company, 1911.

The Tea Room and Coffee Shop. Scranton, Pa.: Woman's Institute of Domestic Arts and Sciences, 1932.

Terborg-Penn, Rosalyn. *African American Women in the Struggle for the Vote, 1850–1920.* Bloomington: Indiana University Press, 1998.

Thompson, E. P. *The Making of the English Working Class.* New York: Vintage Books, 1963.

Thompson, Ruth, and Chef Louis Hanges. *Eating around San Francisco.* San Francisco: Sutton House, 1937.

Thorne, Robert. "Places of Refreshment in the Nineteenth-Century City." In *Buildings and Society,* ed. Anthony D. King, 228–54. London: Routledge and Kegan Paul, 1980.

Through the Years to a Greater O'Connor, Moffatt and Co. San Francisco: O'Connor, Moffatt and Company, 1929.

Todd, Frank Morton. *The Chamber of Commerce Handbook for San Francisco, Historical and Descriptive: A Guide for Visitors.* San Francisco: San Francisco Chamber of Commerce, 1914.

———. *How to See San Francisco by Trolley and Cable.* San Francisco: San Francisco Chamber of Commerce, 1912.

Tong, Benson. *Unsubmissive Women: Chinese Prostitutes in Nineteenth-Century San Francisco.* Norman: University of Oklahoma Press, 1994.

Torre, Susana, ed. *Women in American Architecture: A Historic and Contemporary Perspective.* New York: Whitney Library of Design, 1977.

Trowbridge, Edwin. "New Shop Fronts." *The Brickbuilder* 16, no. 8 (1907): 136–40.

———. "New Shop Fronts II." *The Brickbuilder* 16, no. 9 (1907): 158–62.

True, Ruth Smiley. *The Neglected Girl.* New York: Survey Associates, 1914.

Underhill, Paco. *Why We Buy.* New York: Touchstone, 1999.

Union Pacific Railroad Company. *Diagrams, San Francisco Theatres.* San Francisco, 1888.

Unna, Warren, and Bruce Rogers. *The Coppa Murals: A Pageant of Bohemian Life in San Francisco at the Turn of the Century.* San Francisco: Book Club of California, 1952.

Up to Date San Francisco and Vicinity. San Francisco: Aug. Chevalier, c. 1913.

Upton, Dell. "Architectural History or Landscape History?" *Journal of Architectural Education* 44, no. 4 (1991): 195–99.

Upton, Dell, and John Michael Vlach, eds. *Common Places: Readings in American Vernacular Architecture.* Athens: University of Georgia Press, 1986.

U.S. Bureau of the Census. *Historical Statistics of the United States, Colonial Times to 1970,* part 1. Bicentennial ed. Washington, D.C.: U.S. Government Printing Office, 1975.

U.S. Department of the Interior, Census Office. "Table 1: Population of the Cities on June 1, 1890, by Ages, with Distinction of Sex, Color, Nativity, Parental Nativity, and Birthplaces of Mothers." In *Report on Vital and Social Statistics in the United States at the Eleventh Census, 1890,* pt. 2: *Vital Statistics, Cities of 100,000 Population and Upward.* Washington, D.C.: Government Printing Office, 1896.

Valentine, Gill. "Images of Danger: Women's Sources of Information about the Spatial Distribution of Male Violence." *Area* 24, no. 1 (1992): 22–29.

Vance, James E. *The Continuing City: Urban Morphology in Western Civilization.* Baltimore: Johns Hopkins University Press, 1990.

Veblen, Thorstein. *The Theory of the Leisure Class: An Economic Study of Institutions.* New York: Macmillan, 1899; reprint, New York: Penguin, 1967.

Vest Pocket Memoranda and Directory of San Francisco. San Francisco: Doctor Sweany, c. 1895.

Vibert, Paul. "Shop Fronts and Windows." *Architecture* 32, no. 1 (1915): 171–73.

Victorian San Francisco: The 1895 Illustrated Directory. Sausalito, Calif.: Windgate Press, 1996.

Wachs, Martin. *Men, Women, and Urban Travel: The Persistence of Separate Spheres.* Los Angeles: Graduate School of Architecture and Urban Planning, University of California Los Angeles, 1988.

Walden, Keith. "Speaking Modern: Language, Culture, and Hegemony in Grocery Window Displays, 1887–1920." *Canadian Historical Review* 70, no. 3 (1989): 285–310.

Walkowitz, Judith R. *City of Dreadful Delight: Narratives of Sexual Danger in Late-Victorian London.* Chicago: University of Chicago Press, 1992.

Wall, Diana diZerega. *The Archaeology of Gender: Separating the Spheres in Urban America.* New York: Plenum Press, 1994.

Walters, Henry L. "Modern Store Fronts." *Architectural Review* 14, no. 6 (1907): 153–68.

Ward, David. *Cities and Immigrants: A Geography of Change in Nineteenth-Century America.* New York: Oxford University Press, 1971.

Warner, Sam Bass. *The Urban Wilderness: A History of the American City.* Berkeley: University of California Press, 1972.

Weintraub, Jeff Alan, and Krishan Kumar, eds. *Public and Private in Thought and Practice: Perspectives on a Grand Dichotomy.* Morality and Society Series. Chicago: University of Chicago Press, 1997.

Weisman, Leslie. *Discrimination by Design: A Feminist Critique of the Man-Made Environment.* Urbana: University of Illinois Press, 1992.

Wells, Evelyn. *Champagne Days of San Francisco.* New York: D. Appleton–Century, 1939.

Wells, Richard A. *Manners, Culture and Dress of the Best American Society.* Springfield, Mass.: King, Richardson & Company, 1891.

Western Press Association. *San Francisco, the Metropolis of the West.* San Francisco: Western Press Association, 1910.

Wharton, Edith. *The Age of Innocence.* Boston: Houghton Mifflin, 2000.

Wheeler, Marjorie Spruill, ed. *One Woman, One Vote: Rediscovering the Woman Suffrage Movement.* Troutdale, Ore.: New Sage Press, 1995.

Whitaker, Jan. "Doing Good in the Cafeteria." Lecture delivered at Boston University, January 31, 2009.

White, Lydia E. *Success in Society: A Manual of Good Manners, Social Etiquette, Rules of Behavior at Home and Abroad, on the Street, At Public Gatherings, Calls, Conversations, etc.* Boston: James H. Earle, 1889.

White, Mrs. Annie R. *Polite Society At Home and Abroad.* Chicago: Monarch Book Company, 1891.

Whittle, Roland. "The Humbler Restaurants of San Francisco." *Overland Monthly* 41 (1903): 364.

Wiley, Peter Booth. *A Free Library in This City: The Illustrated History of the San Francisco Public Library.* San Francisco: Welden Owen, 1996.

Williams, Rosalind H. *Dream Worlds: Mass Consumption in Late Nineteenth-Century France.* Berkeley: University of California Press, 1982.

Wilson, Chris, and Paul Groth, eds. *Everyday America: Cultural Landscape Studies after J. B. Jackson.* Berkeley: University of California Press, 2003.

Wilson, Elizabeth. "The Invisible Flaneur." *New Left Review* 195 (1992): 90–110.

———. "The Rhetoric of Urban Space." *New Left Review* 209 (1995): 146–60.

———. *The Sphinx in the City: Urban Life, the Control of Disorder, and Women.* Berkeley: University of California Press, 1991.

Wolfe, Albert Benedict. *The Lodging House Problem in Boston.* Boston: Houghton Mifflin and Company, 1906.

Wolff, Janet. "The Invisible Flâneuse: Women and the Literature of Modernity." *Theory, Culture, and Society* 2, no. 3 (1985): 37–46.

A Woman of Fashion. *Etiquette for Americans.* Chicago: Herbert S. Stone and Company, 1898.

Women and Geography Study Group of the IBG, and Explorations in Feminism Collective (Great Britain). *Geography and Gender: An Introduction to Feminist Geography.* London: Hutchinson in association with the Explorations in Feminism Collective, 1984.

Wood, Barry James. *Show Windows: 75 Years of the Art of Display.* 1st ed. New York: Congdon & Weed, 1982.

The World Our Field. Catalog–magazine of Goldberg, Bowen & Company. Summer 1914.

Wright, Erik Olin. *Classes.* London: Verso, 1985.

Writers' Project, Work Projects Administration. *Burlesque.* Vol. 14 of *San Francisco Theatre Research.* San Francisco: U.S. Work Projects Administration, 1939.

———. *Famous Playhouses of San Francisco.* Vols. 15, 16, and 17 of *San Francisco Theatre Research.* San Francisco: U.S. Work Projects Administration, 1942.

———. *Foreign Theaters.* Vols. 9 and 10 of *San Francisco Theatre Research.* San Francisco: U.S. Work Projects Administration, 1939.

———. *The History of Opera in San Francisco.* Vols. 7 and 8 of *San Francisco Theatre Research.* San Francisco: U.S. Work Projects Administration, 1938.

———. *Little Theatres in San Francisco.* Vol. 12 of *San Francisco Theatre Research.* San Francisco: U.S. Work Projects Administration, 1940.

———. *Minstrelsy.* Vol. 13 of *San Francisco Theatre Research.* San Francisco: U.S. Work Projects Administration, 1939.

Young, John H. *Our Deportment.* Springfield, Mass.: W. C. King & Company Publishers, 1882.

Yung, Judy. *Unbound Feet: A Social History of Chinese Women in San Francisco.* Berkeley: University of California Press, 1995.

———. *Unbound Voices: a Documentary History of Chinese Women in San Francisco.* Berkeley: University of California Press, 1999.

Zandi-Sayek, Sibel. "Orchestrating Difference, Performing Identity: Urban Space and Public Rituals in Nineteenth Century Izmir." In *Hybrid Urbanism,* ed. Nezar AlSayyad, 42–66. London: Westport Press, 2000.

Zola, Émile. *Au bonheur des dames.* Paris: G. Charpentier, 1883. Published in translation as *The Ladies' Paradise,* trans. Henry Vizetelly. Berkeley: University of California Press, 1992.

San Francisco Newspapers and Periodicals

Abend-Post (German)
Bien (Danish)
California Demokrat (German)
Chung Sai Yat Po (Chinese)
Crocker–Langley San Francisco Directory
The Elevator
Greeters Guide of San Francisco
La Colonia Suizzera (Italian)
La Voce del Popolo (Italian)
L'Italia (Italian)
Official Hotel Red Book and Directory
Pacific Coast Appeal
San Francisco Bulletin
San Francisco Call (later, *San Francisco Call and Post*)
San Francisco Chamber of Commerce Journal
San Francisco Chronicle
San Francisco Daily News
San Francisco Examiner
San Francisco Guide and Souvenir
San Francisco Hotel Gazette
San Francisco Theatrical Guide
San Francisco Vindicator

Trade Journals

American Restaurant
American Grocer
California Grocer
Dry Goods Reporter
Hotel Management
Modern Grocer
Restaurant Bulletin
Retail Grocers' Advocate

Suffrage Periodicals

American Suffragette
The Forerunner
Progressive Woman
Western Woman Voter
Woman Citizen

Woman's Bulletin
Woman's Journal
Woman Voter
Yellow Ribbon

Manuscript Collections

Susan B. Anthony Memorial Collection. Huntington Library, San Marino, California.

Haskell Family Papers. Bancroft Library, University of California, Berkeley.

Inez Haynes Irwin Papers. Schlesinger Library, Radcliffe Institute for Advanced Study, Harvard University.

Keith Family Papers. Bancroft Library, University of California, Berkeley.

Lees Family Papers. Bancroft Library, University of California, Berkeley.

McLean Family Papers. Bancroft Library, University of California, Berkeley.

Alice Park Papers. Huntington Library, San Marino, California.

Pierce Family Papers. Bancroft Library, University of California, Berkeley.

Selina Solomons Papers. Bancroft Library, University of California, Berkeley.

Woman Suffrage in California, pamphlet boxes of materials. Bancroft Library, University of California, Berkeley.

INDEX

Jessica Ellen Sewell is assistant professor in the American and New England Studies Program and the Department of the History of Art and Architecture at Boston University.